MW01268597

ADVANCE REVIEWS—

"I came to know the island of Karmøy and its people almost as well as the author. I liked the acute observations, the humor and the seriousness in a book that is visual, balanced and full of humanity. Patti Morgan is at her best when recalling chance encounters. They come over so naturally, authentically. One can always *see* the people she describes. She says such important things—'If living in another country taught me anything it was the importance of language' and, 'How can you know the soul of a people if you don't know their language?' But, as she found out, that was just the beginning. We need to go beyond words and her sensitive awareness of being in a strange land makes a profound comment on where we feel we belong ... it reveals, too, the individual's need to come to terms ... with not only being an island within an island, but of finding out how and where we fit ... within the universe. More than a travel book or journal, it is a hymn of praise for all life has to offer."
— **Edward Storey**, U.K. poet and author of *The Winter Fens, Fen Country Heaven, The Solitary Landscape,* etc. (Robert Hale, London).

"Patti Morgan describes life in a Norwegian village as an astute observer, not quite inside the culture in which she temporarily resides, but not quite outside it either. She doesn't presume to know Norway. Her graceful prose instead recounts what she sees and feels as an American living in a culture and functioning in language not her own. She is quick to delight in the gentle, slow-paced, reserved, and unspoiled community. This book doesn't merely describe the physical beauty of the Norwegian country-side, although it does so eloquently. It describes the beauty of a heart expanding to make what was foreign a part of itself."
—**Judith Caesar**, Ph.D. and U.S. author of *American Woman in the Middle East,* (University of Syracuse Press)

"In poetic language, this book gives an American view of island life on the west coast of Norway—the nature, weather, the everyday life of the people. Learning the language was the key to making inroads into the culture. She recalls that, at first, having to speak Norwegian in a store felt like being on stage at the theater. I found the exotic aspect of her trip to the Sami at Kautokeino fascinating."
— **Gerd Manne** (Norway) Author of *Ny i Norge, Vågen till Sverige, Dørene Åpnes, Leva bland människor,* etc. Former administrator of language courses for foreign students at the University of Bergen.

ISLAND SOUL

A Memoir of Norway

Patti Jones Morgan

PATTI JONES MORGAN

ISLAND SOUL BOOKS

Originally published in 2000 by Double SS Press
Reprinted 2004 by Island Soul Books.
Copyright © 2000 Patti Jones Morgan
Illustrations copyright the author.

Printed and bound in the United States of America at Morgan Printing, Austin, Texas. All rights reserved. No part of this book may be reproduced or transmitted in any form or by any means, electronic or mechanical, including photocopying, recording, or by an information storage and retrieval system—except by a reviewer who may quote brief passages in a review to be printed in a magazine or newspaper—without permission in writing from the publisher. For foreign use and translation rights, or other information, please contact Island Soul Books, P.O. Box 843, Wimberley, TX 78676. Fax (713)937-3740. Email: <islandsoulbooks@cswebmail.com> or <islandsoulbooks@msn.com>

Almost all names and some details have been changed to protect people's privacy. The author will correct any factual or other errors in a future edition provided they are brought to her attention.

Book Design: Dorey Schmidt

ISBN: 0-9752782-4-X Paperback

LIBRARY OF CONGRESS CATALOG CARD NUMBER:
2004-091699

Library of Congress has catalogued the 2000 edition as follows:

General Subjects:
Americans–Europe; Norway–Social Life & Customs; Norway–Description & Travel
Dewey Classification: 948.3/4
LC Classification: DL 596.K37M67 2000
BISAC Subjects: Social Science–Customs & Traditions; Travel–Europe–Scandinavia

FOREWORD

It is interesting for me as a Norwegian native to see Norway through Patti Morgan's eyes. I suffered with her in the beginning when she struggled to make contact with the Norwegians around her. Then I rejoiced as she found her way to becoming accepted and valued. In many ways the book provides a recipe for how to cope with challenges in a foreign culture and how to fall in love with a foreign and alien place.

Having been an immigrant myself (from Norway to America), I was reminded of how I had realized early on that I could not expect the environment to change just because my family and I had arrived. *We* were the ones who first and foremost needed to make adjustments. Finding ways to do so without losing one's dignity as well as being willing to risk appearing silly at times are important aspects of the adjustment-making process. Patti Morgan handled that magnificently and that is, of course, why the book is such a love story.

— Liv Dahl, Manager, Heritage Programs,
      Sons of Norway Foundation,
      Minneapolis, MN

ACKNOWLEDGMENTS

Considering the solitary aspect of writing, I was surprised when so many smiling faces came to mind as I recalled everyone, mostly Norwegians but not solely, who contributed to this book in countless ways. All our old neighbors in Austevik, more lately tagged Håvik, deserve thanks, particularly Magne and Kari, and the Austevik and Hansen families. Special friends Astri-Margrete, Barbrø, Jacqueline, Alison, Signe, Letten, Dagfinn and Milli are most cherished even as we live far, far away from them now. Milli helped with miscellaneous translations, fact checks, and cultural clarifications. Signe read my book (and worked *hard*) to help fix my shaky Norwegian. Sincere thanks to you both. People met at bus stops and in the post office, along the lanes, at a business party or in a coffee shop, on a plane or whizzing across the sound in a catamaran, each left their mark—impressions which I share with my readers. They numbered dozens, not counting the children who virtually adopted us, drawing close and helping us feel we were an okay part of the community.

The book's visual enhancements are due in great part to artists with pencil and with camera. Karen Sæther's marvelous teaching skills in drawing helped me wear down dozens of pencils for the pictures scattered throughout the book. Ole Jakob Vorraa, environmentalist and superb wildlife and nature photographer, provided a photographic feast which reflects his love, knowledge and respect for the island he has always called home. I was honored to learn so much from these good people.

Across the North Sea, Dr. Hilary Johnson of the United Kingdom provided an enlightening appraisal of my early, way too long, among other things, draft and I thank her most sincerely for her thorough, multifaceted approach to manuscript evaluation. In those British Isles, too, British poet and writer Edward Storey came to my aid, agreeing to read my book. Without complaint, he put aside his projects, reviewed my work, returned it in a flash, and, I'm glad to say, continues to be a most valued correspondent. Back in the U.S.A., Dr. Judith Caesar sacrificed her own writing time to evaluate my manuscript and, lucky for me, provided a heartening review. I am in debt, also, to Liv Dahl, Manager of Heritage Programs for the Sons of Norway, for agreeing to write the Foreword. She not only laughed at the funny parts of the book, she also lugged the original typescript all the way to Norway and back, reading it during her return flight from Amsterdam to Minneapolis. And, back to Norway one more time, thanks to a combination of cyberspace communication and down-to-earth national postal services, I was able to connect with Gerd Manne, author of *Ny i Norge* and several other language texts, who generously assisted by checking my work's content as well as its accuracy in *Norsk*.

I can't forget, either, Lisa Hamnes of Skandisk, Inc., for believing in my book right from the beginning — thank you!

I am grateful, too, to Dr. Christopher Forrest McDowell and Tricia Clark-McDowell, and to Edward Storey, for permitting me to use excerpts from their own books. Particular thanks also are due to Aleksander Hauge for sharing his stirring Karmøy song, and to singer, Mari Boine, for allowing me to publish lyrics from her *Ørnebror* (Eagle Brother) compact disc, and to Martin Pope for permitting me to present his beautiful translation of The Saami Anthem to an American audience.

No book comes to life without a publisher. Dr. Dorey Schmidt, an unabashed lover of Norway, offered a special perspective — that a book is not only an aesthetic object but also, in many ways, a writer's gift to world. She waved her Hill Country wand over my umpteenth effort and sprinkled it with some mighty powerful magic dust in the form of gentle but challenging suggestions. The book I had always hoped for emerged from under the clutter of a dozen reams of paper and millions of words. Thank you, Dorey. And, thanks, too, to Texas writer, Linda S. Bingham for her friendship, unfailing optimism and writerly support. The Austin Writers' League Marketing Support Group deserves kudos. The input, brainstorming and idea exchanges that evolve from our monthly meetings infuse us all with that vital dose of stubborn optimism that writers need to survive in the publishing world.

And, to all those nice people who kept on asking, "How's the book coming along?"— thanks for not forgetting.

My parents, the late Arthur Edward Jones, a bookseller all his life, who married an inveterate reader, Eileen, both provided me those particular genes which made reading almost anything written on a piece of paper second nature, and having a pen or pencil in my hand at all times a need more than a choice. Our house was full of books, many autographed, and one I always remembered was *Reach for the Sky* by World War II British Air Force hero, officer Douglas Bader, who lost both legs as a result of his courageous exploits. Perhaps it set a standard in my subconscious that manifested itself later in my attraction to the positive story, often the personal struggle to achieve a worthy goal that benefits others, too. Ordinary and extraordinary people, in their work, personal and community ethics, productiveness, and creative endeavors reveal as clearly as possible the human spirit at its best; and America, I believe, is full of people just like this who add to our quality of life.

I thank my mother for saving every single article I have ever written but I officially give her permission to throw them away now. This book takes up less space!

This is where everyone writes last but not least and I shall do the same. My 'last but not least,' most heartfelt thank-you goes to my husband, Mike, who cheers my smallest dreams, embraces my craziest and most improbable ideas, and runs emergency and general trailside service alongside the hilly, rocky, sometimes amazingly scenic path my mind, body and soul take me on. Without him, I would not be free to be me, and there would have been no reason or way to write, or to create this book. He deserves more than thanks; a medal may be in order.

—Patti Jones Morgan
Houston & Wimberley, Texas
June, 2000

Note: As this 2004 reprinting goes to press, I thank all those who have spread the word about this book: readers, book store owners, and amazing Amazon.com. Special thanks go to Lois Shrout, Ph.D. of Austin, Texas, for her regular dollops of wisdom.

—PJM
April 2004

For Mike,
for everything.

A Song to Karmøy

Proud you rise from waves in motion
green fields facing sky and ocean,
beaches white as ivory.
Boknafiord, the ships are sailing
while the Sirafiord is wailing
sloopy rocks in spray of sea.
As a wall against the water,
you protect each son and daughter
and let waves of Karmsund touch you tenderly.

Dragonships in ancient manners
left your shore with royal banners,
silky sails in air did flame.
Gilded shields they shone like fires
as the Viking ships with squires
brought you, Karmøy, wealth and fame.
Once, the fort King Harald founded
Olav saved with crosses grounded
by his church while sacred bells did bless your name.

May God bless you, Karmøy, from moor to strand
May God send good fortune on sea and land.
In village and farm, let joy take place.
Bless woman and man with faith and grace.

—Translation by Marit Synnøve Vea,
Kopervik, Norway, 1995

CONTENTS

"Lowering my eyes from the sky to those more accept-able limits of earth I was struck by the sudden smallness of things. Farmhouses and red-roofed barns now seemed no more than toy buildings. Rows of tilting telegraph poles were as stalks of straw left uncut by the harvesters. It took time to adjust. Such magnificent space. Such beauty."

—From *In Fen Country Heaven* by Edward Storey

Moving Overseas

In January 1992 my husband, Mike, and I left America to spend the following three or four years in Norway while he worked on the Heidrun oil project. I had not wanted to go, to Norway or anywhere overseas, but like any wife, supported my husband's career and off we went on what was to be my first expatriate sojourn. The worst part, I thought, was leaving the familiarity of our Houston, Texas, neighborhood and having to quarantine my three cherished pets for four months, just when I most needed their companionship. But the hardest part was to surprise me. It was being unable to read, speak, or understand the language around me. Conversations, newspapers, even labels on cleaning products, were unfathomable and every face was someone new. Overnight I changed from a competent and fairly sociable woman to a helpless, isolated one in a completely foreign land.

In Oslo our neighbors smiled but with reserve, and my longing to be invited in for a cup of coffee and friendly exchange was rarely satisfied. I made conversation wherever I could, but it was not enough and, besides, it was limited to English—their foreign language. I made few inroads into the culture, fewer friends, and withdrew into a separate, expatriate world.

In desperation and hope I joined some ongoing Norwegian language classes only to drop out in frustration when I couldn't catch up. My future in Norway looked bleak. Handicapped by English-only communication and unable to make friends with the very people I wanted to get to know, how would I survive for four years? My welcome reflected the January weather—beautiful to look at, but cold.

After almost a year we learned that Mike's part of the project would be based in Haugesund, a small fishing town on the West Coast. There, far from the city, I was sure we would get to know the real Norway. Our house hunting expedition revealed a cozy, picturesque world where townsfolk went about their business looking relaxed, shoppers in warm coats marketed on foot, boats bobbed in the quays, and life followed the hourly chimes of the clock tower. It promised the time and the place for us to experience daily life in a culture we had been on the edge of for months.

One December morning we took to the air and crossed the mountains to our new home, the area my husband's employer termed a remote site and for which we had been lightly prepared. Our family consisted of two adults, two dogs, and a cat, the latter severely indisposed to any kind of travel including air. Forty-five minutes of furious meowing accompanied the journey and we bowed our heads, hoping never to be remembered or recognized one future day by anyone, especially those who might be our new neighbors.

Long after the main landmass had run out, our plane skimmed over rocky waters toward a small, gray mass in the middle of deep, cold ocean. The island seemed an afterthought in the Nordic creation plan. I eyed the North Atlantic with alarm. It lay unnervingly close, close enough to swallow small planes. Miraculously our craft snatched at the runway and when the pilot applied his brakes, I felt my internal ones engage too. We were there. I had done all the traveling I wanted to do. Everything that bothered me was far, far away, and all Mike and I needed to do was get to the house the company had leased for us a mile or two away.

A strong, ocean breeze cleared our lungs as we stepped on to the tarmac of Haugesund airport on Karmøy. Flags whipped furiously, and my husband and I smiled at one another. At last we had made it—almost anyway. And we were going to live on an island! Beauty and quiet summed up the little world we had joined, but first things first. We needed to retrieve the animals. Pets add another degree of difficulty to air travel that only pet lovers understand. Getting them crated, to the airport, and boarded had been a challenge in itself, and everything else was only slightly easier. When the luggage carousel hiccuped into action and presented our motley three in their crates, plus numerous bags, our taxi driver summed up the needs of the Morgan traveling zoo. Wordlessly he tore apart his maxivan seats and we all squeezed inside. "Håvik, please," we tried several times until one of our least poorly pronounced versions received a spark of recognition and he started off.

We had seen the house and neighborhood earlier that fall when the owner had showed us around, pointing out the impressive ocean view. Everything felt good about the place and we decided on it quickly. Moving now for the second time in Norway was a last hurrah for me, however. I was tired of the roving life of an oil company spouse or the lonely life of one left behind while the other is away. My dream had been to improve the quality of our life in Houston and to advance my modest freelance writing career there. Yet here we were, following the siren call of the Heidrun oil project, a job too good to turn down. In my more optimistic moments I justified the upheaval with the thought that the sheer length of the assignment meant my husband and I would spend more time together, and that once in the Karmøy house, no one would ask us to move again for a long while.

Only seagulls' cries in the wind heralded our arrival. Wooden farmhouses dotted the rough fields beneath a wash of transparent blue sky. Stone walls divided the terrain like ropes of beads, and distant mountains loomed out of the sea. The scene evoked a sense of peace and sanctuary. Carved by centuries of sea, winds, sun, and storms, the island outpost stood sturdy and serene. Her people, I sensed, would match her enduring temperament, not standing for any disruption from city folks, foreigners into the bargain. Life would move at a quiet, slow yet rewarding pace and came with an unspoken caution. Respect the island people's ways and traditions and you just might be accepted. Deep inside I made the place a promise: we Americans would try to blend in as inconspicuously as we could.

Once I saw the house on Liarveien, with its door propped open in a shy invitation to enter, my tensions fell away. Something about it looked odd, though, until I realized it was the first front door I'd seen which opened outward, hinges exposed. In America this would have invited burglars, but evidently Håvik residents didn't give such matters a second thought. Half afraid it was the wrong house, we held back for a few minutes, then walked inside.

Music blared from the large den where a young woman stood at the top of a ladder painting energetically, and in the hall a man busily assembled a wardrobe. They nodded at us quickly as we picked our way through a wrangle of tools, cords, and electrical wires. Roomy and bright, our new house contained two main floor bedrooms, a central kitchen with deck, a long den with a wall of windows overlooking the sea, and a corner entertainment room with built-in bookcases. A spacious pine-paneled room in the basement seemed perfect for our bedroom. Other small rooms downstairs would serve as work areas, guest room, and storage. The latter was critical because, with the exception of large electrical appliances, we had brought everything we owned to Norway. Take all your belongings, things are hard to get and expensive, we were advised, and so we did.

Before long voices upstairs announced the arrival of our landlords, Håkon and Grethe Henriksen. Over hearty handshakes they apologized for the not-quite-ready state of the house. No problem, we assured them. Our plans were to spend the night in a

Haugesund hotel. The seaport, half an hour away, over a bridge, and located in the county of Rogaland was home to HMV, a local ship and rig building company where Mike's offices would be located. "But could I leave the pets here overnight?" I asked. Nicky and Rudy the dogs pricked up their ears. Calypso the cat ignored us all. Grethe smiled warmly. "Of course! It's your house now!" The way she said it made me feel she understood the travel-weary wife in front of her. Later I learned that she herself was married to a husband who traveled internationally. Her English might have been hesitant, but her intuition was on target. "Your house now" had a permanent ring to it, and relief washed over me. Now, with no more moving on the horizon, we could settle down.

Next morning we found the house transformed. Immaculate, painted, no speck of dust to be seen, and pine floors reflecting the sunshine. It was as though the previous day's disarray had never existed. Our considerate landlady had left us fresh *julekake*, a type of raisin and dried fruit loaf, and a cheery red Christmas poinsettia. Both our stomachs and our souls had been taken care of. I felt our house was primed for being a family type of place, unlike our short-term Oslo house with its history of bank repossession. Nice surprises continued since the dogs had left me none in the basement. They dragged us outside to explore the wild, cliff-side garden while the wind gusted its hellos. For the first time in a long time we felt caught up by nature, open spaces, and prospects of discovering a brand new world.

The moving truck was due at ten o'clock and tensions ran high. Any street noise sent us rushing to the front door. On one excursion I discovered two neighbors chatting. One went indoors and the other came over to say hello. "Liv" introduced herself, speaking fluent English. The maneuvering of our multigeared moving truck clipping the hedges in the narrow lane soon squelched our conversation. Shaking our heads helplessly, we promised to continue later. Before leaving, she asked, "Do you speak Norwegian?"

"No, not really," I apologized. "Well, just a few words," I added, feeling inadequate.

As the crew unloaded the conspicuous abundance of our possessions, her question rang in my head. Did I speak Norwegian? The problem had trailed me like a shadow from Oslo. I would not be able to get away with not speaking Norwegian on Karmøy either. The woman spoke English well and yet clearly preferred that I spoke some Norwegian. Visions of being like another corporate spouse whose Norwegian neighbors refused to speak English to her or her children came to mind. Four years would be long and lonely if I could neither read, write, or speak the language. I didn't want to be locked out of Norwegian life. I needed to learn their language.

Fortunately an Oslo restaurateur had already prodded me in the right direction when he complimented Mike and me on our fledgling *norsk*. "It's good that you want to learn," he said, "because, after all, how can you know the soul of a people if you do not know their language?"

Sipping my coffee, I had pondered his words. "Soul?" All I wanted to do was be able to understand a bus schedule or find the right section in the *gule sider*—the Norwegian Yellow Pages. But the grand philosophy sparked my imagination and I tucked the idea away. Maybe I would do it—be the one to uncover the soul he spoke so earnestly about. But it would have to be when I got settled, wherever that was.

Now, almost a year later his words came back to me as I glanced across at Liv's house. Was she worried that we would disrupt the neighborhood, place demands, i.e., English language conversation, on her?

If we could speak her language, her life and her family's would remain more normal. Maybe I could try to learn it one more time? The prospect threatened like an impending storm. The language seemed hard, yet not to learn it would be a waste of the overseas experience. As a writer, I surely owed it to that part of myself which needed to communicate to try to do it. It would be a passport into a world I knew nothing about and needed to get to know. Unless I got involved in the daily life of the place, how could I ever write about it? I would have to meet my new hosts halfway. Conversation would lead to friendships and friends were what I needed, women I could laugh with, share confidences and worries with. How would I find some and how long would it take? And did it all depend on my learning Norwegian?

My thoughts cast a cloud over what had started out as a bright, exciting day. Clues about what my life should look like on Karmøy were popping up, but how to get there? I tore open a packing crate, and with it a page from Scarlett O'Hara's diary. I would think about it all tomorrow.

Two weeks later it was Christmas, and our living room filled with our familiar furniture plus Christmas decorations looked comfortingly normal. Inside our house we still lived in America; outside was Norway. But nonetheless the soaring pine ceilings, contemporary wallpapers, and sunset hues created a perfect ambiance, and I already loved what I could see.

Miles of water and an impressive mountain range seemed close enough to touch. From the deck we watched marine traffic traversing the coast along the Karmsund waterway. Below the wall of windows lay an untamed, craggy garden sprouting a few bushes and remnants of summer's flowers as well as a friendly forest of mostly leafless trees. Our house was next to last on a lightly traveled lane which dead-ended at an old quay and union hall, so we rarely needed blinds. The majestic outdoors flowed in through three large windows to our living room. Ours was what I later called a "million-dollar view" and one not even the president of the United States could enjoy. Best of all, it had become mine, twenty-four hours a day.

The world outside pledged a never-ending change of seasonal elements: foliage, weather, different water shades, birds resident and migratory, flowers. Over the first weeks I stationed myself at the windows. Nature pressed her abundance on us to smell, touch, speculate about. Ships floated by; nights turned black earlier. I coveted the darkness, absorbed by the mystery of the cold beauty of the sleeping world, anticipating the next sparkling sunrise over the sound. Watching, waiting, wondering, absorbing it all became my calling. First in contemplation and silence we would take each other's measure, then the place and I would talk. December did not bring the snow I expected. Central and northern Norway received generous long-term snows, but ours were wetter and windier, with few really icy drops in temperature. Haugesund and Karmøy's coastal climate was more like Scotland's, moderated by the Gulf Stream. Somehow or other a Scottish radio station came in occasionally on my little kitchen radio and I wondered how many other foreign listeners tuned into it. Although the BBC never seemed to broadcast anything Scottish when I grew up in Britain, I liked the Scots' melodious accent. I tuned and retuned the radio trying to improve the reception, anxious to keep these friends in my new house where, with my husband gone ten or eleven hours a day in dead of winter, I suddenly felt very lonely.

Christmas Day demanded a semblance of cheer though, and for entertainment Mike and I videotaped ourselves opening presents, as our dogs and cat chased ribbons and rolled in discarded wrapping paper. When we replayed it, laughing at our staged silliness, our numbers doubled. With us as players, then as audience, plus double pets, it seemed we'd become a substantial group over Christmas, and not a lonesome bunch at all.

Once in awhile we peered out of the window looking for signs of Christmas lights. A few twinkled from windows, but it was our decorated tree in the window which created a stir. A handful of pink-faced children pressed against the glass to get a good look at it. To their surprise, our statuesque black and white cat hiding under the branches stared back. They burst into delighted giggles, chattering in another language. The tree and the cat enchanted them. I turned to Mike, laughing, feeling relaxed. We weren't invisible after all. The neighborhood knew we were there and a junior advance party had bravely investigated our goings on. Now, surely, a parent would drop by? To my disappointment, however, our doorbell remained silent over the holiday, indicating that for us newcomers, fitting in would likely take time.

The Language Class

As I unpacked boxes, my thoughts went over my experience thus far. Like it or not, coming to Norway had been a traumatic experience. I had dropped everything and followed my husband to a land neither of us knew much about. His focus was work, where he had no worry about language; his Norwegian colleagues spoke English in the office. He came home at night for dinner just as he did in the States. I, on the other hand, felt completely unfocused. I had no idea what I was going to do. I could barely grocery-shop; felt confused, aimless, frustrated; and hated having no control over my life, particularly my future, since the company was in charge of every aspect, including where we lived. Each time I turned on the computer to write, I gazed at the screen, noticing a creeping heaviness in my arms and fuzziness in my brain. Thoughts and words mixed themselves into a useless tangle and I threw away pages of unfinished bits and pieces. It was a relief to turn the machine off. It was best that I had no writing commitments or goals because I couldn't think.

But that was the past; the new year had arrived and with it my decision to make a new, optimistic start. We were living on a little island that had enchanted us from the beginning, and we would be residents for a long time. I had to learn the language of the people if I were to find fulfillment in Norway, even though the prospect was daunting. Taking the easy way out and just speaking English sounded so much easier, but I feared that my beautiful house would turn into little more than a lonely prison that way. Gathering up my courage, I called a community school for Norwegian language class information.

The person who answered spoke excellent English. To my surprise, two classes were scheduled in January, which meant there had to be many "foreigners" like me in the Haugesund-Karmøy area. I chose one, verified the place and date, and we hung up. I also, not entirely altruistically, signed up an English woman whose husband and mine would be working together. She had agreed that taking a Norwegian class made sense, but that did not prevent me from feeling a little like a wolf in sheep's clothing, however, for I had a secondary motive. I needed her companionship in class for my own selfish comfort. Pauline had a down-to-earth, bright way about her which would deflect my own insecurity and anxiety in the uphill struggle, and we could discuss it all in English. It didn't hurt, either, that I had lassoed myself a friend who shared my British heritage.

The letter from the school astonished me. For some bizarre reason it was all in Norwegian, a language I could not understand. Since that was why I had enrolled, I couldn't imagine why they sent it that way. Scanning it over and over, I tried to guess at what it said. It looked as if I might be enrolled and class would begin the second Monday in January. I would have to take the bus, so I pored through various categories in the phone book in search of a bus company. Ten minutes later I finally reached one office and was referred to another where a man read bus times, in English, over the phone. The whole procedure took forever, prompting me to wonder for the umpteenth time if I was making the right decision and if it all was going to be worth it.

I wished I felt as peaceful as my sleeping cat who buzzed contentedly from the chair. Outdoors everything was quiet—too quiet. Gray skies, children in school, and neighbors away at work all underscored how lonely life could become without people to talk to and be with. The dogs wandered in and gave me a friendly nuzzle. "Well, guys, look on the bright side," I announced into their understanding eyes. "Starting in just a couple of weeks, I will be out in the world every day and have people to talk to, not just you." Unoffended, they wagged their tails genially. If truth were known, they probably welcomed a change of pace and I wanted to oblige.

The first morning of class began in a claustrophobic crush of what seemed like a hundred people squeezing into a dingy-looking, two-story building in town. Swathed in winter coats and parkas, our disparate group of nationalities was bound by one common goal: learning a new language so we could fit into a new culture. A black tee-shirted young man hesitantly led eight of us into a small classroom where we sat in a U-shape of tables. Sincere and crumpled, he looked as though he had only recently risen from his bed. He appraised us expectantly from his spot in front of the blackboard, and I supposed he was an aide, helping to get the milling group of students into their particular rooms. Surprisingly he was our new teacher. Thus, inauspiciously, we met Tor.

After his introduction he asked for ours. We started around the room, a little shyly, and learned that Li was from Beijing, China; Hasan from Turkey; Gísli from Iceland. The women consisted of Nadya from Russia; Mary and her daughter, Olivia, who were from the Philippines; and Pauline, the lady whom I had signed up, from northern England. I rounded the group off as the only American, albeit one who still carried remnants of her British accent.

We were as diverse as my occasional language classmates in Oslo had been alike. They had been mainly American and British expatriate women who drove to school in Mercedes autos, wearing nice clothes and pretty footwear. American togetherness became such an internalized 51st state, one could rest in its familiarity. But on the streets of the city, away from familiar enclaves, I was just another lost foreigner. We foreigners had to register at local police stations as *innvandrer,* a word which meant "immigrant" but sounded like "invader." I equated police stations with criminals, and when I came away with my "person number"—the identification number everyone had to have—I felt I would be scrutinized until the day I left the country.

Language and feeling helpless in another country were always the issues; when groups of Norwegians chatted on a sidewalk, their words closed me out. When I bought the wrong food and products because the labels confused me, I sighed and clucked irritably, and when I saw every written word in a language I could not automatically understand, frustration raged. During my heavy-hearted bus trips to visit my poor, quarantined pets for our once-weekly, thirty-minute visits, I felt like lashing out at the world. It was not long before Oslo and I were at odds in every way.

But all that was behind me. Life in a small, coastal town felt easier, more my speed, and my classmates represented a very different, less affluent cross section of the community. Since most of us came by bus or on foot in winter, our clothes were sturdy, lumpy-looking things and so were we. Our mission was to learn Norwegian and meld into the culture. Certainly, if I were to survive and be happy in Norway, it was the only way.

Class began with Tor directing us to our *Ny i Norge* (New in Norway) textbook, and we stared at *Leksjon en,* Lesson One. We met a cast of immigrants who learned to greet one another, find out what country each was from, say where they themselves were from, and bid one another good-bye. We did likewise, using our new language. "Jiyy arrh frah OO-ESS-AAH," I gasped out, surprised at how similar it sounded to U.S.S.R. As of that day I was *amerikansk* with a small "a." We learned new vowels, the Norwegian alphabet, and to wrap our lips acrobatically around the new sounds, a little embarrassed. Peering out the windows, we practiced ways to talk about the weather. *"Det er kaldt! Det er sne. Det er overskyet,"* we chorused against the chilly elements and overcast skies.

The first hour and a half seemed to last half a day, and break time came none too soon. Like wild ponies released to the hills, dozens of students stampeded out of confining classrooms down the halls to the pastures of the lunchroom, jostling to be first in the food and coffee line. Language and cultural differences paled against the communal need for sustenance against the cold conditions we battled getting to school. Hot drinks, carbohydrate-laden snacks, and sandwiches were devoured in a fast twenty minutes, and snippets of conversations indicated that, despite the many tongues, people were finding some common communication lines.

Over the weeks our group exchanged more and more personal information. Pauline and I tried to tune in to our classmates' accents and struggle with them on word searches to express something. Hasan was quiet, speaking just a few words here and there, but quite quickly shared that he and his Norwegian wife were expecting their first child. Li was a math teacher whose wife studied elsewhere in the country. Nadya had married a Stavanger man who lived temporarily in Haugesund. Mary had come to Norway to be with her Haugesund-born husband, bringing their teenage daughter, Olivia, along. Young Gísli, the Icelander, had moved to Norway for better employment opportunities, he said.

January offered a cold, windy introduction to West Coast life, and having to relinquish my cozy nest each morning for a drafty one-mile or so walk to Håvik bus stop, developed into a daily battle. I preferred to contemplate the world outside my picture windows, marveling at the daily sunrise across the water. One morning a surprising, momentary flash of green sparked from behind the dark outlines of the mainland mountain peaks. I found my camera too late. But could I have seen bright *green?* Later someone confirmed it was not a mirage. A luminous flash of green light did, occasionally, accompany sunrise. Cold weather

magnified the sound of throbbing boat engines and, from seven
o'clock onward, double rows of lighted windows whizzing across
the rough water marked the fast boats, the catamarans, shuttling
people to jobs or school. Fascinated, I curled up in a soft chair in
front of the window with coffee aroma wafting into my nostrils
and a stream of excuses for why I did not need to go to class
grinding through my brain like adding machine tape. I kidded
myself I would not go to school that day. Guilt won out, however, and Monday through Friday, off I went.

If the winter elements weren't daunting enough, grappling with new words, grammar, and pronunciations certainly
was. As an emigrant to America from England in the '60s, I had
not had to face learning a new language, and in that regard,
functioning in a new land had not felt different. I coped quite well.
My mother tongue had provided me an almost seamless transi-
tion into a new, yet not foreign, culture. But trying to make
headway in Norway was much more of a struggle.

I glanced at my studious colleagues with a twinge of
shame. Some would argue that I was just playing at learning
Norwegian whereas for them it was deadly serious. Yet I felt
equally lost at having to abandon linguistic assurance for near-
baby talk in Norwegian. Six people had put their lives on the line
for this and, although my circumstances always allowed me the
luxury of dropping out and just treading water until I returned to
Texas, I felt a shared responsibility for the group's success.

My strained attention span and curiosity about everything took to detouring. Mostly I ventured on paths of specula-
tion about my life, everyone else's, and how on earth we all
managed to find ourselves in that classroom, miles away from the
people and places of our past. We kept on with *Ny i Norge*,
reading dialogue in small stories about immigrants, studied
grammar and read out loud, all the while longing for two-thirty
and blessed release. Some days I plotted to quit and tell myself it
didn't matter, but by that time the school had promised us a
certificate for an absence-free attendance record and I wanted it.
A certificate of competence in anything sounded wonderful to my

tattered ego, so I signed the agreement and, with that simple action, let my dream of abandoning class slip through my fingers.

For the next five months class and classmates held the key to communications *på norsk*. Mornings drew us to school, bundled in thick coats, boots, hats, and—Texas thin-blood that I still was—heat-retaining silk underwear. All except Gísli, our Icelander and the second youngest in the class, that is. Genetically or geographically infused with heartier blood than most, he favored instead a body-hugging short, black leather jacket, jeans, and cowboy boots with no room for extra socks. For him, break-time nutrition consisted of coffee and a cigarette, followed by a cough or two and hippopotamus-sized, oxygenating yawns.

Winter clothes notwithstanding, a natural antidote to the chilly weather was Nadya. Her periodic furrowed brows, pouts, and skeptical looks laced with contentiousness guaranteed a hot surge of blood through the veins of the coldest person. I searched her face and body language for some invitation for light conversation because I was very curious about her. She was from a country whose people had been cut off from me for most of my life, and I wondered how she felt about her society—and my American one. I feared my overtures might make me the target of one of her exasperated looks. Fate had once again treated me unfairly. The uphill struggle of learning a new language in a different culture was surely character-building enough? Now my first contact with a Russian looked shaky. I would have preferred a less volatile subject and a much larger room.

During the Cold War, Russians and Americans never shared the same landmass, let alone in the same room, unless they were government spies; at least that was the way I had seen it in the movies. Real life made things more complex. Times had been simpler back in Texas where, even if there had been some, I had never met any Russians. Now that I had found one, I was afraid to ask anything. Driven away perhaps by political and economic turmoil, she was trying for a better life. I wasn't sure I liked being in the position of watching her adapt and struggle. A happy endings person, I would have liked her to live happily ever after with a Russian man, but it hadn't happened. To me, hers was the face of all of Russia's young women, and I wondered if they all wanted to leave. When we exchanged a few words, I picked them carefully, not wanting to sound too sure of myself and feeling guilty about my favored life in America. But as happens in all matters where there is unfinished business, never a day passed that she didn't fail to provoke my interest and curiosity.

The lives of the immigrants in *Ny i Norge* were bland in comparison to ours for they did not have Nadya. She regularly sought battle and challenge in its innocuous paragraphs and our classroom conversation. When not confronting Tor, she stridently demanded Pauline give her the "Engleesh verd" for something or vehemently argued the benefits of the informal Haugesund dialect against formal *Bokmål*. The sparing use of "please" and "thank you," combined with her brusqueness, chafed me. I had been raised around politeness: the English apologizing when you trod on their toes, sandwiching all requests between "please" and "thank you" and courteous Texans politely addressing women as "ma'am." Such niceties oiled the mechanisms of daily life, and their absence reminded me how raggedly gears can grind without them.

My angst was unnecessary, for Nadya harbored me no ill will whatsoever for being an American. I counted my blessings to be on her good side. Statuesque, with thick, auburn hair, she was hard to please and harder still to fathom. Given to asking personal questions and making controversial statements, she was all that a diplomat should not be.

"Why you no have children?" she demanded of Pauline and me across the lunchroom table one morning. We blurted out responses which failed to satisfy her, so we rephrased them, hoping to stave off the frown which trembled near her eyebrows. Her skeptical expression indicted me for inadequacies past and present and she remained unconvinced, as usual. We raised the volume of our explanation as though that alone would clarify our answers. Aware that several dozen total strangers in the lunchroom were now privy to our most private reproduction beliefs and thoughts, I small-mindedly gave Nadya the same opportunity to broadcast far and near.

"What about *you?*" She looked surprised.

"Me?"

"Yes, do *you* want any children?" I persisted. Nadya pouted, dropped her gaze, and mumbled something short, fast, and unintelligible in her thick accent. The conversation was over.

Another time she delightedly copied my muffin recipe and invited Pauline and me over for pizza. Waving happily at her pastel-colored wall phone, she cried, "There, I can dial Moscow!" My classmate accepted many American ideas, but we could never convince her that bribes weren't a part of everyday life. Firmly pro-American about the U.S.-Iraq Arabian Gulf crisis, she dragged me into a subject I avoided, war. "America went there and stopped them. That's right, Patti? America did it all!"

Pauline interjected, clattering her teaspoon around in her cup in a noisy whirr of irritation.

"Britain was there too. Our men were over there! Several nations sent soldiers, in fact. NOT just America!" Pauline's sharp, patriotic retaliation put an end to further discussion, and I, for one, had not the gall nor guts to disagree. I dived for something deep in the recesses of my bag while Pauline stood by her statement, looking fierce. Nadya could not be shaken so easily. She withstood Pauline's reprimand, looking unconvinced, discounting it with a slight arching of her eyebrows and a flippant nod of her head. As I busied myself in my books, I felt unexpectedly proud of her certainty and a great deal less worried about our stock in Russian hearts. Maybe we could be friends and have a normal conversation one day?

Despite the recent acquisition of a Norwegian husband, learning his native language appeared to be a reluctant mission and definitely secondary to improving her English. And when class was over, since a mighty holler to where he waited for her across the road got him careening his car to her side like a drag racer, spraying up gravel en route, who was to say she needed the Norwegian anyway?

Resident Russian included, each of us brought our individual and national beliefs, styles, and cultures to class and to the new country. Our faces told only part of the story. We were dark and fair-haired, bespectacled and not, medium to short, plump and skinny, just eight ordinary people, yet with Tor included, we embodied the majority of the world's beliefs, governmental systems, and socio-cultural influences. Catholic, Lutheran, Protestant, Moslem; rule by royalty, presidents, communists, democrats, semi-military. We were products of various classes and educated at schools, religious institutions, colleges, and universities where we learned different versions of the world's history and where religion was taught, obsessed about, or kept in its parochial place. From countries where bribes got you everything or your accent did, where goods were dirt cheap or prohibitively expensive, where the government took care of you or encouraged you to strive for independence—we eight were now tended by socially democratic, mother country Norway, who liked her citizens not to get too many fancy ideas about themselves or to fluff their own nests too luxuriously and not need her.

Our diverse group was bound by such frail ties and divided by such enormous differences, I guarded against saying the wrong thing. Potential for a chance remark to escalate into an insult lurked like a burglar around the fragile walls of our encampment, waiting for an undefended moment to pounce and cause havoc in our international group. Hurt feelings would strangle us all in the tiny room we had to share for many months so, like a polite guest at a party, I steered a neutral, cautious path away from trouble, rarely mentioning much American and studiously avoiding mention of the treacherous three: money, politics, and religion. "Loose lips sink ships" could have been adapted to our crew's voyage across choppy linguistic seas.

In time, confrontations on the larger issues remained blissfully unplumbed while any beneficial astrological aspects, coffee, and who had control of opening and closing the windows and turning the heat off or on assumed vital importance. Our power struggles were reduced to the bizarre and the basic, and these alone drew us representatives of eight nations together or pushed us apart.

Nadya was the main power broker since she sat next to the heaters which were illogically placed directly under the windows. Clucking with disapproval at any drafts, she regularly descended upon the heaters, instructing her new personal assistant, Hasan, to apply a few appropriate twists to the knobs. In a short time the rest of us were sweltering, falling asleep from lack of oxygen, or praying for break time when we could open the windows. Nadya's departure was regarded as prime time for flinging them wide open and adjusting the heaters. Our triumphs were brief. The second she returned, the parallel slams of the two windows closed off our fresh air.

Nadya's questions often surprised me for the implausibility of what they were and where we were. How could I be sitting across a table from my first Russian friend in a dreary school in Norway in the midst of winter, the world around us afire with wars and political tensions and hear, "When iz your birzday, Patti?" delivered with an expectant glint in her eye. "The Goat!" she exclaimed, and continued her quest with the others. If this was *glasnost,* it seemed deliciously innocuous. We children of Pisces, Capricorn, Libra, Leo, Cancer, and Taurus exchanged a few more planetary tidbits, but Nadya's sun in Cancer, opposing mine, bode poorly for us even if the missiles had gone.

I drank my coffee in what had become my permanent dazed state, wondering just what else would prove we were complete opposites, destined for head-on collisions. Meanwhile Nadya demanded Hasan tell us his sign, and she prodded his arm until he gave in, still rubbing his sore spot.

Hasan's forte, nonverbal communications, meant he

could produce performances worthy of any professional actor. Smiling confidently at his audience, he sat up erectly, stretched out his neck, chin slightly forward. Then, while angling his head to one side, raised his arm, bent it at the elbow, drew back an invisible bow and freed an invisible arrow. Ah! Sagittarius! A proud smile almost split his face, his brown eyes twinkled with satisfaction, and in surprise and admiration we fell about in our chairs laughing. His special talent put us all in the shade.

Along with our astral houses, socio-cultural-economic backgrounds, beliefs, and educations, we stirred Turkish, Tagalog, Icelandic, Russian, Chinese, British-English, and American-English into a bubbling bouillabaisse of communications, using English as our basic stock, highly spiced with accents. I had to admire a language so elastic and accommodating.

Nadya's accent loaned itself impressively to both English and Norwegian. She sounded like a husky-voiced Russian spy in a movie, and her trademark downcast eyes with long sweeping lashes, matched with disconsolate pouts, rounded out the persona. Hasan's deep voice delivered English and Norwegian in an abrupt monotone totally ignoring commas, periods, and beginnings and ends of paragraphs. I wondered if Turkish grammar had pauses, commas, exclamation marks, etc.? Once she got into it, Pauline confidently attacked Norwegian passages, British style, her clipped accent sounding like a box bouncing across a ship's deck in a force-ten gale. I hoped that Pauline would drop the clip and try to slur and sound guttural, but I knew that violated her chosen enunciation style. Li's rather difficult-to-understand Chinese-accented English developed into just as difficult-to-understand Chinese-accented Norwegian. Mary's Filipino-English took a bit of getting used to, spoken in a rhythm my ears often failed to discern, on first or subsequent tries.

Of course, I had no idea how I came across but hoped my gutturals made me sound somewhat authentic. On the downside, focusing so hard on phonetics meant I often had no idea what I was actually saying. But whatever it was, saying it properly seemed the most important thing to do. We progressed daily through *leksjoner* and the dreaded *arbeidsbok*, workbook, gradually overcoming our major hurdles, a foreign language, and cold, windy weather. Our future success as citizens of Norway rested on our respective bottoms. As long as we attached them to our chairs two and one-half hours a day for one hundred days, we would make it.

Tor inspired us to study. *"Flott, flott!"* he would say. Why he was saying "Cream, cream!" confused me until I checked the *ordbok*, dictionary. *Fløte* was cream whereas *flott* meant generous or good. Like unsteady walkers on a circus high wire, we tried to keep our balance in a new world, swaying and tense as we inched forward, dependent on our trainer's encouragement. Would we make it to the other side? He beckoned us, smiling, *"Flott, flott!"* Yes, yes! We were doing well in Norwegian, he said, and we so wanted to believe him.

Laboring through our book tired us, however, and we lingered like frogs on lily pads for any excuse to break the seriousness of class. One day we learned the names of fruits and vegetables and practiced singular and plural, *en banan, to bananer, mange bananer*. For some reason bananas were funny that day, and a laugh here and there broke out in Nadya and Hasan's corner of the room. Pauline soon incited more civil disobedience. "Did you say he was *bananas?*" she inquired facetiously, deliberately misconstruing a conversation from Turko-Russian territory.

Tor interceded, *"Nei. Bananer, n-e-r. flertall.* They're just saying *bananer."* He cast a watchful glance at Pauline. We were developing into an increasingly mischievous and unruly group of adults as our confidence with language clashed with our boredom from sitting, but Tor had our handling down to a science and knew our game would have to take its course.

His logical answer about bananas' plural was ignored in favor of Pauline's witty "being bananas" inquiry. The phrase appealed to those who knew what it meant and those who thought they did. Although it was unworthy of teaching to others, it was gaining popularity by the minute. Hoots of laughter burst forth from the Filipino contingent, a sure sign that we had built up a head of steam and were off and running. Li, the math teacher, connoted being bananas with another idiomatic expression.

"Don't they say 'You're a turkey' in the U.S.?" he called out, a big smile wreathing his face. Throwing my usual caution about making proclamations about America and Americanisms to the wind, I prepared to answer. After all, his was such a funny, benign inquiry.

"Oh, yes!" I called back over the racket. "People *do* say that—they say 'You're a real turkey!' My loud turkey! resounded around the little room as all conversations faded and all eyes turn toward Hasan, our own Turk. My cherished, saint-like uninvolvement in the cultural minefield of international relationships exploded. I was the culprit whose voice rang out loudest and last.

I sunk guiltily into my seat. No wonder the world needed the United Nations to maintain some semblance of peace between diverse nationalities. News at Five: Joke starts war. Safe old *Ny i Norge* lay open in front of me and I wished it would swallow me up. Miraculously Hasan was smiling at something Tor was saying, continuing on the fowl theme. A look of immediate comprehension provoked a nod toward me and something about the U.S. Maybe *we* were considered turkeys in Turkey, I thought, glad to take some punishment in return.

My maligned classmate, now under attack from both Nadya and me, it seemed, rose above it all by performing an award-winning turkey impression, flapping his elbows out and up and down and adding the theatrical fillip of a realistic turkey call. Hysterical laughter ripped through the silence, and Tor waited for us to get it out of our systems and settle down. Patiently he got us back to what we were supposed to be doing, learning Norwegian.

Foreign Accents

When people at school or anywhere asked what brought me to Norway, I told them that my husband's job had. I felt uncomfortable, ashamed somehow, of not having a separate identity. My visa safely tagged me as a housewife, not freelance writer. In Norway I wasn't anything in particular because I wasn't allowed to be; working was forbidden at that time as jobs were scarce enough even for the country's own residents. Also I disliked the designation "expatriate." It sounded too close to "ex-patriot," which cast doubts on my national loyalty. Troubling me further, the label "expatriate" implied a defined state of affairs to what was, by its nature, an undefined one. The abbreviation, "expat wife," sounded particularly, annoyingly, glib and light-weight. "I'm just an expat wife. Don't expect much from me; don't take me seriously. As soon as my husband's job's over, we'll be off again." The inference of very comfortable circumstances and easy international travel seemed to guarantee alienation from everyday people. I felt the word repelled rather than attracted others.

If I wasn't allowed to call myself a freelance writer and do some work, what was I?

Sometimes I believed that if I just searched long enough for the perfect, defining term, I would uncover one that described someone like me leading a purposeful existence in a foreign country without any creative or work-related identity.

My comfortable background hurt me at the language school when a fellow student drew me into conversation at the bus stop. Filipino and married to a Norwegian, she wanted to chat. Was I married? Where did my husband work? My ambiguous response about Mike's work in a shipyard sent her speculating that he was possibly a welder there like her own husband. Forced to, I added something about him being a manager. "Oh! Boss! boss!" she cried, clucking with alarm and disapproval. She scurried out into the street, staring impatiently in the direction of her bus which would release her from a situation where she felt inferior. The chill which permeated our little attempt at sociability felt every bit as cold as the day. No chance of a relationship with her now, yet we had important things in common. Both of us struggled with powerlessness in a new country, inadequate language skills, not driving, and marriage to men who had brought us to a foreign country. We were more alike than different.

Relocating, transferring, emigrating; what made people move? As a one-time emigrant, I had moved to improve my prospects, which was exactly what happened. The girl I had just spoken with wanted the same thing. In any event, here I was again after multiple moves in my life, in yet another place. Was moving an American trait—the constant redefining of the perfect place for job, family, or retirement and setting up a home for that purpose, after which you evolved and moved on to yet another neighborhood?

Maybe I only thought I knew what home was. I still clung for comfort to Houston, but the fact was our old house had been sold, so we had no home there. Norway was forcing us to start from scratch, almost, and not for the first time nor the last, I felt

confused and ill at ease with issues of relocation. How long would
it take for me to feel at home and secure again?

After three months I was on automatic pilot going to
school. The usual excuses for not going lined up each morning
like wayward children, demanding attention, insisting no one
would notice my absence. But our group was so small, the
anonymity afforded in large classes was reversed. By not coming,
the absentee was missed every minute for two and a half hours.

During a slow morning when even our coffee break failed
to invigorate my brain or enthusiasm, I was stuck on the verb *to
be.* Tor looked pained as I struggled, but Gísli came to life with a
snuffle and assisted me in an unforgettable way. Usually not
inclined toward scholarship but rather, by self-reputation, to
removing his clothes for interested young women, our young
disco king proceeded to outdo even Hasan for dramatic performance.

"Å være eller å være ikke. Det er den spors-malen!" he
parodied Hamlet's "to be or not to be," addressing the group and
sweeping his arms through the air. Being entertained was our
favorite pastime and we demanded an encore which, bolstered
with a few more flourishes, surpassed the first. He had our total
attention and, for the first time, really shone. How would I ever
hear "to be or not to be" and not think of Gísli, our man in black
leather? Taking a deep bow, moment of leadership past, he
returned to his late-night-induced lethargy not to be heard from
again for the rest of the lesson. His spirit was clearly alive and well
but not in the classroom.

As the weeks went by, Gísli showed up less and less,
usually looking worse for wear. Massive, frequent yawns were his
trademark as was his head-in-hands position over the table. His
favorite expletive regularly punctuated the proper and quiet
atmosphere. Later a friend explained the "s—" word was innocuous, used to express surprise, dismay, or pleasure in Norway. He

and Olivia, however, as babies of the group, benefited from a big brother-little sister relationship.

Classroom questions revealed our needs and interests. Li asked over several lessons the way to say, "You look beautiful! You look wonderful!" His expression lit up as he faithfully memorized them. He was looking forward to having his wife visit and I trusted she would not come down with a headache. Olivia asked about *gymnas*, the type of school she would soon enroll in, and Pauline wanted to know the word for drivers' licensing bureau. For me, *forfatter, datamaskin,* and *redaktør,* or author/writer, computer, and editor, encompassed my mothballed writing concerns.

The tedium of learning got to us all, especially by week's end when mentally drained from training in *konjunksjoner* and *preposisjoner* and the challenge of tagging *adjektiver* with the appropriate masculine, feminine, or, sadly, neuter identities, we stayed alert for fun digressions. Gísli informed us that Reagan in Icelandic sounded like "kick out," but Nadya's version was funnier. When she wrenched her damaged umbrella closed on drizzly days snarling at the rain, *"regn, regn"* which sounded like "Reagan! Reagan!" I found it bizarrely amusing.

Li added an interesting digression from an innocent story in our *Ny i Norge.* According to him, the Norwegian word *"sa"* sounded like the Chinese word for kill, and he leapt to his feet and swung an imaginary rifle across his chest to make his point. I speculated that perhaps, in Chinese, when you had said good-bye, it meant forever.

We learned that the interjection *uff* was Norwegian for "Oh, dear!" and, to say it authentically, you needed to bite your upper teeth down on to your lower lip and blow the extended *eff* sound through the gaps. A positive *ja,* or yes, required a noisy inhalation on the last letter. The party was not choking as Hasan feared when someone *ja'*d with a noisy gasp in a restaurant. He mimicked the sound and we all followed suit, concurring that both *uff* and the sucked-in *ja* were peculiar Norwegian interjections and very, very funny. If Tor let slip an *uff* or gaspy *ja* during the lesson, we deafened him with a chorus of multi-accented versions to provoke his look of mock hopelessness. Our ensuing fits of laughter let us handily escape *Ny i Norge* for a few blissful minutes because, when not clowning or getting ourselves into and out of potentially tricky cultural-political waters, we were actually studying and learning.

Our book chapters in *Ny i Norge* followed the daily lives of immigrants as they attended language classes; discovered the library, grocery store, and the movies; and visited one another's homes and families—and we did the same. Textbook pages curled beneath our fingers, and the ancient class pencil sharpener ground unceasingly. Marginally easier than writing in Norwegian was reading sections of dialogue out loud. Unfortunately it often fell on Hasan to take on a heavy load of extra dialogue, unfortunately of the female variety. Preparing myself for his voice only helped a little as I hunched over the book.

Hasan's heavily accented, deep Turkish voice rumbling forth as a Betty, Fru Eriksen, or Indira echoed incongruously in our tiny room. Our faces remained expressionless and our lips showed no twitching as we maintained our polite facade. Nadya, bored, decided it was time and her responsibility to do something about such an unnatural situation. Fidgeting in advance of her move, she picked her moment. Hasan's monotone reading style of no pauses for commas or periods had barely started when Nadya looked at him askance, giggled, and thumped his arm. As he turned to look, she snatched at his curly hair. "Hm! Indira!" she snorted, playfully. Hasan stopped in midsentence, glared defensively, and leaned back in his chair. We held our breaths, waiting for something to happen. But, impervious, numb, or unable to defend himself against the probable sole cause of the Cold War, Hasan kept his thoughts to himself and returned to his dialogue. And, although Nadya was, Hasan was not smiling.

Hasan's stoicism tickled Li. Nadya's perpetual unhelpfulness, confrontational behavior, and devotion to tweaking the status quo usually perplexed him, but today her outburst sent him into hysterics. His high-pitched laugh rang out, and he nearly overbalanced him off his chair. Before long the class was a chorus of laughter, with no sign of a let-up. My eyes streaming, I blinked gratefully across at our classmate. Only she gave us the excuses we needed to run away, laughing, from *Ny i Norge*.

With school in the morning, food shopping—often on foot—dogs, and homework, not to mention husband and our shared activities, mental challenge was not my problem, but feeling left out of Norwegian life still was.

I shared the fate of all immigrants, feeling myself in a sort of no man's land. My own language and home were miles away, yet it was there that we were validated and knew people and they knew us. We knew how and where we stood in a culture; we felt sure of ourselves. In this country we remained everlasting pupils, always carrying a dictionary. Back home seemed, in retrospect, so easy, so perfect, simply because of automatic language skills.

Creating something solid and secure for my soul to lie upon and rest in Norway often eluded me. It was like knitting or crocheting an afghan from contrary-minded yarn where every so often all the intricate little loops spontaneously unraveled, leaving me staring at needles with nothing hanging on them. Back at the beginning again, all signs of progress gone, any ideas that I had been actually getting somewhere evaporated.

In class I was unnaturally brave for we were insulated and nurtured, helping one another. Together we corrected our errors and moved on to the next chapter toward success, completion. Outside school it was quite different. We were one, often alone, often lonely. Sometimes worried, nervous, unsure. We missed the news because we could not read the papers properly, wished we could work but didn't know how or what was involved. We depended on others for too many things. In America I knew the steps and where they led. In Norway I often could not even find the place where the steps began because I did not understand the culture.

The loneliness of being a foreigner showed up in small

ways. At break time Li sat alone, reading his Chinese newspaper. Weekends offered little relief as he could not drive as yet and his wife still lived in a far-off city. Sometimes he rushed into class at the last moment without his sandwich. If the coffee cart rolls vanished in the first flurry, he looked crestfallen and I felt sorry for a man so thin, a candidate for one of my mother's fattening-up campaigns. He must have felt the cold for he never discarded his neat wool sweater. In that regard, my natural padding had its benefits. When Li shared a dream about being home with his parents, it was evident he was homesick, and I wished he *could* be back with them.

Nadya killed time downtown to avoid going back to an empty house when her husband was offshore. Gísli had been driven to Norway, he told us, by high unemployment in Iceland. "All my life I've worked in restaurants," he said with the jaunty assurance of a twenty-one-year-old. His evening shift as a cook meant he worked until the early hours of the morning.

Nevertheless, he was never short of friends. His questions and interest in Old Norse, Viking words and language pointed to an inquisitive intellect. Gísli sadly was the first and only casualty in our language team when he finally chose work over school.

Separateness and confusion affected our new situations. Hasan came in shaking his head one morning. "Rah-cism, rahcism!" he stormed, looking upset. Some foreigners like himself had experienced affronts over the weekend and the papers were full of it. Although I did not know the people involved, I considered Hasan a representative. He was devoted to the class and never missed a day. What more could he, an immigrant, or any immigrant, do? His well-thumbed Turkish-English dictionary and class books served as a testament to his commitment to adapt to the new culture. He had the burden of untangling such varied tongues as Turkish, English and Norwegian, no small feat. Through him I learned the Norwegian word for key, *nøkkel,* after he had accidentally locked up his bicycle at school and left the spare key at home. Pauline was not immune to disappointments either, the most constant one being the lack of friendship with her neighbors.

I thought I had things under control, but not so. Awhile before, I had managed to gather up my tattered writer's ego and confidence, insisting they pull themselves together and try to get back to normal—interviewing and writing. I had been working on a great article idea—a story about the community's successes, failures, and experiences in general with immigrant and language programs. I wanted to interview various administrators, students, and former students and produce something useful and pertinent, written from the perspective of a class insider. I imagined the idea would be well received and that the local newspaper would happily translate and publish it.

But I was wrong about it all. The newspaper accepted no English language articles nor would they translate it, and the administrator showed no enthusiasm for my project. Was I writing a book, he wanted to know. I replied, no, just an article. My heart fluttered anxiously as I scanned his face for some sign of interest. Would he view it as good publicity as an American would or something quite different?

"I can't talk now; I'm too busy," he muttered disinterestedly. "Maybe some other time." He returned to his hurried lunch and I studied his back, knowing I was dismissed and he wanted nothing to do with me or my idea.

Feeling ineffectual as a foreigner felt disturbing and familiar. Failing to accomplish anything concrete was becoming the norm. My expatriate status had lacked purpose, passion, and creative contribution, and I had tried jolting myself back into writing. The adrenaline surge of beginning work on a story had lifted me out of my psychic doldrums and creative lethargy. My old self jumped back into my body, and the feeling of being alive, stimulated, and full of hopeful energy crowded out all the emptiness and struggle of the months since coming to Norway as though they never existed. But after the letdown, my newly emerging confidence crashed and my writer self, seeing no glimmer of hope, vanished. After her flying visit, I reacquainted myself with the vacated quarters. Like it or not, my new self had the place all to itself again, so when I got home, I told her to curl up under a blanket, eat some chocolate, and try to forget making grandiose plans.

As is the way in life, however, the man's words—few that they were—planted a seed. A book? For the time being though, I returned to *Ny i Norge,* safe from the real life I had wanted to write about. The people on the pages could have their disappointments or personal failures, but they wouldn't touch me. Yet the experience left its scars. Was I an educated person with something to say or just another foreigner taking up a person's time and easy to shake off ? What was it about me that made the fellow freeze me out? Just that I was a non-Norwegian, an American, a threat, or a nuisance? Whatever it was, trying to express a need or desire, to gain information or help, meant we people from other countries had to work harder.

At school I met a Vietnamese girl who spoke in Norwegian and English—loudly. Extrovert and vocal, she held the floor while we capitalized on her occasional pauses to squeeze in a few words ourselves. Her hands danced around in time with her rapid-fire delivery while her thick, long hair swung across the shoulders of her red dress. When we learned her story, it was clear why she had developed her assertiveness. Resident of a refugee camp, she had gotten out only thanks to a Norwegian delegation's visit and even then she had had to stay in the Philippines one more year before coming to Norway.

"Refugee camp" conjured up television pictures of nameless people clawing at chain-link fences. How a young girl could exist there offended my belief that privacy and dignity are innate human rights, but how could one have privacy in such a crowded place? Had she been one of the faces I had seen on the news once, one of hundreds of skinny Vietnamese penned up like animals? The girl's hyperactive nonstop talking and fingers fiddling with her thin, red passport shocked me. That passport was her ticket to freedom, won with the generosity of Norwegians. With it she could enter all lands, except Vietnam. She was only twenty-two, an age at which her life should have been starting, not when a whole history had already imprinted itself, cruelly, on her. After that, I would never see refugee camp pictures without seeing each face as a real person with needs and hopes, remembering her and her already storm-tossed personal life.

Another refugee, short and with somber eyes, repeated where he was from over and over again, but neither Pauline nor I could catch the word or figure out the place. Later a browse through an atlas unearthed that his country had long ago been absorbed into a kingdom of the Middle East. "I am Christian, Christian," he said. The emphasis seemed unnecessary to me, having come from a multi-ethnic land, but to him it was important. Friends back home were killed, he went on, due to their religious beliefs. His complex reasons for leaving his country were probably known only to him, I guessed, and none of my business. All that did matter was that he was safe and free in Norway.

One man in our school, a civil engineer, spoke wistfully of going to Chicago, where he had many relatives. He had no such ties in this town in Norway, and he told Pauline he felt lonely. A solid-looking man, he could have fit into an office anywhere in the world, and I wished I could have made a phone call and gotten him an interview. He was qualified and needed to get back to work before he lost heart. What a waste, a grown man—an engineer at that—demoralized by endless, unproductive time on his hands, no job. He was one of several I had often seen wandering around town during the day, waiting to return to the work force. He too showed us his new, thin, red Norwegian passport, looking pleased and proud of it. But his past, present, and future were summed up in four words, written in spidery black handwriting, words I would never have wanted to write, casting a person away from his own land. *Alle land untatt Irak.* All countries except Iraq. He could not go home, ever again, just like the lady in the red dress.

One day everyone congregated outside for a picnic-style lunch, our faculty promoting interchange and *norsk* conversation. A tall, slender, handsome Somali and a young, athletic Yugoslav drank coffee across the table. I had seen CNN that morning. Somalia, Bosnia, fighting and death everywhere. What could I say to them? How did you start a conversation with "I'm sorry"?

They were interested in where I was from, but their eyes showed no recognition of Houston or where it was. Their response disturbed me, perhaps because I visualized the immense activity of Houston—a people-laden city, crisscrossed by twenty-four-hour streams of traffic, anchored by downtown high-rises stretching up into the Texas sky. How could it not be known? In any other place, on vacation perhaps, I would not have felt so irrational, but after so long away from my own country, I desperately needed them to recognize it for my sake, to remind me I had real roots somewhere. Their not knowing added to my insecurities. Like a refugee, I belonged nowhere for now—just like them.

I struggled to focus on our cautious introductions, feelings in turmoil. All I wanted to find out was what was going on in their countries, how they got to Norway, what were their families doing, what about their own futures and prospects? How did they feel about being safe in a peaceful, little Norwegian town while their families suffered? Their eyes hid their pain and secrets and I was afraid to ask. But it was the only thing I wanted to talk about. Anything else would have been superficial given the political climate. But Tor had warned us earlier, "Don't ask people too many personal questions. Some have left children and families behind." I would not let Tor down. I would not hurt anyone by asking anything of significance.

Chilled, I pulled my sweater around my shoulders. Everything seemed to be a pretence.

The season was too cool for a picnic; the sun held no real heat, a facade too. I went along with it all—pretending the men had no pasts—and made small talk with a classmate. The day of the picnic was supposed to be fun, but for me it was tense, orchestrated, and not fun at all. Every face mouthing a few attempts at neighborly introductions or smiling to a total stranger represented loss and pain, and I felt a deep, aching sadness for such ordinary citizens who wound up paying the price for their leaders' mistakes and power plays. And their numbers horrified me the most.

Under the trees three women began singing in Spanish, eyes large and sad, strumming guitars to a Latin tune, emotional and patriotic. Two tall, robed, and turbaned African women sang, in high, little-girl voices, with wide, toothy smiles. The Middle Easterners danced like Greeks, in a row, arm in arm, kicking forward with a slow, low step, joined unexpectedly by the Chilean coffee lady. A dozen Vietnamese posed in family photograph precision, tall folks at back, short ones at front, singing and strumming a guitar. Two Filipino girls delicately swayed to the music in a national dance. Petite, in colorful native dresses, they sashayed slowly down in front of the crowd, pointing their toes like ballerinas and pinching their full skirts out and up into butter-fly wings.

People called for the school caretaker to increase the volume of the stereo which played taped music for the dancers. He tried without success, shaking his head every few minutes as requests mounted. No, something *var feil*, was wrong; it would not play any louder. The uncooperative equipment reflected the real problem. Nothing was really right. When you're a thirty-five-year-old refugee with no job, how do you dance? How do you sing when you're sad or lonely, can't get hired, and have to depend on the government to feed your family? The problem was reflected all the way to the stereo. Something *was* wrong; something *var feil.*

Outside, over the walls of the compound, did anyone else know or care? Innocuous as they looked, the festivities, because of the reason they were there at all, were terribly serious. I pushed my cooling pizza around the plate, keeping my eyes moving, never catching anyone's gaze for long, pretending to look as though everything was fine.

On the way home a thousand angry, frustrated feelings stormed in my heart. My voice, where was my voice to say something? People torn from their own lands. Killings. Was this what human beings did to one another? The enormity of their problems overwhelmed me.

The *Avis* duly reported the ravages of Balkan wars. Photographs showed escapees from the border Balkan states requesting asylum. Norwegian Lutheran churches offered refuge, and church leaders lent financial and spiritual support. No police came to drag the desperate people out, and I doubted they ever would.

Considering its small size, maybe Norway was doing all it could because the flow of displaced people was like a torrent. The country's humanitarian stance of accepting large numbers of them stirred up controversy among its own citizens, yet where could the refugees go and weren't they entitled to live humanely and in freedom *somewhere?*

"Were it possible for us to see further than our knowledge reaches, and yet a little way beyond the outworks of our divining, perhaps we would endure our sadnesses wtih greater confidence than our joys."
—From *Letters to a Young Poet* by Rainer Maria Rilke

4

A Wonderful, Windy Winter

All winter ferocious winds had blown heavily across the sound, pouching in our picture windows. Whining like predators against our protesting refuge, they jettisoned the dogs' bowls across the deck at night so that the eerie thumping woke me. Out on the deck I struggled to secure everything nature was blowing away—lawn chairs, tables, flowerpots—managing after much effort to force open a shed door and squeeze everything safely inside. All the while I worried the kitchen door might slam itself shut, and I could wind up locked outside in minus degree temperatures, in my nightgown, with no chance of my husband hearing me banging to get back in. Unrelenting, the storm raked everything on and around the island: the seas, trees, trash can lids, and old leaf piles.

Next day, Nicky, my Newfoundland-mix, and I edged along the crumbling concrete and steel jetty, nervous but exhilarated by being part of the roaring storm. The spray spewed warnings to get back, and we did, letting the wind power us back up the hill. My dog's long black coat flattened in the wind, and he glanced up happily as we scrambled up the slope, with me almost breathless. He was back by my side, thank goodness, and memories of his four-month quarantine were fading. In the safety and quiet of indoors, Nicky gulped his water while I settled in the corner, lights off, to watch the picture show.

The onslaught against our windows kept up for hours and I imagined they would explode inwards any minute, but our landlord's father, Einar, had assured us they would not. Nevertheless, watching the glass pressed in night after night, I expected a breaking point. Nothing seemed secure enough to withstand such constant tugging and buffeting. Perhaps some surprised lady in northern Norway would even find someone else's laundered drawers on her clothesline next day?

Evenings came early still, at four or five o'clock, and light did not return until almost eight the next morning. Distant lights moved across the water; two ships slid north to Haugesund, another south to Kopervik or Stavanger. Who was on board, and what did the ships carry? It was all so new to me, living on the water, and I took to it like the proverbial duck. I had my personal MTV outside my windows—Maritime Television.

When North Sea winds scoured the coast, vessels sheltered in our cove for a night or two. One January night the number of lights fore and aft indicated three ships at anchor, swinging in line with the waves and tides, colored dots of light sketching their positions. Mike and I began rating storms on a one to five scale; five for a five-ship night, four for a four-ship night, down to a paltry one for a one-ship night. Nights and mornings were so charged with delicious mystery about the ships in our marine parking lot, I became addicted to their business. Telescope and binoculars were keyholes into their world. We observed crews on deck, men fishing over the side. One night a red flame danced in the darkness and I feared one of the boats was on fire, but our telescope caught the serious expression of a lone crew member tossing debris into a bin and watching the sparks fly up into a moonless night.

At daybreak or sooner, if the winds had abated, the ships prepared to leave. They awaited the pilot boats which roared into the bay like race boats. Almost on top of a ship, the small vessels eased back, slid alongside, lingered for a momentary caress, then sped back toward the pilot's station at Kopervik, streaming a bubble of water. If a ship managed to slip away before I got up, I felt cheated as I loved watching the process of departure. Perhaps a big, old Russian vessel with a Cyrillic name, deck glinting with a mini car park—vehicles acquired legally or not, locals hinted, would be heading off, or a container ship or ships we couldn't identify at all. Whatever their missions were, each left silently, swinging around after puffing smoke with the exertion, maneuvering into position, then cut forward frothing at bow and stern. I whispered the captain good-bye, regretting I still knew nothing about his life on the sea, although it had touched mine for a few hours. For all their sense of freedom and intrigue, ships promised a hard, risky life. Were the men out there Russian, Filipino, Romanian, a few Norwegian? Would many return to homelands short on basics and luxuries? The ships left, leaving me to flounder in a wake of unanswered questions.

When this you see
Remember me
Tho' many miles
We distant be.

— Writer unknown (written on an antique milk jug
in Haugesund Museum)*

* All 'Sea Poems' are reproduced exactly as they were written on various pieces of old china in Haugesund Museum.

Getting to school and back each day brought me back to earth as it required a physical workout. Struggling to remain vertical and warm, off I went each morning, over icy ruts, through slush puddles, zapped by sleet or lathered in snow, leaning into or away from the wind. Bundled in layers galore and a scarf long and sturdy enough to be used as an escape rope during a prison breakout, and squinting my eyes half closed to protect them from snow, I could barely see where I was going. By the time I closed in on the bus stop, late, I turned into a sort of runaway missile. A few times I watched the bus disappear, its driver oblivious to the fact I had risked cardiac arrest to get as close as I did. None of the passengers saw me through the steamy windows, so nobody buzzed the bell for him to stop.

I waited an hour for the next bus, stamping my cold feet and doing my previous night's homework in the cell-like bus shelter. Although I was able to shine with linguistic brilliance when I finally did get to class, everything fresh in my mind, I couldn't quite shake the deep body chill.

After school one afternoon I bought two bottles of wine from the state-run wine and liquor outlet, the *Vinmonopolet*. They would add a warm touch to dinner, I felt, despite the expensive price. Clanking past a neighbor, however, in the home stretch and with my guard down nearly ruined everything. The red, plastic *Vinmonopolet* bag swung on my arm and the telltale sound revealed my unfortunate habit. The man's eyes bored through the plastic bag and then away. He tugged his child closer and away from the Demon Drink and Drinker, ignoring my sociable greeting. I felt sure our reputation was ruined forever with the teetotalers in our neighborhood. The first chance I could, I slipped the symbol of our depravity into my book bag hoping its proximity to *Ny i Norge* would redeem me civically if not morally. Next time wine bottles would go straight into an innocent white plastic supermarket bag so I could walk home with my halo shining.

At home, jacket and bags dropped to the floor while I hid my loot behind a wall of liter-size soda bottles. Best to take no chances. The German white wine did enhance our meal later on, but regrets lingered. How I would have liked another chance to explain to our neighbor. "We are not party people. Surely you can forgive a little Blue Nun?"

Fortunately the sad-eyed man kept our lapse to himself because people still nodded and smiled at us, and the children waved. Perhaps my disciplined school habits exonerated me. We were on the right track and all we needed were friends, people to come inside our lovely house on the water and talk to us.

The universe heard my wish and, as became a regular pattern, fulfilled it in an unexpected way. Our house came with an unreliable wiring system, and Einar was an expert in its foibles. When the house went dark after a powerful storm had raged all day, we called for his help. Using a flashlight and after much squinting inside the breaker box and up in the attic, he clicked all the right switches and we had light. A celebratory drink of wine seemed in order, and our landlord's father was of a different school from our other neighbor.

"That would be very nice, very nice indeed!" he said, slipping out of his warm jacket and cap and leaving his shoes, Norwegian style, next to the front door. Our cache of wine lurking in the shadows was tapped. Einar was our first real visitor, and we were ready to celebrate, especially on a wild, windy night, new in our house and not knowing how it worked under pressure. As well as being our landlord's father, our guest was also a neighbor—and neighborly relationships were what we wanted. Tonight was a start. We three entered the room with the big windows overlooking the water and did a polite shuffling dance until our guest eased down onto our couch with the gentle sigh of a man about to have something nice happen to him. It must have felt strange for him to sit in his son's house with an entirely new set of people and furniture. But the times and economy dictated it. His son's work, like Mike's, centered on the energy business and had caused him to abandon his home temporarily. Family ties were loosened and I was sure our neighbor must miss his grandchildren.

If Einar felt at all uncomfortable, he hid it well for he was relaxed, genial, and easy to talk with. Softening evening shadows washed across his face, and his deep, resonant voice filled the room. He possessed a marvelous depth of character and the same ability to appreciate the funny side of life that my father-in-law did. I began to feel he was family. Perhaps we could adopt Einar if he were willing? We celebrated the evening's fellowship against the elements by opening our cherished Texas Messina Hof port put aside for very special occasions.

Nicky plopped his big, black head, unasked, across the visitor's lap, and Einar stroked him, complimenting him in a low, pleased tone saying he too used to have a dog and liked them. Two hours slipped away as we three found comfort in one another's company. Over the wine and conversation we got to know Einar and get a feel for everyone else in the neighborhood. I hoped our friendship would transcend our rental agreement. The storm could do its worst; we were warm and content and had nothing to worry about as long as Einar was there.

Mike stretched back in a leather recliner while I sat in my favorite corner by the window. Einar, who was a big man, almost six feet with a full face topped by a balding head, made himself comfortable among the loose sofa cushions. Winds howled against the windows, forcing jets of cold air in through ventilation ducts built into the wooden frames. Ebbing and flowing conversation cocooned me like a soft, wool blanket.

In a room facing a windblown, boiling fjord on a small island, hardly a dot on the edge of the Scandinavian landmass, we had left the realm of any world I had ever known. No satellite could even begin to find us. Places we used to call home were lost from my heart or memory. Did we even exist? We had dropped off the American map, the world map, and were invisible.

Yet we were tucked away in a tiny hamlet in Norway hearing stories from an old sea captain. Sea captains and Norway, tales of the high seas! It seemed more storybook than real.

Our guest's seafaring history went back years, and his vast, general knowledge of the world and its peoples was entertaining and thought provoking. Strangely the body of water that bothered him the most wasn't the rough North Sea. "The Mississippi River!" he said. "That's the one I didn't like so much." His reminiscences from sea and land were just a taste of what we would come to expect from him. Interspersing our stories, we three strangers traveled through one another's personal diaries and feelings vitae. Mike and I had no need to struggle to think of a "foreign" word either for our guest was comfortable with English and did not expect us to speak Norwegian. Karmøy people had strong ties to America, he said, and English would not be a problem. He failed to tell us about his wife, Else, however. On telephoning their house soon after, we learned that she spoke only Norwegian.

Darkness and shadows, soft lights and fellowship drew out words, freeing us from daylight's urgencies which trim conversations down to short, superficial news bulletins and polite exchanges. Time was our free luxury that night, being together, talking, exploring one another's character and experience, really reading one another's eyes. Voices and laughter blended. We smelled the melting candle wax, tasted the rich red wine, felt the storm's strengths, curled our fingers around our drinking glasses, examined the texture of chair cushions, caressed the silky haired cat, studied one another's expressions, listened to Nicky grinding his bone, touched hands in friendship, felt brotherhood. The enactment and interaction were almost art: aural, spoken, emotional, and tactile.

Despite his compliments of it, Einar's wine was mostly for nursing and I wondered if he didn't like it and was too polite to say anything. When he drained it half an hour before he left, my concerns vanished. "Hmm. Very nice! Very nice!" he commented. He pressed the lingering flavor to his tongue, nodding approvingly, remarking that it tasted like one of his own homemade wines. As we got to know him, we learned that this was his style—waiting until it was almost time to leave before really drinking it.

At a quarter to ten he unfolded his arms and legs from yielding cushions and prepared to leave, bidding good-bye to the dogs with regret and as nicely as he did to us. I felt we had passed the test. He liked us and our animal family. He thanked us for the pleasant evening, assured us we would have no more problems with the electricity that night, and retrieved his shoes by the front door. He unhooked his flat navy seaman's cap and pulled on his warm jacket. With a final smile he took off into the blustery wind and rain for his two-minute walk home. I felt sad watching him go. It had been a long time since we had had people in or stood with them on the doorstep, saying our good-byes. The night had been a good omen that it would happen more often.

Inside, our den was still rich with the residual atmosphere of cozy intimacy, three glasses marking our places. At last our house had a lived-in feel and all because of Einar's company. His visit had also given us our first few hours in months actually to talk about something other than moving. I missed him already. We turned off the lights, blew out the candles, and went down-stairs to bed. As I fell asleep listening to the wind, I felt his visit pointed to a change in our fortunes. We could not afford to live outside Norwegian life any more, and shouldn't. For the first time since we had arrived in Norway, I felt quite certain that Mike and I had a chance to belong, and with our neighbor's kind help, we might make it.

For those who enjoy winter as I do, perhaps part of it has to do with watching rain pelting the window or hearing the wind rattling the roof from the comfort of a warm and safe living room. Norwegians are masters of warm homes. Heated bath-room floors and skylights placed so that you can lounge in your bathtub watching snowflakes land not six feet away on the cold glass surely merited some practical type of Nobel Prize.

Thanks to a massive shopping spree before we left Houston, I was well supplied with warm clothes, and I bought more in Norway. Coddled against chills both psychological and physical, I had been in a sort of hibernation at the very time Karmøy had been too.

Over the months I tiptoed over her snowy fields, watched ponds turn into ice and thin sticks of trees and bushes droop with snow. I felt her steady breathing all winter when wild winds tore across the little island and strummed eerie solar music from strings of giant electricity cables. When the Atlantic raced inshore at Åkrehamn, I felt the beach dissolve under my feet while the sea flung sand crystals at my cold cheeks and bonded with salt on my eyeglasses.

Mike and I gave up trying to walk into the wind when it bent us nearly double. Crouched, almost flat, behind some dunes, we struggled to keep our eyes open in the gusts. Almost blown off our feet, we finally left, letting the storm have Åkrehamn beach to herself. Winds and sea action; beaches blown and rocks thrashed against; grass and rain steeping into soup with salt and manure seasonings; soils freezing, melting, and mushing into mud, and freezing again imparted the Nordic air with a bite of continually changing odors. Each morning I checked the bay for ship traffic, then sniffed the air, testing it like a wine steward.

Most days began with a walk across the fields, in wet weather or cold, before class. All the little corners, shrubs, trees, ditches, ponds, and creatures along my path became familiar friends. The island's natural garden of mountains, water and wind, birds and nature was mine alone during those walks, awesome and absorbing. The breeze carried my heart and soul through the northern universe. Mind and spirit reached for that elusive chord into eternity, came to agreements and understandings, and received answers to things I had not known I was questioning. In the face of nature's perfect order, my own conflicts and anxieties shrank. All yesterday's mistakes were forgiven; she gave me a new day, another chance. "Morning time has gold in her mouth," the Viking saying went, and I believed it.

A fisherman, dressed in orange oilskins, worked in his dinghy out in the cove. Bent over his nets, he believed he had the world to himself. His tiny boat bobbed gently with the tide, the majestic scene an uncertain ally. Like thousands of fisherman before him, and that day like thousands which had passed before, he fished in surroundings which had not changed for centuries. The sky could hurl rain, snow, or gale-force winds, depending on her mood, driving his boat against rocks, sinking it, even drowning him, yet experience had taught him what he could and could not do with dangerous and beautiful nature as his landlord; he was completely at home on the living, breathing Mother Sea.

My Lad is far upon the sea
The bark that bears him far from us
I hope he will safe Return
And from his earnings I'll save up
If lucky he should be.
And then when old with me shall stop
And go no more to SEA.

—Writer unknown
(Words inside an antique bowl, Haugesund Museum)

I admired his self-reliance and methodical toil. It confirmed that wise men should never totally count on technology. As long as people and armies destroy lands and livelihoods, we might only be left with the natural bounty of the ocean to survive on.

What if we have all forgotten how to feed ourselves like this—or if we ever knew in the first place? Certainly I have never caught a fish and would have to rely on a man like him to keep me alive.

I walked on. Total certainty that I was quite safe walking alone was almost a revelation. In Houston concern about personal safety had always held me back to some degree and I had always chosen my walking routes carefully. It was not until I lived on Karmøy that I realized that this limitation, and worry, had also stifled my creativity.

My daily route took me past our mailboxes, past the last few straggling houses near some farms, then across Norsk-Hydro's main entrance on to graveled roads across the fields. On the way I might catch sight of neighbor Gudrun's cat sitting motionless, pretending not to care that an enormous, swaggering bird was stealing its food from a saucer.

Audaciously the bird passed in front of the cat again, a nugget of food clamped in its beak. Some days the cat got its revenge, though, by darting low and determinedly across our lawn to intercept scraps meant for the birds. This sent flustered, squawking avians up into the safety of the trees, where they watched their rival sniffing the food even though he didn't want it. It was the surprise attack, the streaking out from the bushes at top speed more than serious eating that he enjoyed.

Nature was full of surprises: A blur of black cats streaking across the low horizon materialized into a low flying flock of long, black birds. Snow, gray clouds blending with the landscape, rocks, taupe-colored boulders, black cats, or birds? Hidden elements teased the imagination, reminding me of some of American Bev Doolittle's beautiful camouflage-style paintings. And on foggy days, land, mountains, and water appeared to dissolve into a veil of gray and a cruise ship's white swan-like hull looked smeary and nicotine-colored.

One morning two crows flew close to one another, crying out warnings. Landing on a rock, stabbing at the air with their beaks, heads chopping up and down like hammers, they vied for control of something invisible, maybe territory alone. A third bird swooped in between the quarrelers, forcing them back. The angry cries ceased simultaneously. The two fighters stalked stiffly

away, backs turned, then flew off. The mediator lingered a couple
of moments to make sure the squabble didn't start up again, then
he flew off too.

Watching birds resolve a dispute reminded me how
poorly some politicians and governments handle problems to do
with property rights. Land, the plot of earth you stood on, were
born on, or wanted was, according to human history, both the
source of all security and the heart of all warfare. People fought
for it. Yet with the approach of the twenty-first century, could
men still not accomplish what simple birds instinctively knew and
utilize negotiation instead of aggression? The natural way to do
things was never so obvious as on Karmøy, where the island lived
and breathed peace.

5

Neighbors, Nicky & the Children

Re-engagement with nature offered solace when friend-ships remained elusive. School camaraderie was all I had, and Einar waved at us from his driveway, but where was everyone else? Winter's cold, short days contrived to keep our neighbors hidden, and cultural assimilation remained torturously slow. On bad days I wavered between raging internally about the situation and gritting my teeth and hanging on a bit longer. I found the thought of just going back to Texas, buying a small house, and living there for periods of time popping into my mind as an answer to a problem I was losing patience with.

Fortunately things were about to change. My doorbell rang one morning, and a woman smiled and introduced herself. "Hello! I am Hanna, your neighbor," she explained, waving at houses across the lane. "I live over there."

"My friend and I would like you to come to lunch," she announced. I tried to contain my total look of surprise and gathered my manners. "Thank you! I'd love that. When would you like me to come?" I replied. "Today," she answered as though it were assumed—"now." I snatched up my coat and followed her.

Over at the corner house, two doors down, I recognized Liv's voice ringing out from the main living area. "Hello! Come in!" Cinderella going to the ball could not have felt more pleased than I was to be asked to lunch. Since it was so unexpected, I suspected Einar was at the bottom of it and, if so, he once again proved a valuable conduit and friend. Sit down, they urged, and we arranged ourselves around the kitchen table. They put me at ease right away, and over hot fruit tea and open-faced sand-wiches, we got to know one another. Liv was a nurse, and her empathetic attitude matched her avocation. She talked about her children. We'd seen two teenage girls, and I knew her two boys from their activities around the lane. Hanna, small-boned with a head of thick, curly brown hair, had a bright, sparkly way and a quick smile. She too had a brood of youngsters, but I wasn't clear how many.

Liv and Hanna were childhood friends, close as sisters, and both spoke English well despite their protestations to the contrary. Liv's first question on move-in day still worried me though, so I explained how my Norwegian classes were going and that I tried hard to use their language whenever I could. They seemed to make sense of my Norwegian and my confidence soared. Maybe I *was* pronouncing words properly. When I shared some recent blunders in Norwegian, Liv promptly shared one of her own, in English. "When I was working at a hospital in Stavanger, we were treating an American patient. I said to him, 'You must wait for a moment. I have to put a snake down your throat!' He looked scared! The correct word should have been *tube*, but I didn't say it right!"

She replayed the drama vigorously, trying to duplicate her apologetic expression and the man's horrified one, and Hanna and I laughed uproariously. That first good laugh was medicine to me and released months of built-up tension from worrying about how I was doing and if I could cope in Norway. We had something in common, these ladies and I, and I felt less isolated from their society. When we parted later, I floated home on cloud nine. I had acquired some *friends!* And having tested out my school-style Norwegian, I was thrilled that it worked!

The following week Hanna came over for lunch. She eyed my tuna-stuffed pita breads with restraint and I was glad I could offer cheese rolls as well. Was she used to eating tuna fish? I inquired. "Yes, but ... I've never seen it made like this. No. I would never do this," she stated, eating bravely. During lunch she told me her husband, Thomas, had been born in the United States, of Norwegian parents. Sometimes they went over for visits or on business.

"I was in Memphis and went to Elvis Presley's home, Graceland, once," she related between mouthfuls. "We went around it, saw everything."

The King's passionate croonings and lifestyle seemed hard to reconcile against her family's conservatism. Did they tour Graceland because they had a certain number of hours to kill on a layover in Memphis? I would never know. Still, Hanna astonished me that day as being my closest encounter to Elvis's world to date, and that this unlikely contact lived in an equally unlikely place, a little Norwegian island, surely merited inclusion in a record book somewhere.

She also inadvertently awarded me an undeserved compliment when I mentioned my regular habit of exercising to a videotape. "Oh," she commented with a touch of admiration. "I do not have the character to do that." "Character" was not exactly the right term, and I leafed through my dictionary later. It showed a number of interchangeable words and meanings in Norwegian concerning character, principles, and self-discipline, but I had warmed to her definition and tried it on for size. To have character, that prized attribute, thrust upon me even when I did not merit it felt remarkably good and stabilizing after feeling unsure of where I stood for so long.

Before she left, my new friend agreed to evaluate my

Bokmål-style reading from my textbook. She listened attentively, commending me afterward. Additionally, she volunteered to help me out with the country's other official language. "Would you like me to read the same piece to you in *Nynorsk?* Even in *dialekt?*" I clicked on my tape recorder. None of the *Nynorsk* registered at all. Why was I even learning *Bokmål* in school if Hanna and the other local people used a different one? Trying to read along was useless. No sooner had I found a word that looked and sounded vaguely familiar, than she had almost finished. She looked at me expectantly and I tried to hide my confusion. All told, this lesson over tuna sandwiches proved way beyond my capabilities. Rather conveniently, the tape of Hanna reading from my book mysteriously disappeared soon after she left and I never found it again.

Buoyed by my acquisition of two Norwegian friends, I subscribed to the *Haugesunds Avis,* the local newspaper, although I could rarely understand the headlines unless there were helpful photographs. But at least having the orange saddle-bagged boy spin his bicycle into our driveway daily to throw the *Avis* elevated me from my role of illiterate outcast.

As it turned out, spoken language proved easier for me than the written, and when I visited Einar's wife, Else, she gave me all the practice I needed since she didn't utter a word in English. *"Du er flink! Du er flink!"* she would insist, looking thrilled, assuring me I was good in Norwegian. During the months ahead I visited Else often, watching her knit or sew for an hour or two, with Einar popping in and out. I nibbled on homemade delicacies in her flower-decked living room and dragged up all my *norsk* vocabulary, hoping I was not the worst conversationalist she had known. Every *flink* was a stamp of approval, and I wanted to believe a nice lady like that could never lie, could she?

Just as I was getting the hang of the language, Mike dropped a bombshell. He and some others at work would start an intensive, accelerated, Norwegian language course. The material looked slick and sophisticated and, when he told me he would achieve this expertise in twelve full days plus homework assignments, I felt under attack. Up to that point I had been sole reader and speaker of any Norwegian in the family and gained a modest claim to fame from it. All the winter days of class had earned me that right. How could my husband steal victory from me, his poor spouse, when he already had something important to do? Managing part of the construction of the world's largest tension-leg oil platform and the first using concrete surely was enough. All I had was my language class, and I wanted desperately to succeed in that. The worst part was the twelve days. I had yet to finish twelve weeks and was nowhere ready for tests of any kind.

Tor consoled me the next day. "The guy running that program must be a miracle man," he said, shaking his head in disbelief. I agreed. I felt a burst of fierce loyalty to him and our low-budget community classes. *We* didn't *need* any fancy programs; the basics were tried and true—and working, I triumphed.

Guilt clouded my joy. Mike deserved my support, but he was on his own. His fast program would not intimidate me. Plodding progress was better than none, and justice would surely be mine. As in the fable of the tortoise and the hare, I hoped I would reach the finishing line first.

Not long after, Liv invited me over again, this time for a church-related evening. Whether it was something to do with the Norwegian Seaman's Church, a local evangelical church, or some overseas missions, I didn't know, but getting invited inside a Norwegian's home twice in one month was a heady experience, far exceeding anything that had happened in ten months in Oslo. We "foreigners" were integrating, and I felt that being happy in Norway at last was a real possibility.

Liv had exited her daily cocoon of sturdy winter jacket and loose jeans to reveal a slim figure in a flowing skirt beneath which high-heeled dress shoes peeked out. Only in the nick of time had I changed out of slacks into more appropriate dress, thanks to my husband's suggestion. About a dozen women, many older than I, found seats under the sloping eaves of Liv and Egil's rustic home. Unsure of what was expected, I sank into a large armchair hoping to blend into the furniture. My hostess introduced her friends to me and their happy-you're-here expressions indicated they weren't surprised about the stranger in their midst. A few spoke to me in English until two ladies made some announcements and read aloud from letters, from missionaries in faraway places, I speculated.

Afterward the group pulled hymn books from their purses as neighbor, Gudrun, sat at the piano. Her energetic playing infused the atmosphere, stirring each voice to sing and praise. I went into quiet shock. We were singing hymns, but nothing from my childhood, and the effect of singing in a confined space touched on the claustrophobic. Private spirituality took a back seat. No matter how I felt, I was committed for the evening.

A tall lady next to me glanced at me with concern and quickly saw a way to remedy my discomfort. She thrust her songbook into my hand, pointing out where we were and singing with gusto into my ear. If her powerful voice were any indication, she was a Christian who would brook no nonsense, so I tried obediently to get a grip on the tune and my emotions. My mouthing of word-like sounds in Norwegian pleased her for she began encouraging me with "Good girl!" This lady's rather forceful attitude and several "Good girls" later made me feel she would be a perfect maternity coach. "That's right! Breathe! Push! Good girl!"

Slowly the aura of warmth and goodness overcame my initial guilt and regrets that I was unworthy of being there. In the small room, filled with good-hearted, friendly women, I was safe from the cold, dark Nordic night, from unnamed fears, the world. Nothing bad could get to me through the sturdy wall of their kindred spirituality which permeated every body, soul, and thing there. I felt blessed to be part of such powerful company. My anxiety about being in a strange country where I knew so little about the people subsided. Later Liv started plates of food around, and no one made any special fuss of the visitor. Merely sitting around a table, sharing food, meant more than almost anything. I felt I belonged. I had been in Norway for what seemed a long time, but it was only then in an ordinary living room that I had felt cared for by its people. My long stretch of separateness was at last, thankfully, coming to an end.

Neighbors at that gathering included Elise, whose home overlooked our local monument, the mailbox where the children liked to play and chatter to us as we passed by. Mike and I grew to appreciate Elise and her husband, Karl. Their comfortable home with flower-decked windowsills calmed and nurtured, and Elise always welcomed us at the door with a smile. An invitation to coffee would be a treat—sandwiches, delicious homemade cakes, and *vafler* served on pretty floral china displayed on a hand-embroidered white tablecloth. Fresh flowers brightened the table. Elise invariably lit a tall table candle and, after a nod from her husband, led the sung grace. *"O Du som metter liten fugl, velsign vår mat, O Gud."* O Thou who feeds the little bird, so bless our food, O God. *Aaah-men!* This grace, to me, was her signature, and I joined in once I knew the words. Before we left Norway, Elise and Karl presented us with a picture of a child saying that prayer and it hangs today in my kitchen in Houston reminding me of these two very special people who reached out to us.

I didn't understand it at the time, but there was symbol-ism in that picture from Elise. Children took a starring role in our new life overseas. They clustered around us whenever they saw us outside, giggling, asking questions, practicing their English. Conversations about pets, mail, and where we came from forged a foundation of trust in which language could be explored with no fear of embarrassment on any side. They couldn't understand why we had no children, but soon the novelty of our foreignness and, particularly our dogs, took over.

Liv-Marit, a freckle-faced, blue-eyed eight-year-old, was the first to speak to us as we walked the dogs. Fascinated with 110-pound Nicky, she dropped to his side with an adoring look, asking me his name. The child pressed her small cheek against his massive head.

"Nicky!" she repeated with delight. "Beautiful . . . beautiful!" She stared rapturously into space, running her hands through his shiny coat. Nicky's expressive eyes filled with happiness and he gave a doggy smile, tongue flopping. I glowed with pride as he soaked up the attention. "Beautiful" was a mighty compliment from the petite girl who had never had an English lesson but whose dreamy look more than eloquently summed up her feelings about Nicky.

Our big dog charmed the children and they fussed over him lavishly. No matter what we said, they insisted our pets had to be pedigrees. Perhaps they just looked different from those they were used to, but it was only an accident of emigration that had elevated our Greensheet fifteen-dollar Cockapoo, abandoned Newfy-Chow-something-mix, and stray kitten to possible purebred status. Whenever we walked the dogs, the children dropped their bikes and climbed out of yards to pet them and chat with us. They were kind and patient with us newcomers and of course it didn't hurt that we had a dog like Nicky, an amiable, international ambassador.

Nicky quickly adapted to the kinder, gentler world of Håvik and immediately forgot his watchdog duties, so he barely opened his eyes when the daily *Avis* whizzed through the hallway over his head. Our paperboy always opened the front door and tossed the paper indoors. This relaxed attitude about security was new to us but common on Karmøy. Residents exchanged keys and information on spare keys and sometimes left basement doors unlocked. Liv added my house key to her special pot of secret keys around the house. Just about everybody knew where everybody else was hiding their keys and their neighbors' keys, and I suspected that Brinks Security in the United States would have been alarmed, both literally and operationally, had it heard of such a system.

One day the door chime announced a giggling Liv-Marit and best friend, Kristine, thrusting a bunch of wild flowers into my hands. Their loving ways touched me, but triggered troubling thoughts about my former city world. Why couldn't American children be free like this? American children seemed to live in cars, buses, their houses, and fenced yards. Even on Halloween night, parents trailed their children, scrutinizing the "trick or treat" candy. Americans in cities did not trust their neighbors and, accordingly, couldn't trust their children to be around them either. What did this say about the society?

The girls peered into the hall. Big happy barks echoed behind the inside door, and the real reason for their visit was clear.

"Oh! Nicky!" they chorused and I was putty in their hands after the bouquet. *"Vil du komme inn?"* Would you like to come in? "Yes!" they cried and rushed indoors, hands out-stretched to the dog. They stroked him affectionately as his tail swished with joy. Their little fingers lighted tentatively on any part that stayed still as he performed some kind of happy sideways dance trying to make sure he got the maximum amount of attention. Liv-Marit's voice danced up the scale with apprehension. "Ooh! O-o-o-o-o-OOO!" finishing on a very high C as Nicky pushed his face next to hers.

Ten chaotic minutes later everyone had calmed down. Their first date was a success and real love, not the puppy variety. The ooh's and aaah's and Nicky's ear-to-ear smile promised that my love-struck dog and his admirers would be going steady from then on.

The two girls became regular visitors and brought others who became regulars too. Their natural curiosity about our foreign knickknacks helped banish their initial shyness. Before long they settled into a routine of showing up after school, saying hello to all the pets, peeking through the telescope, and cluster-ing around the coffee table to draw, flip through books, and play with gadgets and games. Little neighborhood girls' faces became so commonplace at our house mid-afternoon that when a totally unknown little creature rang the bell, hurried inside, and began slipping off her jacket and winter boots, I assumed that the grapevine had established us as okay people who never turned a child away. Many days four or more might be camped in our house, playing, teaching each other the Tiddly Winks game, or engrossed in their favorite pastime, drawing. We all spoke in a mixture of Norwegian and English. Liv-Marit, however, almost preferred to speak in English, a great help to me, and she translated things the others said. Kristine understood English but, unwilling to speak it, she limited herself to "Yes, no, thank you," and a wonderfully formal, enunciated and exuberant "GOOD-bye!" which I felt she must have picked up from British films or British school text books for older grade students. One of our little visitors spoke no English and reacted blankly to my old reliable *"Hvordan har du det?"* How are you? Repeats and different inflections did not help, and later one of the girls happily clued me in.

"Next time ask her, *'Kos har du det?'* She understands dialect." They were right. Monika's big gray eyes lit up just slightly as she softly answered *"Bare bra,"* the standard phrase meaning "just fine." When I asked it again, just to be sure, she looked at me as if she couldn't imagine what the fuss was about, making me feel rather foolish.

Tor adamantly shunned any teaching of dialect, but had he done so, I could have better understood an electrician. When the man launched into a sentence beginning with egg-something-or-other, I wondered what his choice for breakfast had to do fixing our outlets. Our confused exchange had us scrambling our eggs until his colleague stepped in. The *"egg"* sound was Haugesund dialect for the first-person pronoun "I,' spelled as *jeg* in *Bokmål* and pronounced *"yiy. "* Clearly dialect was very different from our textbook *Bokmål.* No wonder I had been unable to decipher any of it despite Hanna's valiant effort.

Mike's intensive language course soon went by the board, and secretly I was glad. I held onto my hard-won and rightful position as the main Norwegian speaker in our house.

My schoolbook's predictable realms supplemented by

casual conversation with the children proved a perfect combination. They taught me word and thing combinations and correct pronunciations, and in their sympathetic company, if I failed to improve, it was through no fault of theirs. In a homey atmosphere over cookie-making sessions, vegetable choppings, drawing, playing with the pets, or just hanging around, we eased in and out of language. The older ones benefited too by balancing formal classroom English with the Morgan household's variety, all the while learning our customs. I felt more relaxed with the children than I did in the adult world. Children's honesty too opened up our different lifestyles to one another. Kristine insisted on helping set the table one evening but kept glancing at the clock. *"Hvorfor spiser du så sent?"* Why were we eating so late? Six-thirty was late by local standards, so I had to explain that Mike worked a long day, ten and eleven hours.

Mike's absence from seven or so each morning until six o'clock or later was a fact of life. He had his job, his life at work, and I had to deal with that. Fortunately I was self-motivated and independent and wanted to fill those hours productively. The expatriate company spouses I had known in Oslo—not all were women—all seemed to share a sort of stalwart independence. Whatever their transferred spouses did, their partners managed to operate their lives accordingly, almost genetically predisposed to self-containment. They managed in new countries, created new homes, and kept smiling. One friend had moved fifteen times in twenty-five years. Many expressed both excitement and regret at transferring overseas and ensuing upheavals. The hardest part was leaving family, friends, aging parents, or grandparents who would miss the grandchildren, yet the upside was seeing Europe and Asia, meeting people from different cultures, and developing new interests and hobbies.

One Norwegian woman shared how she felt when her husband told her he had accepted a job in Houston. "I cried at first! But we enjoyed it and felt sorry, in a way, to go back afterwards. But three years was long enough; I wanted to get back to my parents as my father was old and quite ill." Another, an

Australian, moved abroad on only the most skimpy of corporate relocation information. "They really don't tell you all you need to know. If they did, they're afraid you won't go!" she said, trying to sound more lighthearted than she felt. A native of Mexico City explained that her German husband's career had taken them from Mexico to Switzerland, England, and the States, and each time she focused herself and their children on adjusting to new cultures, schools, and lifestyles. "I wish my boys hadn't abandoned their Mexican heritage, but when I say anything, they say, 'Well, Mother. It's your fault. You shouldn't have married Dad and moved us all over the world.'"

For the moment, though, the miles of cold, icy water between me and the mainland symbolized how far away I felt from everything and everyone I knew. With no previous experience with transferring overseas, no clutch of expatriate friends to compare notes with, I was certain that my problems with acculturation and adjustment were unique. I tried writing my way out of the complexities of physical, cultural, and emotional isolation. Pages of typescript piled up but failed to find form. When I stuck stamps on the envelopes, I wondered if my article queries even left the post office.

The night wrapped us in blackness as Kristine and I waited for Mike. Her dismay at the lateness of the dinner hour meal prodded some nerve. He did work a long day and who was right? The Norwegians who "worked to live" and got home at a reasonable hour or the Americans who often "lived to work" and found themselves eating later and later?

When words failed, the children turned to the dictionary. Liv-Marit became quite adept at flipping through the Berlitz English-Norwegian Dictionary to help me out, but almost shivered when handling the formidable Einar Haugen *Norsk-Engelsk Ordbok*. After she got over her fright she was able to run her little fingers up and down its imposing columns in search of some word that gave me a problem. Before long, the children had more than compensated for their size in what they contributed to my quality of life. Subconsciously my ears were tuned for the sound of the doorbell in the afternoon, and if it were silent for two days in a row, I missed them. They had become *my* little companions, a family, verification that we were a part of the Norwegian community.

The little girl who had been unable to understand my *hvordan har du det?* eventually made her mark. She had meandered over to my rising pile of typed papers one afternoon and wondered why she couldn't read a word. *"Hvorfor skriver du på engelsk?"* she inquired accusingly as though I were trying to complicate my life. Why had I written in English? Her exquisite question sent me into orbit. Obviously little Monika hadn't figured out I was English-speaking, and that surely meant my Norwegian, such as it was, had passed her scrutiny. That she was barely in school was irrelevant to one starved for linguistic success, and I preened like an exotic bird for days. Monika's talent for memorable questions did not stop there. One was a quiet *"Mike, er du gravid?"*—are you *pregnant*—as she noted his slightly protruding stomach after dinner. This sensitive little girl proceeded to whisper her way around our house on Liarveien, always brightening our days with her innocent little questions.

6

Language, Lambs, & Popcorn

Since much of my life was spent on foot—walking the neighborhood, hiking across the fields to the post office and shopping along nearby Kopervik's pedestrian high street, I took advantage of meeting people face to face. Most of the time I initiated the conversations, often with a salutatory comment about the weather or some small question. Those who made time for me were generally the youngest and the oldest, those with patience to stop and listen. It occurred to me that retirees, as well as children, had been invisible in our former Texas suburb, where even neighbors were virtual strangers, hidden behind shuttered windows and tinted automobile glass.

I chatted with neighbors, children, downtown shop owners, and an obliging lady with an unpronounceable name whom I dubbed "Rex's mother" because of her adorable little dog, Rex, who greeted me like an old friend. "Rex's mother," and Else, Einar's wife, were both Norwegian-only speakers, so it fell to me to speak their language if anything were to happen.

Another lady, Hilde, at our only grocery store soon joined the list. She and her husband ran a one-room grocery business attached to their home. For a long time I had avoided the store. I dreaded being a lone customer and unable to understand enough Norwegian to buy anything. Eventually I summoned up my courage and went in. The door slammed hard behind me and both my heart and the walls vibrated in unison. I looked around nervously. The small place was empty, and the nasty hinge, an effective watchdog, had already announced me.

Fortunately a friendly lady, Hilde, magically appeared from a back room. My little stream of "Hello, how are you, I'd like to buy so and so," and "Thank you," seemed to make sense to her and I left with some groceries and a tremendous boost to my self-confidence. Once I mastered this shopping expedition, I felt brave enough to repeat it another day.

"*Hei! Hvordan har du det?*" I inquired a little half-heartedly, hoping Hilde would not tell me exactly how she was. There was much we had not yet covered in our textbook, and I could quickly end up out of my depth. Fortunately her *bare bra!*, just fine, was easy to understand, so I risked a little more. "*Hmm, jeg trenger ... um ...*" I tried, but after a brief struggle to come up with the right words, I simply pointed at the things I needed. We wound up our affairs with amiable nods and a multiple "*takk*-ing" finale on my part as I left. Going into that shop was like going on stage at opening night of a theater production where I acted without benefit of whispered lines from a stand-in, and sometimes my nerves weren't up to it. On those occasions I took the cowardly way out by shopping in the supermarket in Kopervik. But as a stretch of cold days and icy streets continued, I knew it was safer to stay close to home and inevitable that I would audition again, soon.

An absence of Mike's evening staple, popcorn, sent me back in search of Micropop microwavable popcorn, Orville Redenbacher's distant cousin. With luck the popcorn would be in sight and I would not have to ask for it. I frantically scanned the counters and shelves. A slight sound drew my attention, and I found myself the focus of Hilde's husband's steady gaze. He looked ready, willing, and able to serve with an efficient-looking apron around his wiry frame.

"*Vær så god?*" he inquired. Gathering my full complement of literacy skills, I responded to his genial request to be of help.

"Mee-crow-pop? *Har du* any 'Mee-crow-pop?'" I enunciated. Unoffended by my brusque manner, he obligingly turned to survey his shelves, hand to his chin.

"*Nei!*" he said with the little intake of air that Norwegians do and shook his head as though he could have sworn he had just seen some somewhere, but it was all gone. The weighty quiet demanded I buy something, something right there in front so I could get out. I reviewed a cookie display, a row of canned fruit, and many mysterious packages.

We weren't totally alone. An elderly lady was surveying me quizzically. Her serviceable gray wool coat and wraparound hat fit snugly. She nodded and I smiled back, praying she wouldn't say anything, but she took it as an invitation to address me in a stream of unintelligible Norwegian while she waited for her groceries to be sacked. Dialect-laced words flew by, and all that was clear was that we were far from *Ny i Norge* territory. "*Jeg beklager men ...* I'm sorry but ... *jeg snakker bare litt norsk.*" I apologized, adding raised eyebrows and shrugged shoulders, all international sign language, I believed, for "I sorry. Me no understand, can't speak language. Very sorry."

The shopkeeper distracted her with a barrage of words which, I gathered, explained my situation—that I was new in the neighborhood and American. I felt like hugging him. A foreigner could not be expected to start answering questions she did not understand—or so I thought.

Undeterred, the lady asked me something else equally incomprehensible. In desperation I fell back on our little classroom technique. I would say something in her language just to prove that, if I had a chance at understanding a question, I could answer. I launched forth in my best memorized Norwegian.

"*Jeg er fra Amerika, jeg er på norsk kurs hver dag. Mannen*

min jobber her i Norge, vi bor at *Henriksen's hus,"* I explained,
clarifying who I was, my daily language class, my husband's work
bringing us to Norway, and where we lived, followed by an
apology for speaking *"litt norsk."* I felt sure I had laid to rest
further questioning, as well meaning as it was.

The lady nodded and the owner filled in the gaps as he
knew them, including a reference to *Håkon og Grethe's hus,* which
pegged me geographically at least. While I started edging toward
the door, she engaged me yet again, sounding matter-of-fact and
clearly assuming that now that we had those details out of the
way, she could just get back to what she wanted to talk about in
the first place.

My repeated apology, *"Jeg beklager men,"* failed to deter
her. She pointed at the ceiling and repeated her statement and I
stared up there too, hoping heavenly guidance would come to
my rescue. Unless I figured it out soon, we would be stuck there
forever. Again she tried, her gaze moving from ceiling to me,
willing me to understand. A desperate idea struck. Maybe there
was a little apartment up above the shop and she lived there?
"Oh! *Du bor* o-v-e-r t-h-e s-t-o-r-e," I stretched out the syllables
trying to sound both confident and skeptical, no mean task. She
stared back blankly, but the owner looked as frantic as a hockey
goalie intercepting a fast, hard puck.

"Nei!" he said, jabbing the air above his head for emphasis, "Water. Lots water!"

Water? Now I had a word clue. Water—a leak perhaps?
The subject had me drowning and coming up for the third time
when it hit me what water came from above, from way above
ceilings. "Rain?" I asked, hardly daring to believe it.

"JA! Regne," he said, sounding both exasperated and
relieved.

"Regne!" she repeated, smiling hesitantly as though it
should have been perfectly clear all along.

"Oh, rain! *Regne!"* I repeated just in case. "Yes, there's
been too much lately. That's why I'm carrying this!" They looked
rather astonished as I pulled out my umbrella and brandished it in

a mad sort of way. *"Ja, for mye regn!"*

Now that it was over, the three of us smiled, the shop-keeper and I with relief and a minor feeling of success under trying circumstances, and the lady, just because I finally understood. The few minutes it all took seemed forever. Such a lot of trouble and effort had gone into a little exchange about the weather. I made for the door and escape, but the persistent lady joined me on the doorstep and accompanied me along the lane. Naturally she continued talking to old chatterbox me and I caught a couple of familiar words: *"... Henriksen's hus ...?"*

I replied as intelligently as I could, *"Mmm, jah, umhumm."*

We reached a point in the path where she stopped and nodded to the right. I pointed out my path to the left. "I go this way," I explained, straight, cave-woman English being all I could muster at that weary point. Her understanding smile told me of course she knew that. We wished one another a cordial *ha det bra* and went our respective ways. At home I raided the candy jar to soothe my nerves.

These little complications weren't going to stop me from talking with Norwegians. If I was serious about talking to people, learning about their lives, I had to keep it up. The payoff was feeling tremendously satisfied when things went right. Fortune had smiled on me with Hilde in her grocery shop. When I managed something understandable, her face lighting up was my reward. From her I learned that *det var det* meant "that will be it" and that, in her store, eggs were sold loose by the kilo. Remarkably, they always stayed secure in the little paper bags she placed them in. One day I decided to try to conduct a real two-way get-acquainted conversation asking how long she had lived in Håvik, how many children she had, simple questions patterned after our classroom practices. She had already credited me with my favorite compliment *flink!* so how bad could I be?

Hilde's store was empty so I did not need to worry that I was slowing up a customer line. There would be enough time to try to think of the words I needed. I began with some light conversation, knowing that only a pinched expression around her eyes would signal I was speaking gobbledygook. When this happened, I usually dropped the subject and moved on to something else. Hilde had latched on to this odd routine well, looking quite unsurprised when we continued our conversation on a different subject. Today I was planning to expand my territory.

I began with an inquiry about her day. *"Hvordan har du det?" "Bare bra!"* she replied, indicating all was well. Pushing my wares across the counter, I said, *på norsk,* that I was going home to make dinner for my husband. She understood and said she would be doing the same shortly and we chatted about that. Hilde threw in a *flink* somewhere which acted like a multivitamin to my perennial case of low confidence in expressing myself. *Flink* was a funny-sounding little word, reminding me of "click" but meaning skillful, smart, or clever, and I cherished it. Now was my moment. I took a breath and started on the first of the questions I had practiced on the way there.

"Hvor lang har du bodde i Håvik?" (How long have you lived in Håvik?) She answered eagerly with a number which sounded like thirty or forty years. Certainly, it was many years.

"Har du barna?" (Do you have children?) I went on.

"Ja, to jenter" she said, two daughters. Did they live in our neighborhood? Well, one did, it seemed, while another lived a few miles away in a village on the way into Haugesund. My inquiries sent her whisking back behind the shop into her living room, and she returned with a formal photograph of the one who lived close by. She asked me the same question about children. I told her we didn't have any, but that my pets were almost the same. Hearing about my dogs, she disappeared again into her private quarters to get a photograph of her dog.

"Hun var så snill, så snill!" she said lovingly of a contented black lab in the picture who fitted her description of "so gentle" by acting as a pillow for a tiny baby. Hilde's voice and eyes filled with love as she looked away from the photo and back to me repeating how good-natured the dog was. She died at fourteen,

she told me, and I tried to say something in Norwegian that was appropriate. Hilde questioned me about our dogs too, and we overcame our language limitations by reading one another's feelings. She wanted to know where we kenneled our two when we went away. Once I dropped the word *hundepensjonat* (kennel) as well as the name of Torhild, who owned the doggy home-away-from-home in scenic Bjoa, Hilde looked relieved. I was so grateful we had our pets. Bringing them to Norway had been the right thing to do, no matter how complicated the government quarantine had made it. To them we owed much of our success in integrating into country life.

Later Hilde counted out my change, expressing the small number first, the larger one second. *Ni og tjue* was nine and twenty to me, but twenty-nine to her. I always sensed her disappointment in not being able to say anything in English, but she did the next best thing by patiently allowing me time to speak and time to discern her responses. Conversational-speed Norwegian still went too fast for my untuned ears, but if it were spoken slowly, I had a chance.

I said good-bye while my stock was high, clutching my little paper bag of eggs. Hilde always led me a few more steps towards language competency. The process was hard on my brain but nourished my soul. When I wanted an easy way out, I just shopped wordlessly at the supermarket, but when I wanted a kind person who would help me, I went to Hilde's.

Another lady helped me too; she was Anna, one of the neighborhood's oldest residents. We had met out walking when she streamed an incomprehensible remark at me which I answered with my usual apology about being able to speak only a little Norwegian. *"Jeg beklager, men jeg snakker bare litt norsk."*

Her bright, wise eyes understood, but she had more to say and I strained to understand.

"Hmm," I replied.

"*Du* … something, something … *gå tur?*" she asked with a friendly smile.

Now I understood two words, *gå tur*, going on a walk. "*Ja, jeg gå tur!*" I replied and she told me, I guessed, that she planned to join me. Off we went together with me wondering how I could hold up my end of the conversation and if someone so well advanced in years was up to doing a couple of miles.

Despite her age and outwardly plain country appearance, Anna sparkled as she forcefully took my arm and led me down the lane, bursting with lively chatter. Anytime I caught a couple of familiar *norsk* words, I frantically tried to get the gist of the sentence. Plumbing the depths of my Norwegian language skills, I doubted I ever came close to matching her remarks correctly or intelligently. My sole mission was to fill the air around us with any Norwegian words which seemed to fit and fall back on English ones only in desperation. This way we maintained a semblance of a two-way conversation.

An hour later I had learned she had diabetes and lost a great deal of weight and celebrated her ninetieth birthday the previous January in style with a party and dozens of cards and gifts. She had never owned a *bunad*, folk costume (too expensive, she said) and one of her peeves was that Hydro had not paid local people enough for the land when they built their aluminum processing factory. To my delight, the lambs that were just sticking their heads out into a new spring were hers, and she pointed them out with pride as we returned to her farm.

Her farmhouse sat back off the road behind a cluster of pines, and I had passed it dozens of times. Her property came to life in the spring with fluff-balls of lambs which I loved to watch and wished I could touch. She lead me into her lamb barn. Inside, five newborns sucked contentedly on an obliging row of plastic nipples. A young woman was crouched inside, taking photographs, and she looked a surprised to see me. Apparently this was a granddaughter. To reassure her that Anna had not picked up some oddball foreigner, I made a few intelligent inquiries about the feeder. The device apparently came in handy when ewes had several lambs. "These lambs will get more milk and grow better than the ones that stay with their mothers," the young woman explained.

Afterwards Anna ushered me into her dollhouse-neat farmhouse and proceeded to introduce me to generations of her family who smiled out from photographs hanging on the wall and propped up on shelves. My few basic words in Norwegian for relatives came into play, and I used them all with as much confidence and courtesy as I could, repeating familial connections to make sure I had them right. Her family was very important to her, and I felt honored to be introduced to them all. How trusting she was and could afford to be. Not fearful that I would harm her, not resistant to a foreigner, not set in her ways nor closed to new people, she stayed alive by participating in life, even welcoming newcomers into her home as she went about raising her heaven-knows-what group of new lambs in her barn. Many city people in the States might envy her independence. Fear of intruders or dependence on social services weren't part of her life. In Håvik she still managed her affairs, lived peacefully, and felt secure in inviting me in.

Anna was eager to show her interest in the original home of the English language and intently searched through drawers for ancient travel brochures from England, a place she had visited and where relatives still lived, as far as I could tell. Animatedly she recounted feelings and experiences to do with some distant trip. When words came at me too fast, I reverted to "*Hmm, Aah!* Wow! *Det var bra!*" and plenty of smiling. What she spoke of was from many yesterdays ago, yet alive and vibrant to her. We hunched over an increasing mound of books and souvenirs.

I drew forth all my Norwegian vocabulary and fell back on simple staples, amazed that she hadn't tired of me and my garbled conversation yet. Feelings and instincts drove us and her constant excursions to other parts of the room, and different cupboards produced many unused picture postcards from Britain. The number dissatisfied her, however, and she seemed bent on finding another, disappearing into other rooms and returning with more flyers and brochures.

My watch showed me time had flown. I needed to get home for dinner.

"Vil du ha kaffe eller te?" she invited, wanting me to join her for a cup of something, obviously happy for me to stay for hours more and give her more time to search for more things to show me. Her eyes sparkled with warmth and enthusiasm, and I felt she could go on for hours. My *norsk* vocabulary, alas, had its limitations, and by then I was missing too much and getting confused. I needed to make a polite escape. I shook my head apologetically.

"Nei, takk." I'm sorry. *"Jeg beklager, men mannen min kommer hjem snart og jeg må lage middag."* Saying that my husband was due home shortly and expecting his dinner was a legitimate reason to leave. Anna smiled as I mentally straightened my homemaker's halo. She nodded understandingly only to dart away and return with another handful of brochures and post-cards. Evidently we were not quite finished. The places and pictures depicted Britain from a simpler time.

She proudly handed me a stiff travel flyer, art work dark and dull with age, printing heavy and large. A yellow circle, two slash six, two shillings and sixpence, dated it from perhaps the 1950s or '60s. The dusty-looking booklets and brochures reminded me that my whole week's salary in 1962 had been only three guineas, or three pounds and three shillings. Daily bus fare from Kintbury in Berkshire, where I lived at that time, to the local market town of Newbury was about two shillings and sixpence round-trip fare. Years, progress, and decimalization had turned that old life on its ear. She did not see my fear and sadness at the passing of time and an era of my youth. I could not say, well, Anna, there are no shillings anymore. The country you remember has changed.

Adrift in past times, hers, I feared, predicted mine. I wanted to hurry through, afraid the oldness was contagious and the papers would spread something on my skin and make me catch being very old too. But they were just dulled brochures, nothing to be afraid of. Anna's eyes danced as she enjoyed her memories, riffling through her brochures and explaining them as delightedly as if they had just arrived in the morning's mail in advance of a trip.

My fidgeting, standing up and sitting down, and attempts at explanations convinced my hostess I had better go. To my surprise the ninety-year-old lady helped me on with my coat first, then escorted me back along the path past her sheep and garden, through the trees to the very intersection where she had found me so I would not get lost. Two strangers, from worlds and ages apart, we gave one another's arms a friendly squeeze as we parted. Then she turned back toward her little house where she lived alone. Pleased with myself beyond measure, I followed the stony path home.

"You won't believe it," I announced to Mike like a week-end hiker who found himself atop Everest, "but I've just spent the past two and a half hours with a ninety-year-old lady and I spoke Norwegian the whole time!" He put down his magazine, appropriately impressed. "Who is she?" he asked. I relayed the whole story as I contentedly prepared dinner. My husband had *his* project and I had mine—to speak to the people around me, in Norwegian if I could, and I was doing it, and not too badly!

Tor's eyes lit up when he heard the story. I hoped it repaid him a little for the effort he put into equipping us with language. Without him I would never have had the confidence to march off with a lady of Anna's age and try to keep up my side of the conversation. But I knew too that Anna had generously forgiven my stilted words. My maturity and experience had a long way to go before glowing in wisdom like hers.

Later I mentioned the visit to Einar. "Ah, yes, Anna. I have known her for many years and she's almost like a mother to my wife," he said. "Once I was going away to sea for two years and I was feeling bad as I left here. She, Anna, was weeping, Else was weeping, and I was too," he said, his deep voice trailing away. I pictured Einar as a young man facing months away from his wife and children and wondered how he survived it—and how Else managed too, almost raising the children alone.

Sailor's Farewell

Sweet oh sweet is that sensation
Where two hearts in union meet
But the pain of separation
Mingle (s) bitter with the Sweet.

—Writer Unknown (words inside an antique
bowl, Haugesund Museum)

Everything about Anna's home was pretty—gauzy curtains, flowers and vegetables in rows in the garden. I half expected *Claire de Lune* to waft out of the cottage's windows for it could have been a music box. Nothing difficult or heart-wrenching could happen there. But behind the storybook door a still strong woman busied herself. Did she still remember the good-byes from those days? She was there for Einar's family and for her sheep when they had too many lambs to feed—and even for me, someone who needed conversation. I wondered if God kept her in suspended aging as there was no reason for her to go and she was still needed. Certainly she was strong enough to maintain her cottage and garden and tend her sheep, remaining curious about people and the world. Perhaps she could go on for another ten years. Anna had the hang of life, and I admired her openness and spirit.

After that I watched hopefully for the marvelous lady, but I never saw her again around her farm or on the footpath. Two years later someone said she suffered a stroke and I studied her cottage even more intently. From the outside nothing had changed, and when the familiar seven-candle ornament lit up her window at Christmas time, it symbolized her beating the stroke just as she had everything else. But I steeled myself for the absence of lambs that spring. Maybe they would be too much for her. To my delight, they were there as usual as was she, somewhere behind her curtains.

At Liv's one afternoon a totally new little girl appeared from behind the mounds of washing, coats, and jackets which distinguished my neighbor's first-floor laundry room and entry hall. *"Kan jeg snakke med Liv?"* Could I speak with Liv, I asked. She called upstairs to the family room while I observed the volumes of linens and clothes with bemusement. Liv accomplished heroic amounts of work in this room, whipping her contrary and stubborn machine to finish the next load much as a rider urges his exhausted horse to finish a race. Taking "no" for an answer offended her principles and capabilities. Once I found her sitting on the laundry room floor, flushed with exertion, applying a wrench to her washing machine's throbbing innards. Hadn't she better just call someone to come repair it? *"Nei!* I like fixing it myself," she countered, eyes bright with challenge as though I had tried to take some pleasure from her. Occasionally even her strenuous machinations failed to revive the overworked appliance though, for once I actually saw a repair truck parked outside.

The little girl's sweet expression provoked my curiosity. "And who are you? Where do you live?" I asked. She looked mystified. In the meantime my friend popped into view upstairs in the living room. *"Kom!"* she called out, motioning for me to join her. The little girl mumbled her name to me, glancing up rather desperately at Liv. They clearly had a connection, but what?

"I am Irene. I live here," she answered, looking a little confused.

"*Her? Du er en dotter?*" I shot back.

"*Ja,*" she said tentatively.

"And you are Liv's *daughter—Irene?*" Again a *Ja!* Hanging up my jacket with a sigh, I slipped out of my boots. It seemed impossible to have missed a whole child in all these months. Her name had never even come up in conversation when older sister Anne-Lise visited us or cat-sat. Apparently our neighbor was mother to five, not just four, and had banished one as scullery maid to toil in the laundry room all winter.

Liv's voice urged me to come up. I knew if I just followed my nose I would find my friend in her usual position—in the *kjøkken*, kitchen—stirring something on the stove. Around suppertime it was likely to be soup or stew and in summer enormous quantities of *saft*, or fruit juice, even jellies, after the family's annual berry picking forays. Liv had even generously given us several frozen cartons of the vitamin-rich juice concentrate.

"I'm coming!"

"*Kom! La! Kom la!*" she shouted urgently.

"I am coming, Liv!" I yelled back, wondering what was the hurry, and what the *la* meant. Egil, Liv's husband, was chuckling and I knew something was afoot.

"*Nei! Kom-le! Komle!*"

I translated as best I could. "*Kom la!* Let me see. *La*—lie down, past tense? Do you want me to lie down? Or, is *la* or *le* past tense of laugh?" Am I supposed to lie down or laugh? No? What are you saying to me, Liv?"

Egil was rolling in the couch, laughing helplessly, by the time I appeared upstairs and Liv's eyes sparkled with fun. "Patti, *kom.*" She led me into the kitchen where we inspected the contents of her giant soup pot as though in search of some amazing hidden mystery.

"*Komle! Har du hørt om komle, har du prøvd?*" Had I heard of *komle*, or tried it? She scooped up what looked like an innocent dumpling from the bubbling liquid. So this was *komle*, nothing to do with coming, lying down, or laughing, past tense. It was a thing, food, and no, I hadn't tried it. "*Nei. Jeg har ikke spiste det!*" I confirmed, accepting my role as ding-a-ling as well as someone who lived in a fog, unable to figure out who their children were or how to differentiate between "come in" and the little Norwegian dumplings under my nose.

"*Komle,*" she repeated. "*Du og Mike,* have some for *middag,*" she insisted, ladling some out. Liv could not let me leave without a sales and promotion pitch for the island's famous dish and, judging by her reverent tones, I was remiss in waiting so long to try them. Apparently *komle* was a West Coast delicacy, and real Karmøyans even set aside a particular night of the week to eat them. Before leaving, I begged for clarification on one more subject: the extra child downstairs, bringing the number to five. I reviewed them by name: Anne-Lise and Rebekka, the teenagers; Toralf and his brother; and now Irene? "*Oh, nei!*" she hastily corrected me. Little Toralf's constant companion was not a brother at all but her friend Hanna's youngest boy. She and Egil had the three girls and just one son. Young Toralf was a cheerful little fellow and I told his mother so, hoping to be forgiven for my abject confusion. "Yes," she agreed with a resigned, loving look. "He's a happy little boy. Happy and dirty!"

I had to vouch for the former for he sang his way into the world each morning. The ten-year-old greeted the day with an operatic high note timed to coincide with the door slamming behind him. Holding the quaver, he threw on his rucksack and peddled off to school with his best friend, Hanna's boy. Liv looked astonished that I once actually complimented Toralf on his singing. "You like to hear it?" she asked. I contended that singing his heart out on the way to school reflected his happy family life. She lost no time in setting me straight. "He does it because his sisters won't let him sing in the house! He has to wait until he is outside!" So that was the reason! Nevertheless I admired how he circumvented this rule by internalizing his music as he hurtled downstairs each morning, only releasing it as he reached the front door. Calypso and I always waited in suspense for his optimistic, loud, sometimes off-key blast to vibrate the sleepy day into life, a unique signal that all was well in our little neighborhood.

Back home, I eyed my three *komle* with curiosity. They looked appetizing, shimmering in hot gravy. Despite their modest size, they had obviously earned a substantial reputation. And substantial is what they were. The compact little dumplings made from grated raw potatoes, salt, and a little pork fat in the center filled you up quickly. At dinner Mike and I ate one and a half each. Now we knew why Norwegians stayed slim all their lives—one or two *komle* at dinner eliminated evening snacking. *Komle* had nothing to do linguistically with lying down, but after you had eaten one, you might feel the need to do so.

HOW TO BAKE A CAKE
(. . . with toddlers underfoot)

First, turn on the oven. Butter the cake pan. Set out bowl, spoons and ingredients. Clear building blocks and toy cars off the kitchen table. Measure two cups of flour and find sifter. Take a young child's hand away from the flour. Wash off the child. Measure a new cup of flour to replace the one that landed on the floor. Answer the door. Remove boots and rainsuit off the little 'friend' who wants to come in. Run back to the kitchen. Find out what has broken. Get out the broom and dustpan. Throw the rest of the broken bowl into the trash. Take out another bowl and start again.

Separate 4 eggs, yolks and whites. Answer the telephone. Turn around and clean off the egg mess from the table and floor. Remove socks from two sets of boys' feet that are all sticky from egg whites. Wash socks in the bathroom. Hurry back to the kitchen. Retrieve plastic toy from the bake oven. Scrape the oven clean. Beat a new amount of egg whites until they are stiff and measure 3/4 cup of milk. Add baking powder and cardamom to the flour and sift together.

See who is ringing the doorbell. Open the kitchen window and call two barefooted boys back into the house. Wipe up the flour that spilled from the sudden draft. Find clean, warm socks for the boys. Finish making the cake batter. Check to see why the boys are screaming. Separate the young 'fighters.' Return to the kitchen and pour the batter into the pan. Dispose of the batter when egg shells are discovered in it. Clean the kitchen. Call the bakery. Lie down and rest.

Originally published by a Moksheim ladies' church group, 1960s. Used by permission of Norheim Church's Kirkeringen's cookbook, **Velkommen inn i våre kjøkkener.** Translation courtesy of Milli and Lori.

Spring wafted into the air and nodding violet-blue crocuses peered out of the embankments. Hills that were recently sledding heavens greened up. White bathtubs sprung up across the landscape as water troughs for cattle, moving with the herds. The delicate contrasted with the utilitarian. Baths and bulls sharing muddy pastures. Not for these tubs a double-page spread in *House Beautiful*. All they could hope for was a mention in a farming newspaper. But I was a fan, of sorts. Who could *not* notice a white bathtub in a field?

Migrating birds returned to sing in stereo, their chirps, tweets, clucks, squeaks, eeks, and aawks like orchestra players tuning up. Ten hours a day was not enough for them in Norway, and they sang and churckered from daylight to sunset, past seven-thirty when we walked the dogs, a chorale prelude to summer. Fair weather brought out linens to air, and Elise's cheery comforters, *dyne*, puffed from an upstairs window. *Dyne* added unexpected color to the green landscape, bursting forth as brightly as flowers and supplementing nature's greens, grays, blues, and white just as well.

The following year *dyne* inspired my colored-pencil picture, "Karmøy's Colorful Quilt Bouquets." Much to Mike's chagrin, I could never resist stopping to admire a windowful of quilts. While I begged him to let me, please, quickly take a photograph or do a quick sketch, he was expert in numerous reasons why it was impossible: there was a car behind us, it was a bad corner, where could he park anyway. They masked his real reason. "People don't want you staring in their windows!" he admonished. He may have had a point for housewives retrieved them before we could turn around. Was there a giant sign on our car warning people I was cruising for *dyne*-window pictures? All I could do was stir my memory and imagination to recall how the different colors fell and draped, ballooning softly in shadowed folds in the breeze.

Near the highway some pregnant sheep chewed slowly. One was as round as a wine barrel; the other a lady of droopy pear-shape. Others were tall, dark, and rangy-looking creatures, unpregnant and sporty looking. Sheep were skittish animals. Human attention sent them scattering, bleating worriedly, so I watched out of the corner of my eye, pretending they were invisible. Farmers' sons played in their driveways on suitable toys: miniature tractors. Two girls in our lane acquired their first suitors that year, each having chosen a boy with a hair color that matched her own. Blonde with blonde, brunette with brunette. One girl had perfected a technique only first love brings about: sort of standing still while alternatively twisting the upper and lower parts of her body like some off-center drilling machinery while her young man perched and fidgeted on his bicycle, transfixed by her very presence.

Transportation for them was feet and bicycles as it still was for me, and I took to the lanes on a newly purchased snazzy pink bike with good brakes. Norway's culture promoted bike riding, and a local lady, quite elderly, was a regular mobile feature of the landscape. She attacked the coastal breeze wrapped knees to chin in sturdy clothing and a large hat. Her headwear always overpowered her small face, and one favorite, a purple wool *chapeau,* hung low around her forehead like a small umbrella. Glancing neither left nor right, she pedaled across intersections with resolute purpose, plastic grocery sack swinging from the handlebars like a pendulum. Her face hung in tight, lightly tanned folds over good bones, and she nodded at me with bright, lively eyes the first time we passed. A little greeting might have been in her mind, and I hoped she would say something, if I could even understand it, of course. But she pedaled by on that day word-lessly, leaving me and my curiosity behind.

FØR BARNA KOMMER HJEM
Patti Jones Morgan
1994

On the Road Again

As much as I loved to be outdoors in the elements, I knew I needed to apply for my Norwegian drivers' license and regain more control of my "foreigner's" life. Both Mike and I had overstayed our legal limit for driving on our Texas licenses, and fear of a ticket kept me from driving very far. I studied the rules of the road which included many references to Norway's king and what *he* wanted from his drivers and especially what he *didn't* want.

Rules included no right turn on red, and giving way to traffic entering from the right unless you were on a "diamond" road. You also always gave way to pedestrians. Pedestrians held a place of honor in Norway, unlike in Houston where they were considered, at the least, annoyances. In some major U.S. cities, pedestrians wielded enormous power, negotiating traffic flows like well-choreographed dancers, confidently hailing down cabs. Haugesunders approached things less subtly. While they never waved down taxicabs—they had to telephone or go to the cab stand—they regularly stepped right in front of moving cars on their way across the street. Their intent to reach the other side in such risky fashion almost promised a sooner-than-expected arrival at the real Other Side if a driver failed to brake in time.

Not for them the old adage, "Look left, look right, look left again." Nadya scared me to death for she must have come from a country where pedestrians shared Haugesunders' disregard for moving vehicles. She invariably marched straight into a lane of traffic calling out to me, "Why not? Wha's matter? We GO!"

"But, there are *cars* coming, Nadya!" I replied, viewing them as thundering buffalo, nostrils steaming, while all she saw were silly car drivers who would just have to stop.

"Come!" she commanded, ignoring the ragged chorus of screeching brakes. But for pedestrians and their kamikaze-like habits I might have applied for my Norwegian drivers' license sooner. Running anyone down while I lived in Norway seemed an awfully high price to pay for the convenience of driving. Still, I needed to get back on the road legally.

It was no coincidence that I waited so long to apply for my license. I wanted all traces of snow to be gone. It was part of my secret plan. Exchanging my Texas license for a Norwegian one was not difficult, but since Texas was considered a no-snow state, we would have to be tested on our ability to drive in icy conditions—except, I thought, when there was no snow for fifty miles. All winter I plotted to outwit the system, yes, the king too, I suppose. Without snow I would not need to do that which I feared most—take the ice driving test.

I was wrong. Norway knew about people like me and had contingency plans. The test drive track would be slicked down with oil, our instructor, Gunnar, cheerfully informed us and we would practice our skids perfectly well on it.

This ever-smiling taskmaster, a part-time military man who taught rifle marksmanship to new soldiers, combined these duties with the equally risky endeavor of teaching people to drive. Threading the steering wheel through competent hands and tapping the brake with a pumping motion, he talked me through what he actually wanted me to do when I hit the ice, or slippery patch, and started to slide. As he shot us into a terrifying skid, I doubted we would get out of the car alive. Pupils dilated, he worked the wheel energetically, the car lurching sideways with a sickening crunch before coming to a shuddering halt. If the exercise affected him, an expert, that way, what chance did I have, an amateur in the skid department? I wondered as my heart pounded.

He joked with us for a few minutes before asking me to take the wheel. I was so petrified there was no chance for me, like a passenger placed in the cockpit of a 747 and told to fly it. "Speed up, then hit the brakes," he advised calmly, pointing to a red stop sign some yards ahead. With Mike in the back and Gunnar to my right, I drove us forward to certain death, only to ease back again and roll to a nice controlled halt behind a plastic facade of the rear of a bus. "There!" I said smugly, glued to the seat.

Avoiding the skid surely was better than skidding? Not so. Gunnar was not delighted. We did it again. He was more pleased but still not satisfied. "Okay. Let's drive back over to the start again," he instructed with uncustomary coolness. "We'll do it again."

During the one and one-half hour of torture I wished for a miracle, I wished I had remained an occasional illegal driver and used the bus for the duration of our stay, and I wished they would have allowed a special restriction on my license banning me from wintertime driving altogether. Mostly I prayed I would not overturn the car. I just wanted it all to be over without my killing anyone. We were on the greased track forever, and even a coffee and chocolate break could not cure my weak knees.

At the end, after three or four skids around a slick corner where yet another inflated plastic vehicle masochistically awaited battering, I stopped the car. Physically and mentally drained, I could do no more—for anyone, even the king of Norway. If what I had done or not done was not good enough, I would forever, gratefully, take the bus.

Then it was Mike's turn and why both men looked
surprised when I declined the opportunity to ride in the back
throughout his test was beyond me. Later on, Gunnar informed
us we had both satisfied the law and could pick up our licenses.
These were optimistically good for 100 years—a truly ambitious
goal at the best of times and even more so for survivors of the ice
driving test.

Norway's rules of the road and constant references to the
king made me view my driving responsibility on a more one-to-
one basis. The title "king" still meant a person whereas U.S. state
departments of transportation sounded like a few clerks laboring
in a depository for printed forms. I had never been around kings
but saw Norway's as a fatherly disciplinarian who could actually
show up and throw me out of the country for poor driving habits.
On the other hand, I felt I could appeal to him personally if I were
unjustly accused. Aside from that, I worried about nosy messen-
gers who might run to the palace and report when I put a foot
wrong, especially a heavy one on the accelerator. Whether I liked
it or not, the king was part of my life.

I came to believe that the king's responsibilities were way
overstretched as main police officer over his citizenry's daily
driving habits. Surely the country and international affairs were
more important issues. Still, every little slip on my part definitely
risked his wrath. He was probably especially vigilant about
watching for ones like me, ones who could make those mistakes
the book warned against. From his palace windows, he could
probably lock onto me with his king-size telescope or mighty
binoculars as I skulked around on the other side of the mountains. He noted my forgotten turn signals, delayed braking,
improper parking, inattention to the road as I searched for
something in the glove compartment, my driving too quickly or
too slowly or in the wrong lane. Oh, yes, it was a matter of time
before my sins and the king caught up with me.

And it almost happened when the king paid a special visit
to the nearby Norsk Hydro aluminum plant. I half expected him to
stop by the house and have me arrested on the spot, but maybe

Gudrun's students distracted him with their songs? Or was it young Toralf's uplifting trumpet solo that made him forget his plan to ferret me out? Whatever it was, he did not come looking for me and I was glad. Now that I knew that Norway's king traveled to distant counties like Rogaland, saw the very fields I walked on, I was *more* careful when I was behind the wheel. Best to take no chances of blowing our residency this early on.

Being a legitimate driver improved life tremendously, allowing me to explore delightful out-of-the-way places. Days were staying lighter longer, and wildflowers and greening bushes softened our brown, craggy hills. The accelerated growth reminded me of New Mexico's, where beige, rocky plateaus produced vivid flora almost overnight. Our lane of colorful wooden houses looked like a child's drawing—a pleasing palette of yellow, blue, white, and reddish-brown, needing only a few, thick, green crayon strokes to make gardens. A UFO-like yellow orb might hover overhead, a wild-eyed woman grin from a window, and an animal of indeterminate species and uneven legs which allegedly lived in the neighborhood could smile out from behind a crooked three-quarter profile. Our neighborhood took on the season in picture-book fashion.

No longer restricted to a bus schedule, I felt more relaxed about school. A quick zoom out the driveway had me en route but not before a quick check of the mailbox, promiser of all bounty, then past the angry dog that lived at a farm, propelling my mobile purse/office/grocery cart to town. I clenched my coffee cup between my knees when I needed both hands to steer, which was not often. Gunnar would have been horrified with my distracted driving habits. After losing valuable time behind tractors, I sped up, practicing how I would explain my speeding to a police officer.

Driving fines were serious money, a needed government accounts receivable, so you paid, period. A friend got caught as she drove too quickly through a Stavanger school zone. Instantly a police office waved her down and fined her 700 kroner, about $100 at that time. "If you had just been going three kilometers less, I wouldn't have had to do it," he consoled her. Hidden cameras snapped motorists speeding through tunnels and along highways, and tardy fine payments accrued late charges.

Fortunately I escaped Norway with just one 100 kroner (about $16) parking ticket for exceeding a prepaid parking fee. It could have been worse; once a police officer waved me down during a routine road block on a teeming wet morning. To my dismay, I realized I had left my license at home after carrying it in my coat pocket as I took a walk. The man stood there, getting drenched, flustered by my English, and trying to control his exasperation. After dealing with several other motorists he ordered me to drive straight home, retrieve my license from the kitchen table where I assured him it lay, and present it at Kopervik police station. "You must go there right away!" he repeated, waving me on. I did what he said, feeling very lucky. Karmøy police were obviously much kinder than Stavanger ones.

I always had one other card up my sleeve, other than speaking English. In addition to the *Ny i Norge* tapes I listened to as I drove was one of Prime Minister Gro Harlem Bruntland's— reading a New Year's message. Her office had kindly sent it to me when I told them that her speeches were some of the few I could almost follow and did they have an old one I could practice listening to? They mailed me an original one, and I was thrilled and honored to have it. In a way, it was my talisman, and I counted on the power of Mrs. Bruntland's voice floating out of my car window to soften an annoyed policeman's heart.

Driving added a new, sometimes frightening, dimension to my quiet life in Norway. Traffic approaching from the left has the right of way on roundabouts, except at the Texaco one in Haugesund. There, anything went, and some drivers seem not to have read what the king said in his book. Before long I distrusted all drivers on my left at that roundabout and stayed well over to my right, just in case. When they noticed my lips moving sound-lessly, did they get the impression I was cursing them? No, sir, not me. I was innocently practicing my *Ny i Norge* dialogue to the tapes, trying to sound like a real Norwegian. Or, then again, maybe I wasn't.

One afternoon Nadya asked for a ride home. I was surprised. Our classmate enjoyed a strong sense of herself as a woman, and her husky voice and sweeping lashes virtually guaranteed her a passage with any one of a slew of obliging admirers. Once that had happened to me. In the New York of the 1960s to which I emigrated, my fresh English accent captivated taxi drivers. They hung on my every word and happily turned off their meters when my funds ran low, usually asking for a date soon after. For awhile I too rarely lacked a ride.

I was happy to help out and asked where she lived. "You go to Karmøy ... it's that way. I tell you." Dropping her off shouldn't be that difficult, but one never knew, and I was glad Pauline was along. Nadya battled briefly with Pauline for the front seat, then squirmed into the back of my tiny hatchback with more difficulty than necessary, casting an irritated look around. My usual paper debris and scattered books revealed my true, untidy nature. She had caught me off guard, and it boded ill for our trip.

On the way she announced she was expecting a Russian friend to fly in that evening. "Oh, that'll be nice for you," Pauline responded. "You'll have someone to talk to, keep you company. How long will she stay?"

"One month without married, three month with married," came the quick answer.

The odd statement grabbed my imagination. "One month without married, three month married." What did this have to do with anything, particularly her friend's marital status? But marital status was the precise issue and Pauline tried to clarify it, "Her Russian friend may marry a Norwegian here."

Long-distance love affairs and arranged marriages of various sorts in various cultures still happened, I knew that. Some U.S. magazines still advertised "lovely foreign women seeking friendship, maybe more." The urge to find a mate, possibly combined with economic and political security, sent people on impossibly difficult paths, and the Russian woman coming that evening was one of them. Judging by the number of foreign-born women in town, the local men were not averse to meeting and marrying nationals from other countries, and Nadya and her friend were part of the bridal trend.

Caught up in the intrigue of the couple-to-be, I day-dreamed as we dropped off Pauline. Nadya hurriedly exchanged her grungy, back-seat quarters for the front, body language broadcasting this should have been her rightful place from the start. Shifting around, she grudgingly snapped the seat belt in place. "I no like, but I do! My friend in Haugesund, she never." Her aggrieved tone implied that smart people did not use seat belts and she was only complying to save me a possible fine. "Oh, you must!" I reasoned, waving at the windshield and tapping it for emphasis. "You would hit this!"

Nadya discounted my advice, casually pointing at the door. "My friend, she say, what if she has to get out?" Debating the issue was less important then than finding out where I was supposed to be driving.

Cruising east, we approached a roundabout and I asked for directions, slowing down a little. "Left, left!" she cried stridently. "I live the way you go." I circled the roundabout and headed south with no idea where she lived or when she planned to give me a specific street or address. She stared calmly out of the window as we joined a heavy flow of traffic. A few minutes later she broke the silence. "One, two, three, four!" she announced, waving her arm at passing buildings. My gray cells, before merely on alert status, now scrambled into action. At the fourth intersection we would turn left?

Friday afternoon was a bad time to be on the main road out of town. Serious weekenders, Norwegians streamed homeward single-mindedly, and I dreaded trying to slow down or stop. No left-hand turns were in sight.

"Where do you want me to stop?" I asked tensely.

"Hyere, hyere!" she cried—but it was too late. We had passed the unmarked spot, and the roundabout out of town was in sight. "Hyere!" she called desperately, twisting back to look at her disappearing residence. Somehow I had to go back. She grabbed at her doorhandle. Under pressure, I made a left into the center of the highway and waited there for a break to get across.

"No, no, 's too mush trubbell for you!" She kept grabbing at the door. I knew her rule book promised that any car coming toward her would have to stop, no matter how fast it was going—but she would get squashed on a Friday afternoon. "Wait, Nadya!" I cried, fighting rising panic. "You can get out in a minute. Just let me try to get across here first," without killing us, I wanted to add.

After making a spectacle of my disgusting driving habits to a hundred people at least, I squeezed dangerously across the road, pulling to a stop at the first available space. Just my luck, it was a bus stop and I imagined a bus barreling into us, horn blaring. "There!" I announced, hoping Gunnar was nowhere around with a student driver. I imagined my instructor's eyebrows arched in horror had he observed me, but these were extenuating circumstances—Nadya surely counted as hazardous cargo. However, now I knew that "One, two, three, four!" meant buildings, not left-hand turns. I learned an important lesson in political history. Nadya's country and mine had been at loggerheads for decades and, knowing she and I barely accomplished even minor things without complications and angst, I could see why.

Once we stopped, my classmate seized her chance to press down the door handle she had clutched for five minutes. In smart leather jacket, short skirt, glossy tights, and knee-length, high-heeled boots, she unfurled her body with labored difficulty out of my little car. Little gray clouds passed across her eyes as she glanced back, almost with sympathy that I was so dim. "*Takk,* bye," she forced a little smile. I replied with a falsely cheerful "*God helg!* "—Have a good weekend—and knowing the former sounded phonetically similar to a more uncharitable American expression I said it sweetly one more time, smiling.

Within seconds I found myself driving the wrong way.

Lord, would I ever get home? Like poor Elizabeth, Hyacinth Bucket's nervous neighbor in British television's *Keeping Up Appearances,* I fell apart around my strong-willed friend. We were destined always to be doing the wrong thing for each other. But unlike Pauline and I, who led intrigue-free lives by comparison, our young classmate was full of surprises and I truly wanted to know her better. Stuffing two chocolate Dumle caramels into my mouth as tranquilizers, I headed thankfully for home.

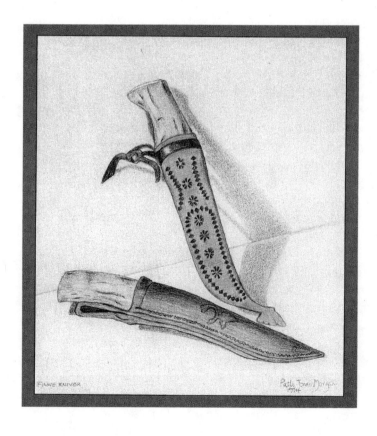

FINNE KNIVER   Patti Jones Morgan
                                                 1994

Driving Down Karmøy

"... to love a landscape you must not first ask if it is beautiful, for beauty often is a thing that passes. Nor can you say after an acquaintance of one season, that it is attractive, for brief affections can deceive with age. To love a landscape you must also know its faults and darker moods. You must know it, not only for a year, but for a lifetime. Only then, perhaps, can you say it is the place you most love, the place where you are most contented and at home."

—From *The Winter Fens* by Edward Storey

Once I got the hang of her winding lanes, I rewarded myself with many drives down Karmøy. On a non-school day, a nice morning at ten was a perfect time to cruise near-empty roads, blessed by blue sky, breezes, and bird song. No anxious ferry-catchers would press me to hurry. Or I could wait until sunset and view the northern part of the island from the center of the almost half-mile-long, 200-foot-high Haugesund bridge as a strip of liquid gold clung to the rocky headland before darkening on its way out to sea.

   After such a dramatic scene, the nearby marshy fields were a letdown, but judging by the hungry, long-legged, black birds which probed the mud, they were their equivalent of fast food restaurants. Right after the marshes, St. Olav's Church at Avaldsnes—the landmark for which the island is famous— loomed up from a promontory like an austere English castle surrounded by a moat. Begun in 1250, it later symbolized the country's unification under King Håkon Håkonson. Avaldsnes lays special claim to being the first capital of Norway. All in all, massive St. Olav's resounded with religious and royal significance.

   The church proved a magnet to local artists; drawings and paintings of St. Olav's showed up at countless arts and crafts shows during the summer and fall. I wondered why there was no public park from which the artists, tourists, and school children could relax and view it. After we left, the *kommune* constructed a Viking center near the church, where ancient life on the island was reenacted. It heralded revived interest in the centuries-old culture and settlement of Karmøy.

   With unimpeded views north and south along the sound, Karmøy has always enjoyed strategic advantage. Early kings taxed ships traveling the coastal route, *nordvegen,* which provided the name "Norway." Excavations have revealed enough ancient artifacts to prove the area was a center of power as long as three thousand years ago. From the beginning I always felt a gentle haunting there which carries a certainty of things that had happened long before, yet I could never size up the island for too much was unknown, or merely hinted at, leaving me with more and more questions. People called her "the Saga Island" for her mention in Saga literature as *"Kormt* (partition or fence), the island which lies and protects the ship's channel, the Karmsund."

   Beyond the bridge, colorful farm buildings and houses thread across the fields, along with muddy tractors and unfathomable pieces of farm equipment, sheep, cattle, horses, green pastures, and bales of hay. To the left the water—teal, silver, azure, depending on weather conditions—flirts with you to stop. Some days she and the mountains gray down to matching shades of 4B pencil lead. Viewed from the top of a nearby steep hill, the wide body of water curving between Karmøy and the mainland mountains looked more like a gentle river valley than a cold, deep ocean sound.

The young teens in my area all attended Bø Ungdomskole, and I always tried to avoid the area when classes let out. The normal country quiet exploded when hundreds of chattering teenagers raced to a quarter acre of glinting bicycles or scrambled into a waiting caravan of blue buses. Their buses took them by the new Visnes roundabout, centered by five tall rocks. Whether the stones symbolized something historic or were simply suitable decoration for a land which appreciates ruggedness and rocks, I never found out. If I could have stopped and touched them, I would have felt more connected. When I half jokingly suggested to Mike one Christmas that little, white decorative lights would make the roundabout more visible and eminently safer on a dark, rainy night—and more interesting, too—he shook his head in disbelief. "They're rocks! You don't put lights on them!"

After several years in development Karmøy Lyngsenter Vignes (historic spelling) opened to celebrate the island's heather culture. Aleksander Hauge, historian and folk singer whose enthusiasm breathed the place into existence, managed the shop, art gallery, and greenhouse. Visnes' old copper mine history and heyday were displayed in the new museum. Once a major industry on the island, copper eventually created an important link between Karmøy and America. For the skeptical, and I count myself among them, a book describes how America's General Electric laboratories, no less, examined and tested Visnes copper and concluded that it had very likely been used for the Statue of Liberty's copper skin. This report appealed to my own immigrant senses. How fortunate that islanders knew that a little bit of Karmøy beckoned them, lighting their way to a better future.

KARMØY-SONG
By Aleksander Hauge

Ut i mot havet langt i mot vest
der ligger Karmøy i skumsprøyt og blest,
med lyngvokste rabbaar og snøkvite strand,
fra Gavel i nord til Skudeneshavn.

Out toward the ocean far to the west
Lies Karmøy facing sea spray and wind.
With heather-covered ridges and snow white beaches
From Gavel in the north to Skudeneshavn.

Og har du vært borte så velkommen hjem
til gamle tufter du kjenner igjen.
Hører sjøbraaket bruser inn over strand
ser Utsira fyret blinker mot land.

And if you have been away, then welcome home
To old fields you will recognize.
Hear the ocean thunder against the shore,
See Utsira lighthouse point the way to land.

Langs torvskjer og myrar mellom braaake og lyng,
der steinsette garder mot sjøen seg slyng.
Her står de husa der vi ble født,
og våre barndoms skor har trøtt.

Along the peat moss, marshes, grasses and heather
where stone farmhouses curve down to the sea,
Here are the homes where we were born
Where we wore the shoes of childhood.

Her ble kongene lagde i hauger som spor,
og viser norvegen der vikinger for.
Om øya ble bgd opp med sverd og med skjold
her blodrøde heiar gitt grøderik voll.

Here the kings were buried in marked mounds
showing the way north where the Vikings sailed
If the island was built with sword and shield,
So the blood-red heaths produced fertile fields.

Refreng:

—Original poem by Aleksander Hauge, Visnes.
English Translation: Erik Sveen, Texas. 1999

PHOTOGRAPHS
by
Ole Jakob Vorraa

Ole Jakob Vorraa is a noted photographer of nature and landscape who resides on Karmøy. His work has appeared in numerous Norwegian publications. Vorraa's poetic renderings of subject, light and season truly capture the soul of the island, and I am honored to include his art in this memoir.

Åkrehamn

Ytreland

© Ole Jakob Vorraa

Fiskere, Åkrehamn

© Ole Jakob Vorraa

© Ole Jakob Vorraa

Sandve havn

Vedavågen

Skude Fyr/Skudeneshavn lighthouse

On my drive I passed a hotel, then Norsk Hydro pumping up clouds of white into the air, steam I was told, and the Shell station at Bygnes. In practical terms the Shell station had assumed the Statue of Liberty's importance as a beacon in our area. To the gas station came all the poor, tired wanderers, huddled in their cars—yearning to be free of confusing signs and dead-end lanes which had enslaved them since they disembarked the ferry. She welcomed them to her telephone and to her pumps.

Twisting left, the road parallels an inlet, leading into the picturesque fishing town of Kopervik. No multistory buildings spoil the view since, in Norway, nature has a mighty lock on height, and the government controls land and building permits. On the whole I agreed with their policy. So much of urbanized Houston had been razed of trees and covered with concrete and brick that nature and the environment were lost. More building meant more flooding, and fewer trees meant fewer birds. Norway resists such improvement—a debatable term at best—of land. Monumental numbers of permissions, including those of your neighbors, are required before you can do any remodeling or construction. A colleague of my husband's spent the better part of a year completing applications, permissions, and paperwork just to obtain a permit to extend his kitchen. One of his neighbors objected to the addition because it blocked his view. Despite it all or perhaps because of it, this society has elevated Norwegians' standard of living to one of the highest in the world, second only to Canada and higher than America's, according to recent data.

Even farmers have to follow strict rules on adding structures to their own land as all land is supposed to be under the plough or used for grazing. One just down the lane from us reclaimed a small rocky area adjoining one of his fields. Over a few weeks he cleared away enormous numbers of rocks, then added a good layer of soil and fertilizer. Finally he raked and seeded it. By summer his crops were growing almost to the water's edge. Imported foods are highly taxed and, although some complain about the continued farming subsidies, the country's history of terrible times of hunger and near starvation hasn't been forgotten. People are asked to give away home-produced fruits and vegetables rather than have them rot.

A delightful detour in my drive was a trip through Vedavågen and Vea, where I took my chances on an arched, single-lane bridge which went over to the tiny island of Salvøy. Driving blind added a little drama for I never knew if I would come fender to fender with another car until I reached the top. I dreaded being the one to back up. Most times I had the bridge to myself and savored the sight of an exquisite little harbor and skies that stretched forever. It seemed all the more enjoyable after having risked a frontal collision to see it.

Had I not needed my shoes resoled and let my fingers do the walking through the *gule sider* to find a repair shop, I doubted I would ever have discovered the island. A cobbler worked out of his home just two minutes from the bridge, but the place was well off any even moderately beaten track. His lane pretty much dead-ended into the sea, and I felt I was standing at the end of the world. No man-made sounds spoiled the moment, just a sharp breeze and wash snapping on clotheslines. Hungry gulls screeched above two incoming fishing boats, their frantic whirring and cries reminding me of the movie *The Birds*. Once a very busy fishing island, Salvøy's name derives from "salvation" or "welcome," a friend told me, and both seemed appropriate.

Around the Fishing Museum in Vea a squiggle of a road takes you back a hundred years in half an hour. Old fishing sheds and buildings lean in so close that you wonder how gravity keeps them up and how drivers avoid hitting them. I toured one with a friend who agreed to help search out some old barrels and ropes for me to sketch. Creaking wood steps led up to bits and pieces, relics, oddments connected with the fishing business—things which once were important to the people who lived there. The owner kindly gave me an old herring barrel, another still-life subject for drawing. My American eye saw many uses for the dusty place which was so steeped in character—a wonderful waterfront lodge, town home, creative agency, or restaurant. Vea was home to my beautician and thus a favorite haunt. I was Ingvild's one and only American customer and, despite our limitations in one another's languages, I always came away with a few more vocabulary words, a little cultural history, and no green or frizzy hair.

Stubby trees, sculpted by the prevailing winds, lined the coastal route out of Åkrehamn, where waves devoured sandy coves. Coastal weather could be unpredictable. Mike and I once drove the thirty or so minutes down to Skudeneshavn on a clear, winter Sunday afternoon only to return in a billowing snowstorm. Scattered alongside, fields of giant boulders looked like renditions of some strange uninhabited planet. When spring brought hundreds of lambs scampering across the rough fields, foals sidling up to their mothers, and wildflowers nodding in profusion, however, the landscape came alive. A lovely, old, white church, a bright lavender blue house on your right, and a post office with a magnificent view of the North Sea each offered unique land-marks. I always wished there were a restaurant or park there instead of a post office, a place to enjoy the startling view of the ocean.

Ferkingstad, a little farther along, just before Skudeneshavn, acquired the name "Little America" when it sent most of its young men there a few generations ago. Also accord-ing to the *kommune*, Ferkingstad people are often known as "Moliners" because in the 1920s many returned from Moline, Iowa, wearing strange, black hats. Many of these men were eldest sons, the ones who by law stood to inherit the family farms, but they began relinquishing these rights so that younger brothers, even mothers, could maintain the family farm.

Still a viable farming community, Ferkingstad, I was told, produced top-quality Langåker carrots. Hoping to support the local economy, I looked for them everywhere in vain. A year after we moved to the island, at the Skudeneshavn Days Festival, a young lady set up a table full of fresh carrots. At five that evening all that remained was dust. I speculated that they must have been the elusive, irresistible Langåker variety and wished I had enjoyed similar success selling my drawings.

Boasting one of the most moderate climates in Norway, southern Karmøy attracted many birds including those migrating from Russia. Ole Jakob Vorraa, local environmentalist, nature lover, and photographer, pointed out some whose long beaks allow them to dig deep into the earth and told me about the *viper*, an early harbinger of spring around Ferkingstad. He pointed out the *prestekrage*, tiny, white flowers resembling an old-fashioned priest's collar, which thrive along Ferkingstad's dunes. Karmøy was home to many unique varieties of flora and fauna, he explained. Seaweed slathered boulders and beaches and, in times past, farmers divided it up for fertilizer. Currently a local factory processes the kelp into a flour for medicinal products, but migrating birds never go hungry; there is seaweed to spare.

Skudeneshavn on the southern tip of Karmøy looked almost too quaint to have real modern-day people living there, conducting real 1990s lives. Perhaps there were microwaves and computers being tapped away on inside old-fashioned wood houses, but I couldn't imagine it. The only clue to electronic wizardry was the occasional satellite dish discreetly placed on a hidden section of roof. Homes and little fences were mainly white, dazzlingly so in summer. The light was particularly beneficial for painters and a sort of artists' colony had developed.

A gift shop was tucked away in one of the alley-size lanes, but although I stared a hole in its window hoping to find it open, it never was. Perhaps it had a proprietor's name, but an appropriate one would have been *"Stengt"* because that what the sign dangling in the doorway always said and "Closed" is how I always remembered it. The town's stillness and order made me wonder was it Sunday or lunchtime, or where was everyone and why did everything seem closed? Apart from festival days when people overflowed through the streets and onto the quay, the missing ingredient in "Skuddnes," as the locals nicknamed it, was always people, yet that very aspect had likely helped ensure its artistic milieu.

The big exception, however, was in the Majorstua cafe. A cozy combination cafe, art gallery, and handcrafts shop, the tiny place offered limited opening hours but convivial company. Their open-for-business signal was a *Diplom Is*, ice cream sign, propped outside the door. Browsing, nibbling, coffee drinking, and conversation were its main stock in trade. Customers shopped for art prints and originals by coastal artists and admired knitted dolls, wood trolls, and a miscellany of handmade items suitable for gifts while waiting for lunch waffles to cook. An open guest book proved that people from all over the world had discovered Skudeneshavn on their travels.

One rainy morning I tugged half-heartedly at the door. A storm had blown in and Mike, his visiting sister, Eileen, and I were getting soaked. The handle didn't budge, so I ran off only to hear the owner calling me back. I entered the shop, dripping all over the floor, and he pointed me to a chair.

"*Sitt ned!*" he insisted, dragging over an electric heater and blasting it against my wet legs, placing a cup of coffee at my arm and fussing over me like a mother. The delicious heat temporarily made me forget my duties.

"*Takk, men mannen min og min svigerinne er med meg. Jeg trodde at caféen var åpen. De ser etter meg!*" I explained, telling him my husband and sister-in-law were probably looking for me. He stuck his head out the door and waved them down. They soon were treated to equal blasts from the heater and cups of hot coffee. Later he showed us upstairs to see his newly begun antique business. When we reluctantly left, he refused anything for the coffee, and we parted as warmly as old friends. Sometimes a mere hot cup of coffee indoors out of the rain tastes like nectar.

Before I began traveling overseas, I had never given much thought about how to get a cup of coffee. It seemed simple enough. You found a coffee shop and ordered what you wanted. In Norway just finding the place was hard. Sometimes you needed to buy a map and make some sense of it, and in Oslo some mapped streets just disappeared and so did foreign drivers trying to follow them. Then you needed to find metered parking spaces and prepay the charge or risk a fine.

Ordering at a coffee shop was harder than it seemed. Foreign words often looked like they might be pronounced one way but sounded quite different with their inflections. Asking for coffee, pastries, or sandwiches—trying to hear the amount due properly, then using "foreign" coins to pay for your order tested your verbal and audio skills. It took a long time before I felt brave enough to add anything extra, like passing the time of day.

But the man at the Majorstua Cafe had an instinct for foreigners, greeting you pleasantly before quietly returning to his newspaper. The first time I tried talking with him and the lady who made the waffles, they both tried their best to figure out what I was saying. I felt my confidence soar. It was my Karmøy equivalent of a power lunch. This man's persona had been captured in a large painting on the wall, and talking to him as his other self smiled out from a picture was uniquely enjoyable. Like Hilde, he was supportive and friendly, and we managed, in a fashion, to enjoy some conversation.

Majorstua was as much a meeting place for friends and travelers as a business, and I took an American friend from Stavanger there. Seven or eight retirees conferred spiritedly in the corner but hushed when they overheard us talking. "Where are you from?" inquired one of the men. Joyce said she was from Colorado, and I replied I was from Texas. Their faces broke into pleased smiles, and soon we were engaged in across-the-room conversations. One lady said she was originally from New York, and she talked about it at length—and the fact she had married a Norwegian and moved to his homeland. Now widowed, she remained in Norway with her children and their families. Her accent was that of a New Yorker and her friends all joined in with contributions about ties with America—trips or guests or whatever. We were sorry when they prepared to leave.

The New York lady was in no hurry and waited back a little. "It was so nice to meet you both!" she whispered loudly as though we three were part of a conspiracy, adding, "And it was so nice to be able to speak in American!" The theatrical stage whisper was designed to be overheard by her Norwegian friends whom she hoped would take the hint. She missed her mother tongue. I was beginning to understand that feeling occasionally myself.

One's identity, even education and intellect, is tied up in one's native language so that seeing it slip farther and farther away is like watching your only life belt disappearing on the ocean. Your history, insignificant memories from childhood, all flow easily in your natural tongue but get discarded in the burden of translation. You are a sort of historyless person. In America the person I was talking to could almost finish my sentence themselves since they knew what I was talking about, and we based that on our common culture. My language and experiences were essential management tools I carried around every day, and I could not function properly without them.

The craving to speak your mother tongue seems to endure no matter how long you live in another country. Language is alphabet and grammar within the framework of a familiar culture, reflecting most accurately and intensely your deepest sense of self. The words you choose and how you pronounce them identify you and membership in a particular society, culture, and land. You don't have to think, translate, or plan how to convert your thoughts to words as you have to when trying a new language. Instead your words tumble out instinctively and in sync, as effortlessly and natural as breaths. Perhaps most people are only truly at peace and happy when expressing themselves in the language of their childhood.

The lady in the cafe was a lost soul, and I wished I could have more time with her. Maybe her friends would agree to a little change of plans—alternating English and Norwegian to accommodate her?

Still, where the majority rules, the lone speaker of another language perhaps finally gives up. A Karmøy friend enjoyed speaking English with me for practice, but her husband, Andreas, refused even when I spoke very clearly and slowly to help him. Marianne confided that she was resigned to his attitude. Her husband was resolute about his right not to speak any English to me although he was kindness itself when we were guests in his home. No one could have tried harder than Andreas to make us welcome, chatting in long streams of Norwegian, smiling broadly, constantly hovering over my coffee cup and offering to refill it. Since he spiced his words with heavy dialect intonations, delivered rapid-fire, he produced much I could not begin to figure out.

After begging a repeat on one statement spoken firmly, I finally understood. *"Jeg bor i Norge, i mitt land og jeg trenger bare å snakke norsk!"* He was stating a truth—that he lived in Norway, his own land, and needed to speak only Norwegian! His eyes challenged me. Unspoken was *i mitt eget hus,* in my own house, in case I had missed that important part.

Sometimes I wished a piano tuner could have tuned my ears since the sounds danced all over the scale and I missed the complete symphony. Andreas refused even the concession of speaking slowly. He reminded me of the Norwegian father-in-law of a newly married Scottish friend in Bergen. Not one word of English passed his lips the first six months she knew him, and he spoke Norwegian at his natural conversational speed while she struggled along in her newly acquired foreign language. Amazingly, when his Scottish in-laws arrived, he spoke English perfectly well but reverted to Norwegian full-time the moment they left. Our friend, Andreas, had more in common with the father-in-law than I had imagined, but I found that out much later.

Visiting Andreas and Marianne was always a pleasure

because they made us feel at home. We were all discussing *hulder*, the mythical and beautiful sirens of Norway who allegedly live in the ground and have tails, when Andreas offered the encyclopedia. If only it had been in English! Another time he turned on CNN so we could see a report on the Oklahoma Federal Building bombing, horrible news that it was. He rocked happily in his living room chair interjecting, answering, and starting new trains of conversation all in Norwegian, of course, while Mike and I tried for thirty minutes to leave despite Marianne's pleas that we should stay a little longer.

We said goodbye, wishing he would speak some English so we would know him better and hear what was important to him. I always worried that he saw me as none too bright since I frequently didn't get the hang of things. Marianne was always the go-between. The following year, when I caught him saying something in English to their visiting American relatives, I was stunned. We regulars from the neighborhood, especially one who was a woman at that, received no such treatment!

A truer test of friendship was when it transcended language, but when I called from the States a year or two later, I stubbornly hoped for a little bit of English conversation.

"Hi, Andreas! This is Patti—from Houston," was met by silence. "May I speak to Marianne?" In a second his voice rang out. *"Marianne! Amerika!"* That was enough for me.

Leaving Skudeneshavn, taking the east coast road north, you have a sense of cat and mouse as you negotiate the narrow road, hoping nothing larger than a car—please no vans or buses—will appear in front of you. The Karmsund sparkles on your right, and many *friluftområder*—fresh air areas—offer drivers a chance to pull off the road, enjoy the brisk air, and take some photographs. In autumn gold and red leaves rustled and shimmered as beautifully as New England's. Smooth, blue, endless horizon seamlessly blended with water and sky—and south across a rough current lay Stavanger. In the midst, however, an ominous, rusting land mine lay silhouetted against a backdrop of sea and mountains. The world stopped until I tore myself away from seeing the beauty of nature and the worst of man horribly united.

Farther north, the Burmaveien, the Burma Road, looped across the island. Built by World War II prisoners, it meandered across the island's heather and peat moors. My friend Vorraa explained that he often photographed red deer and birds while bringing his children on camping trips there. The remote, expansive area had the look and feel of Scotland and contained root remnants of giant trees believed to be five thousand years old.

Stangeland came next, a lovely little place where fields sloped gently down to the shore. An historic house, furnished with the original farm furniture and adjoined cattle barn, hid in a copse of trees. Nearby a deep brook still fed an extinct flour mill whose smooth, flat grinding stone still lay—waiting? Its most recent use was in wartime when people secretly ground their own flour.

By the time I left, I knew at least one person on the sparsely populated east coast, a carpenter. When passing his home, I always gave his workshop an affectionate glance, remembering how the man managed to make sense of my poorly spoken Norwegian requests for art boards and easels. He would pore over sketches, and with words, wood, and the glue of cordiality, always produce some handsome and useful piece of art equipment, tailor-made for me.

After Stangeland the road dipped past a school, then back into Kopervik to rejoin the main highway back to Haugesund. It always felt good to return to Kopervik's bustling little crossroads because her friendly people created a warmth I always felt was missing in postcard-pretty Skudeneshavn. Even their one downtown statue reflected the town's genuineness. They had memorialized their old street sweeper, Gustav, and he stood there, broom in hand, much as he had when he had worked there for many years. The residents missed him so much after his death that *Den Norske Bank* commissioned the sculpture to be presented to the community during its 125th anniversary celebration as a city. Today Gustav remains in the high street, a permanent reminder of a man who made a friend of everyone and brought people together—a real man from a real town, Kopervik.

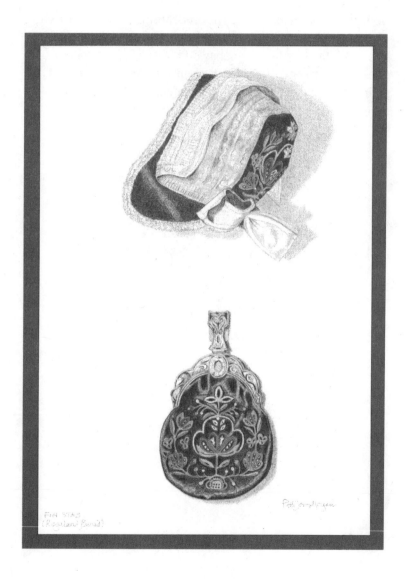

FIN STAD
(Rogaland Bunad)

9

National Day

Easter celebrations, symbolizing the new year, were big in Norway, and were followed by the nation's tribute to their freedom and independence on May 17. Patriotic friend Elaine always made sure her car was freshly washed. Everything had to look its best for *syttende mai*, May 17.

One blessedly bright National Day, the tenth day of sunshine in a row, the children of Håvik and people of the community arose early to celebrate. Women wore their special costumes, Rogaland or Karmøy *bunader*, or those from Hardanger—whichever designs matched their own birthplace or home county, *fylke*. We had woken briefly at 4 a.m. when eager band members had hammered on the front door of the bandmaster's home opposite ours. Paul was well used to this particular ritual and, a few hours later, stood happy and bleary-eyed in his red uniform, no worse for wear.

Silence fell as the flag was raised, and a community leader roused the crowd with a speech. Afterwards people shook hands and greeted one another with *"Gratulerer med dagen!"* Congratulations on the day. Neighbor Einar looked surprised to see us up and about so early. But how could we have missed it? What with horns blasting at dawn and band music echoing throughout the neighborhoods, it was part of the fun of being in Norway. We joined the procession of vehicles heading north to Avaldsnes, flags flapping gaily from cars with floral decorated hoods. Mike and I wore our Sunday best, and with a tiny Norwegian flag at our window, we fit in.

Flag flying was important, as Einar had told us, and on National Day more so. Twenty-foot-high flagpoles announced special days, marriages and anniversaries. Flags in small communities waved like mournful soldiers one week when several men were lost in a helicopter accident. On this day large flags snapped in a brisk northwest wind, and small ones clustered in windows, garages, and patios. Family cars took on airs, purring along the highway like diplomats' limousines, hoods decked with greenery and crossed flags, passengers looking like royalty. A roadside tractor looked ruggedly spiffy decorated with flowers and branches. Even a child's bicycle got the fancy treatment: a boy rode by with green leafy branches entwining his bike's curved handlebars. Only one person was oblivious to all the commotion. In a yard a white-haired lady, wearing a plain blue house dress, bent in half like an old-fashioned clothespin to retrieve something from under a flowering fruit tree.

At Avaldsnes School the narrow roads filled with mothers and children looking like dolls in their matching costumes. Some little boys, briefly calmed, wore boys' *bunader* (short jackets, special britches, and knee-length wool socks with woolen calf bands). In the crowds were a handful of Asian children, one of whom clasped the hand of her blonde Scandinavian mother.

The four-year-old, dressed in a child's costume and white apron, solemnly held up a little Norwegian flag, knowing she was as Norwegian as everyone else that day. Coal-haired girlfriends linked arms, *bunad* skirts swirling behind. A friend's daughter looked like a princess from the Middle Ages, blonde hair falling away from transparent skin, satin-lined cape catching the sun. Teenagers walked in twos and threes, childhood friends, always together.

It was quite a sight to be surrounded by Norwegian women in their costumes, and I wished I was wearing one too for they were so beautiful. Fortunately the weather cooperated. Nothing was worse than having the expensive, hand embroidered costumes ruined by showers. Starting life as young girl's *konfirmasjon* outfits, they were sewn and embroidered by kind grandmothers. The *bunad* skirt was set off by a heavily starched, white blouse and a complimentary vest, lined cape, and cap—the latter hardly ever worn. *Bunad* jewelry was added too over the years. On the practical side, the girl's outfit was created to adapt to her figure as she matured to adulthood.

A fanfare of music announced the children's parade (*barnetog*), which marched right on schedule, not surprisingly for Norwegians are sticklers about time. At 9:45 it was Håvik Skole's turn, each class carrying a handmade banner indicating the year represented. I caught sight of a beaming Liv-Marit and Solfrid before they disappeared into the crowds.

Einar and Else, and Torben and Lone, a Danish couple who had befriended us early on during our stay, waved at us to join the people's walk, the *folketog,* to St. Olav's Church. Hundreds of men, women, and children, baby carriages, and families from the surrounding village communities joined the procession along the winding lane overlooking the sound, the narrow body of water known as the Karmsund. Two *fjordinger,* Norwegian horses, galloped up and down, whinnying, proud heads and strong bodies silhouetted against the sky.

Perhaps one May day Norway's first king had stood on the very same spot, scanning the water, wondering if the distant ship were friend or foe. Even now I felt he would still feel at home on the Avaldsnes hills.

Lone and Torben kept us company later that day at Håvik school's sports hall, the *idrettshall,* where we enjoyed a light supper of *lapskaus*—a meat, potato, and vegetable stew—and fancy cakes made by the students' mothers. Liv and Hanna busied themselves behind the scenes, hoping food sales would boost the band's coffers. The band competed in towns and cities all over Norway and transportation cost money. Costumed women glided around, visiting family and friends, resplendent in silver jewelry. Torben could not resist a wry poke at the Independence Day celebration. "After all, this was once our colony!" he chuckled.

Children's good behavior began to slide after they had been up so long and even the most fastidious struggled to keep ice cream from dribbling down their chins onto their beautiful clothes. I grabbed my camera to catch an informal photograph, but cones got shoved out of sight and chins were hastily wiped first. Years of hearing, "Oh, no, Ingrid! Put that ice cream away when I am trying to take a photograph of you!" had trained them to try to look their best for *syttende mai* photographs, and catching them enjoying their ice cream was impossible. Pictures in my album would tell only half the story. Each innocent, smiling little child was holding a dripping ice cream behind her back.

Life returned to normal next day, *bunader* put away—but not everyone's. A farmer's wife aired hers on a clothesline between the barn and the house. Her elegant skirt and blouse billowed against a backdrop of grassy hills, a silo, and turnips growing across the street. And while the lady's finery awaited its next outing—a christening, a wedding, an anniversary—she quietly tended her garden.

"Every aspect of nature, truly seen and felt through the gesture of reverence, has the power to lead us back to the sanctuary of our soul. . . . We re-envision the world as, perhaps, a more hopeful and peaceful place to live."
—From *The Sanctuary Garden* by Christopher Forrest Mc Dowell and Tricia Clark-McDowell

Drums and trumpets, laughter and greetings filled much of the day on May 17, but the tenor changed after the peoples' procession up to Avaldsnes Church.

When all fell still in the peaceful, green churchyard, everyone took a breather. It was time to count their blessings and take stock of how they felt about their homeland, be thankful, and be reminded that their freedom was hard won from Sweden in 1905, lost during the dark days of the wartime occupation, yet theirs to enjoy again. Expressions turned contemplative during moving speeches, and even children were shushed, left to play quietly around gravestones decorated with fresh flowers.

During the speeches and hymns, my heart and gaze traveled across the cemetery, past the gravestones engraved with Karmøy's familiar family names dating back a hundred years, and stopped at the natural barrier, the mainland mountains across the glistening water. If a giant tidal wave appeared, we might all be swept into the sea en masse, but it hadn't happened yet. For such a small place, thirty miles by less than ten, to be so richly en- dowed with citizens who would rather live there than any place else in the world—regardless of the weather—was a tribute to their devotion. The island had been created by a fortunate accident of geology during the Ice Age and demanded an independent, survivalist people which Karmøyans were. They could survey the high skies and distant peaks, knowing both were out of reach, feeling separate yet safe on their own little island and as connected as they wanted to be.

Studying the people and the days, seasons, and nature had engaged me so fully since I had begun to feel settled on Karmøy that sometimes I could barely keep up with the flow of ideas and thoughts which swept through me like waves. Finally my fingers had begun tapping away happily on the keyboard and I forgot about CNN. I needed America for political protection, but she was becoming irrelevant to my daily life.

Safety was a natural state where days could be spent without a single minute lost to worry about personal security. Everyone knew everyone, and any troublemakers were exposed to public scrutiny. As a friend at the post office explained, our small community was protected by being *gjennomsiktig*, or transparent. Socially and militarily Norway was taking good care of me now. Each time a familiar gray coastguard cutter slid into view, I felt protected. The shiny metal and clean-cut look confirmed that their high-tech detection equipment and armaments were strong enough to scare off an enemy foolish enough to come sniffing around. Interestingly, had we lived on the strategically important Jan Mayen island, a Norwegian possession close to Greenland, we might have had to defend the island ourselves. Or so a young friend of ours said. Applying for work there, she had to agree, in writing, to help fight off invaders. Unfortunately we lost track of her and never learned if the authorities practiced armed drills against foes swarming up the beaches.

Karmøy made no such request, nor had to, as we were part of the close-in Scandinavian peninsula; nonetheless it made me think. Throughout my life I had been incredibly lucky, assuming I would never face enemy soldiers beating on my door, about to take my house, life, and possessions, but how many others had thought it would never happen to them either? For me it was something you read about; for others, the worst nightmare. I rested in the security of the *kystvakt's* benevolent presence under the heaven-high Nordic skies. Our maritime night watchman, at least that's how I viewed him, checked all the dark corners and odd noises, making sure we were all safe before moving slowly on to his next stop. In my heart I always thanked the coastguard for coming to check on us folks in and around Haugesund and Kopervik.

Norway knows its vulnerability from a painful lesson. From 1940 until 1945 invading troops occupied and controlled the majority of the citizenry. Helped by informers and German sympathizers led by the Nazi-established Quisling government, the country labored under cruel hardships. Oslo's Resistance Museum offers sad and poignant reminders of that repressive period. For this never to happen again, Norway of the '90s firmly controls her land and shores. As highly decorated Norwegian war hero Knut Haukelid observed about Norway's tragic position during World War II in his book, *Skis Against the Atom,* "We often discussed the causes of our being in our present situation— having to do our fighting from abroad and live in our own country as outlaws. We always arrived at the same conclusion: if we had been prepared in 1940, if the Norwegian armed forces had had a chance in battle, this would never have happened. We were sure that the Norwegian people had learned their lesson, and that we should maintain our defenses in the future."

Fifty years later national service remains compulsory for all young men, but one looked uncomfortable when we congratulated him for doing his duty and contributing to his nation's security. To him the exercise was rather futile and his part in it nothing special. He preferred to laud America's military capability. I felt he had cheated himself out of feeling good about his own effort. He had learned how to protect his country and his immediate community, if he were needed. People like Haukelid had counted on young men just like him in a time of desperate need. "It was a busy winter ... once again it proved how much easier it is to build up a military force in a country that has compulsory military training for all its young men. All we had to do was show them their new rifles, machine guns, and anti-tank rockets and give them their uniforms," he said.

A young Haugesunder tried to explain our young friend's attitude. "I think there are two reasons for this," he said. "First, they are forced to go. People think it's good for them to be learning some discipline, being on their own. But it's the first time away from home and, well, they miss their mothers! It's boring to them too, with not enough to do, so far away from their families. Also they're so young and they just don't think anything will ever happen. They don't think of World War II. I think if the government made the service voluntary, that would be better. Young men would still go—I believe that—but they would feel differently."

Interestingly Haukelid had nothing but praise for Norway's volunteer militia, which helped prevent national chaos as the war drew to a close. "In May 1945, the most curious army our country has ever seen appeared in the light of day. About 50,000 men of the Norwegian home forces took over control and authority throughout the country. They were nearly all young lads, who for several years had been training and preparing for the day when they would be able to strike a blow for their faith and their people. This army is all the more curious because it was one hundred percent volunteer; not one man had been called up to serve against his will. For several years it had been their daily lot to give ground, and go on giving ground in the face of German encroachments while man after man was taken, and disappeared. Now they came forth in a body. A people which can mobilize 50,000 men in such conditions should always be able to exist as a free people."

Back in Texas no young men in our neighborhood knew the first thing about defending us in the event of an outbreak of war—by air, sea, or land. I feared that the movement of armored tanks into our subdivision would be matched by a fleet of exiting pickup trucks hurrying their owners off to grocery-sacking jobs at Kroger's. We would be left to fend for ourselves. I envied Norway for its national service. Their young men still trekked off north for military training and to be reminded that the price of freedom was often feet on the ground and rifle in the hand, just in case. They would know how to defend their homeland. On National Day we appreciated them all, despite their own misgivings.

I bowed my head in the reverent atmosphere, deep in thought. In many ways I was living on several levels at the same time—all at different, sometimes perplexing, stages. I could function well as a citizen, drive, shop, handle the basics. My language skills were adequate; I was friends with my neighbors. I also noticed I had subtly begun distancing myself from my American world "back home" and even my own British relatives. Something was afoot. There were still many things I couldn't do well, making telephone calls in Norwegian being the main one. Also I hadn't mastered how to conduct any businesslike affairs. Anything official intimidated me as bureaucracy inevitably tangled things up. I had tried earlier to help Olivia get hired for a summer job. My positive attitude and American-style job hunting techniques failed miserably, yet as I listened to the prayers I couldn't understand, my Americanism dissipated. I seemed to belong there, on Karmøy, more than anywhere else. Somewhere along the way I had fallen in love with life there. The people with whom we shared this solemn moment had accepted us and I felt a deep, personal peace. And, at that moment, a question formed. Is this elusive sense of peace and safety important enough to keep you here? I glanced at a little girl in her pretty *bunad* as she carefully placed a floral wreath on a gravestone, and wondered.

10

Beginnings & Endings

National Day was a kind of milestone—our second in Norway—and a new year beckoned. My apprenticeship in language would finish, and I was expected to be somewhat fluent. The land greened up and farmers who had been waiting for Mother Nature's starter's orders descended on the land as single-mindedly as flies buzzing up and down closed windows. Afterwards in unusual-looking pieces of farm equipment, they rumbled the roads, undisputed rulers. When I followed a tractor, my heart lifted, then sank as bus stops and other convenient turnoffs came and went before the driver let the traffic by. Driving home was the time to stop and to smell the roses, or in the case of the West Coast, redolent manure. The thin soil needed coaxing to produce strawberries, turnips, hay, carrots, potatoes, and fruit. The West Coast's special designer fragrance symbolized a thriving spring. Noses remained in their normal position and did not turn up with dismay. During the bustle, farmers waved and nodded obligingly from their bumpy mounts, but drivers of fertilizer tanks seemed less sociable. They averted their eyes when you passed, or more importantly, when they had to pass you.

    An invisible clock ticked and everyone felt it. I couldn't be lazy about my language class; I needed to get my knowledge ploughed in so that I could reap a harvest too. Whenever I managed to express myself clearly and understand any response, my confidence soared. It was all systems go in our classroom and we struggled over our final chapters. At home my unofficial tutors—Liv-Marit; her older brother, Per-Rune; and pals Kristine, Monika, Solfrid, and all the other children in the neighborhood— kept me practicing, practicing. Barrages of words were less confusing, but mastery of the language still seemed far away.

    For a long time my pronunciation of HMV, as "aitch em vee" met blank stares. Since Conoco, my husband's employer, had contracted with HMV, *Haugesund's Mekaniske Verksted*, to build the processing module for the Heidrun platform, I worried that no one seemed to have heard of them. Perhaps "aitch em vee" was just a fly-by-night operation? When I corrected my pronunciation and used the *norsk alfabet*, "hoh-em-vay" was restored to its original recognition. *"Å, ja. HMV!"* confirmed a local man, much to my relief.

    In school we tried to speak Norwegian with authentic accents and after some self-conscious lip puckering for vowels and throat assistance on consonants, we produced our own international versions. For me there were no soft blendings as in American sentences but harder endings and beginnings to words and choppy syllables. We puffed out on *p* sounds and hissed on "Oshloo" to prove our understanding of the capital's favored dialect. Even a little *k* sound took on some fire in Norwegian. *"Kom hit!"* for example meant "Come here!" and I indulged myself using it on the dogs. It sounded too rude a way to speak to a person. Perhaps I could make it more pleasant by adding, *vær så snill?* would you mind? Calypso responded with an icy stare to either version. He, like all cats, responded to the language of food and love more than commands, foreign or otherwise, and ignored me.

One day I felt buoyant enough to try something that always tied me in knots: speaking Norwegian over the phone. Mike and I wanted to treat ourselves to dinner out, and I jotted down a script before calling the restaurant, keeping my Berlitz "handy phrase" section open. A friendly voice responded with something unintelligible, so I just took a chance and said, *"Hei. Kan jeg få en bestilling for to, klokka sju, takk?"* Could I have a reservation for two at seven o'clock? The lady responded with a hodgepodge of words which might have looked like "Hdgdy skdi difg ehen?" and overloaded my mental computer. I sheepishly apologized and asked what she had said, explaining that I was just trying out my Norwegian. "Oh, just what name this would be under!" she explained with an understanding laugh. She took my reservation, but I had disappointed myself. Talking over the phone in Norwegian was the hardest thing in the world for me as I couldn't see the person and read any body language. As a friend told me later, *"Du er flink i norsk, men du får panikk!"* You're good in Norwegian, but you panic!

Panic developed too from a sense of dependence on strangers and having no control over nor adequate knowledge of your environment. So much of a newcomer's life depended on getting help. How do you get somewhere? Where is such-and-such sold? Do you know a dentist? Lucky for you if you could ask clearly enough so that people could indeed help. Even luckier was if you understood their answer. Sometimes responses seemed way off base. A dentist listened carefully to my request for treatment, then quietly asked, "I see. Hm. How old are you?" His society found many reasons for asking your age, probably because of their nationalized health system, but people also volunteered theirs at the drop of a hat. In class we agreed that it seemed unnecessary and intrusive, even silly. When a substitute teacher asked us all to introduce ourselves and expected to hear ages, I grinned then announced in Norwegian that I was twenty-one. She didn't appreciate my humor. Later a classmate suggested it was just a matter of time before restaurants demanded to know people's ages before giving them a reservation. "Dinner for two? We'll have to see. Hm, how old are you?" The possibility had us in hysterics.

Carrying a street map at all times was a good idea in a foreign country, yet classmate Pauline excelled in finding her way around without one and obtained great verbal directions from passers-by. Thanks to her, I firmly grasped *rett fram, til venstre,* and *til høyre* so that, like a mouse in a maze, I went straight ahead, to the left, or to the right, to boat docks, post offices, libraries, enjoying the gyrations of my mouth and tongue in producing the vowel sound ø in *høyre,* right. Accordingly, any directions which involved lots of right turns involved won my linguistic affections. When I managed to get from point to point relatively easily, it confirmed my crazy delusion that people thought I was Norwegian.

Our last test before class ended produced better results than earlier ones. In a prior essay I had written that my parents-in-law had died. "What exactly did you mean here?" Tor had asked very solicitously. Why, I had missed them, I replied. He explained which verb I should have used, not one that sounded like "missed." Still, after more than four months I wondered if I was really getting anywhere. I frequently spoke mixed-up sentences using a bit of this, a bit of that, and if I had been writing for hours in English, then heard and saw Norwegian words in class, the words could have been hieroglyphics for all I could make of them. *"Jeg snakker frokost klokka ni."* I talk breakfast at nine o'clock, I relayed illogically to the class.

The moderating weather drew songbirds and *tulipaner,* tulips, as well as a red-uniformed work crew swarming across our old school building. They webbed the place with scaffolding and tore off rotten exterior boards, replacing and painting them. We replaced our previous weather reports with joyful comments on the sunshine, *sola skinner!* and overall beautiful weather, *det er fint vær i dag!* The new immigrant characters in our textbook had made headway: they sought new apartments, packed suitcases, investigated libraries, and made new friends. I helped Olivia obtain her first library card.

Renewal was forced on Nadya too in an unexpected way. A pair of Jehovah's Witnesses latched onto her, resulting in a frantic cry to Pauline to help extricate her. "They keep talking to me about reliszjion! I tell them I have my own reliszjion!" she stormed, red in the face. By all accounts, these people were committed to high-volume soul conversion in order to guarantee their places in heaven, but Nadya, I could have told them, was not ready to be placed on their "to do" list yet. First they needed practice being locked in a room with an angry bee. Only then would they be strong enough to cope with our fuming classmate.

Local shop clerks became the beneficiaries of our real-life practice sessions. Pauline reported two *"du er flink!"* during just one afternoon with as much glee as one telling of an invitation to tea from her queen. She was clever in Norwegian! Exhilarating times prevailed. *"Vi prøver, vi prøver,* we are trying!"

Making it work—attempting to learn Norwegian, talk with local people, and develop friendships—had been my mission, almost as devout as that of the Jehovah's Witnesses. My survival as I moved into another year in Norway hinged on it. I had to belong where I was. I made it a rule never to go home without having spoken something in Norwegian to someone every day and persevered with the *Avis.* In shedding more of my American skin and speaking and reading the language of my new country, I began to feel like one of its people and really there was no choice. America and American life were so removed from me by then—and I still had several years to go—that it was sink or swim.

In just a few weeks the course would be over. I had already begun writing more seriously and discovered how much the Norwegian style of using lower case for almost everything had influenced me. Anything that made my five-finger typing easier and faster was a plus and this included dropping apostrophes, Norwegian style. I also yearned to use certain Norwegian words instead of English ones; *Filosofy* looked prettier than philosophy and was faster to write. Norwegian simplicity included fewer key strokes. Still, old ways were hard to change, and the words of my heritage marched along in little regulation uniforms fending off an energetic invading force.

During this period I got the gist of more printed material, discerned notices, used the post office and banking *giro* system whereby accounts were debited and credited directly by use of special forms, virtually eliminating the need for checking accounts. Banking and bills were not my strong suit, however. It still smarted to recall having watched an Oslo cable company technician disconnect our television for alleged nonpayment of a bill. It took many minutes of embarrassment and telephoning his billing department to learn why it happened. We had misread the due date; 5/3 meant March 5, not May 3. On the plus side, day to day conversation was easier. My gift of the gab was almost back, even in elementary Norwegian, but I still had difficulty understanding people's answers. If one *"Kan du gjenta?"* (Could you say that again, please?) did not work, I changed the subject or just nodded and looked blank, hoping the issue wasn't critical and that the person was not waiting for a coherent response.

I practiced the language on any Norwegian who would not revert to English to help me out, and the children continued to act as perfect sounding boards. When Mike came home to a houseful of Norwegian kids camped out in our living room, he seemed happy to limit his input to *"Jeg vet ikke"* (I don't know) and *"Hvorfor ikke?"* (Why not?) He assured me, however, he could read his Norwegian thermodynamics book at work. That dubious skill seemed noncompetitive with mine, so I brushed it off.

My whole attitude was improving—not only about where I stood, but how other newcomers were doing as well. Immigrant Algerians were successfully operating a local restaurant, and an *Avis* article featured an immigrant-owned import business. Pauline took a part-time job, taping an English language course, a perfect assignment for one so articulate. Olivia made plans to join a regular school after a year's hiatus to learn basic

Norwegian. Li's life perked up when he passed his drivers' test, bought a car, and had his wife join him in town. Hasan enrolled in a welding course. Positive vibrations filled the air.

Even the school glowed in its new, cheery yellow color by early summer, blossoming into more of a campus setting. At lunchtime students idled under leafy trees, talking quietly. Perhaps even more than the language of words, we students had learned the language of understanding and tolerance. Many immigrants, and the refugees particularly, had traveled a hard road to arrive at this point, and these last days marked their tentative entries into a free, safe world. I hoped I would not forget them.

Siste dag, the "last day" came and we felt happy and sad at the same time. My friends from Britain, Turkey, the Philippines, Russia, and China, even our missing Icelander, had shared in my struggle, lightening my load, helping me not only learn Norwegian but feel less alone. Tor gave of himself as a teacher, encourager, and friend. Because he cared about us, he gave us a wonderful start, including a chance to be around at least one Norwegian every single day.

I stared, unseeing, at my passport into Norwegian culture, my textbook. Was this it? Had I learned as much as I could in these couple of hundred pages? I felt sure I hadn't. Worse, where would we go if we didn't come here the next day? Whom would I talk to? And was my inspiration, the prospect of days of freedom in which to write, really going to happen? I felt sure that I wasn't ready to leave the nest.

I must go down to the sea again, to the lonely sea and sky,
And all I ask is a tall ship and a star to steer her by,
And the wheel's kick and the wind's song and the white sails
shaking,
And a grey mist on the sea's face and a grey dawn breaking.

—From *Sea Fever* by John Masefield

11

Summer on the Water

By month's end beautiful seventy-degree days settled over the island and I soaked them up, caressed by a whispering breeze and serenaded by songbirds. I spent days thinking about absolutely nothing, and loved it. The gentle weather surprised me; Karmøy was behaving like a lady. She let up her meteorological theatrics and allowed the residents to relax. This passive period was necessary to soften their intolerance about what she did to them the rest of the year. For a short time they had no wind to lean into or ice to slip on, no snow to crumble through their fingers or rain beating on their backs. Only an occasional roll of thunder perked up summer's brief stay on the southwest coast.

I forgave summer's blandness only when she doubled up on daylight. Twenty hours or more of useable daylight boosted my productivity and answered my lifelong prayer, a day with no darkness. As midsummer day approached, the sky spread exotic streamers of red, gold, and orange too far north for a sunset. Calypso, jealous that my attention was elsewhere, leapt onto the

windowsill, purring, placing his black velvet silhouette against a
sky as liquid and languid in its colorful transformation as a lava
lamp. Black against shimmering peach, moody mauve, and silvery
gold. Where was the witch on a broomstick?

Several neighbor families planned their annual holiday or
ferie, some choosing to visit Sweden and the newly opened-up
country of Estonia by coach and ferry, others going to Paris.
Paris! From Houston it was light-years away, but from Norway,
Paris was just the other side of lunch. In summer our garden
insisted on attention, and when the grass grew long and green,
Per-Rune, Liv-Marit's brother, paid a call. "I think I must cut it for
you," he announced, standing at our front door, a crooked smile
shining from his round face. Our young friend generally ran over
the grass once and quickly. Tall clumps and troublesome edges or
corners didn't slow him up. If he did not get them on his initial
swipe, they stayed. Cutting the lawn, therefore, was a swift
accomplishment, and the doorbell signaling the job done rang
almost before I sat down. Per-Rune cheerfully pocketed the small
change and a couple of weeks later returned to do more.

When the grass had not grown sufficiently to be trimmed
again, I checked around for another little task. Would he like to
wash my car? "OH, yes, I love to wash cars!" he enthused, "but I
will not take anything for doing it." He looked admiringly at our
little hatchback, and since the whole purpose for the visit was to
earn pocket money, I insisted he accept something. He was off to
a show or exhibition the next day he told me, and they would
have hot dogs for sale! His *engelsk* and my Norwegian sometimes
had us going in circles, and this occurred as I tried to determine
the exact type of show. Often these occasions resulted in *"Jeg vet
ikke."* At first this " I don't know" surprised me, but I learned that
it had more to do with not understanding my question than not
understanding the topic. This issue only bothered me when I
really needed to know about the culture.

Washing my car rapidly became, through various hitches,
a joint effort despite my hope I would just look up and see it

done. Our water hose did not fit the house outlet, so I drove to
Liv's to borrow hers. I left Per-Rune armed with water, cloths, and
a container of unopened automobile cleanser. Three minutes
later he returned bearing bad news. "This stuff is not for washing
the car," he announced. We reviewed the bottle's label together,
discovering that Mike had bought the wrong product. Could he
do anything with it anyway? Somehow he, Toralf, and another
recruit set about the job with much shrieking and spraying one
another with the hose. A few minutes later the bell rang again.
Per-Rune was back.

"I have finished," he stated for the second time in too
brief a spell. My dripping car lagged sadly behind Mr. Carwash's
standards, but at least the shine had returned and the avian
splotches were almost gone. He left with his hot dog *kroner*,
finally explaining that he and his father would be going to a sports
event.

Above our house on Liarveien sea gulls barked like dogs
or cackled madly as they winged over Calypso's territory, the
roof. Conveniently for us Calypso had not figured out how to
jump off and he simply accessed it via the kitchen deck as though
it were an extension of his indoor playground. Birds considered
him no threat. They whirled past like helicopters, hooking pieces
of bread and puffed wheat from the yard. Of all the birds, sea
gulls were the least keen on scraps. They were happiest clinging
to fishing boats which, even on foggy days, failed to shake the
squawking freeloaders.

In summer enormous three- and four-inch-long, curva-
ceous, black, shiny, Texas-sized slugs slipped through the grass,
quite handsome in their way. For some reason I viewed them as
weather predictors. Super-duper sized slugs must mean delightfully warm Junes and Julys; skinny ones, cool? My unscientific
study fell by the wayside after two summers. The septic tank truck
made its rounds midyear, politely ignoring us since we were done
last year, we were assured, and we hoped it was true. June and
July being the national vacation months, it was wise not to plan
anything of importance then. Doctors wouldn't be around to

deliver your baby, and dentists closed their offices, and it was up to you to watch for their vacation ads. Dentist Oddbjörn Eikill never knew how much I enjoyed pronouncing his name, "Oh, I kill!" under my breath as I walked past his office. Friday workdays became even shorter than usual as many Norwegians departed for their *hytter*, weekend cabins, often in the mountains, and Brits headed for their own homes back in the United Kingdom as early as eleven in the morning in order to make sea and air connections.

I lazily watched small craft dart across the bright blue waters. Two neighbors took their boats out of dock. Casual boating had lost some of its glamour, however, as I admired the bigger, commercial ships. They worked the waters year-round, never hanging around waiting for girls with great figures and suntans to giggle all over them. Real ships had backbone. Even the fast boats, the commuting catamarans, were tough. Only the severest of weather would halt them. In those cases they would transfer their passengers to bus and ferry instead. Our friend Torben took the fast boat to Stavanger each day, stowing a bike at the terminal and riding back and forth across town to his office. The most famous ships though were the coastal steamers which ran from Bergen to Kirkenes, taking cargo, honeymooners, and all those captivated by the prospect of awesome scenery and a glimpse of the Midnight Sun.

One summer we joined other vacationers, mainly German, aboard one of the coastal steamers, the *Vesterålen*. We pulled out of Bergen harbor at past ten o'clock in the evening although the sky said it was only six. Before long, four enormous Newfoundland dogs dragged their owners on deck—two very energetic Danes who considered it no hardship to squeeze themselves and the four pets into a small cabin each night on their way to a vacation in Trondheim. When the giant animals wolfed down their yogurt and cereal from special stainless-steel bowls next morning, every camera was clicking. The couple had a good sense of humor, a prerequisite, surely, for those willing to have their arms wrenched out of their sockets each time a hundred-plus-pound dog on a straining leash led them on a frantic gallop up and down decks.

"Now, we are Danish, but when you Americans think of *Danish*, you think of Danish pastries!" the husband chortled.

Danish people had delicious senses of humor. When I inadvertently introduced one as a Swede to my husband, the man corrected me. "Oh, no, I'm Danish!" only to add jokingly, "It's all right, but—don't you ever call me Swedish again!"

Each time our ship eased into port, Mike and I hung over the railing as forklift trucks crept out of warehouses like yellow, robotic mice trying to outsmart a cat. The scary groan of the ship's giant cargo door opening propelled them into nonstop loading and unloading, twirling and reversing, depositing heavy piles of construction material—concrete blocks, roof tiles, paint. When the ship's loading door thundered shut, I held my breath until we pulled safely, gently away and looked forward to our next port of call.

Taking the trip north to see the Midnight Sun almost set was not always smooth sailing even on the capable coastal steamers whose crews were expert in negotiating rough seas. On those days china got flung across the floors and queasy passengers, seasickness skin patches fully deployed, flung themselves on their bunks. Waters were calm for us, but instead of counting sheep at night, I counted creaks while my husband selfishly slept like a baby. That same ship, the *Vesterålen*, sailed into Haugesund later for a fix-up date with *Haugesund's Mekaniske Verksted*. Afterward with a little spray of perfume around her neck, she returned to Bergen to delight more tourists.

I had months to study boats in Norway. Kopervik harbor, just ten minutes south of us, was home to the fishing trawler, *Vea*, and sheltered the *Tingvik, Kvanskjær* from Bergen as well as emergency rescue and fisheries department boats. The *Drett*, the vessels of the black and white *Nor-Cargo* line, others from the *Stavangerske* line, the white *King Oscars,* and the crisp blue and white *Color Line* ferries constantly cut through the sound. On cold days the *Color Line*'s powerful engines throbbed from a mile away as she swept regally back from Newcastle, probably loaded with MetroCenter shoppers' specials and plenty of wine from Sainsburys. The *Color Line* was all business, ferrying people and cars between England and Scandinavia in all but the most inhospitable weather.

My closest encounter with the ferry was ironically from my friend Ruth's living room. Ruth's home nestled alongside the Haugesund bridge, and the monster's heavy heartbeat vibrated the whole house. The ship slipped by like a great metal blade, blocking out the sky, endlessly long. Keep straight ahead; don't veer left! I prayed, heart pounding.

When the living room stopped shaking, Ruth and I resumed our visit as though nothing had happened, but she must have seen my shocked expression. The *Color Line* went up several notches in my book after that for anything that powerful and which took North Atlantic crossings in its stride deserved my utmost respect.

Even tough, noisy ships succumbed to repairs and renovations though and often wound up waiting for service at Kopervik Slip, scraping noisily against one another. Large ones lodged in dry dock, in a rugged landscape of rock and trees, looked like Noah's Arks in a forest. Old ships suffered the indignities of reweldings and chemical dousing in lieu of champagne. Welders and workmen labored into the evening under powerful lights, providing ships new looks, new identities. Plastic tarps stretched across work areas snapped in the wind, straining and ballooning against tie down ropes.

Boats were everywhere; many a Karmøy garden offered shelter to some whose landmark proportions helped lost motorists. The family pleasure craft took root in yards, migrating only briefly in the summer for maritime follies. By fall beached boats adopted the less glamorous persona of weed control device, defying anything to grow in their shadow.

A Håvik teacher devised yet another imaginative use for a boat by setting it in a kindergarten playground. Little boys scrambled in and out, pretending to row, absorbing a subtle lesson not addressed in school books; on Karmøy a boat is equally at home in the garden as on the sea.

Life's like a ship in constant motion
Sometimes high and sometimes low
Where every one must brave the Ocean
Whatsoever winds may blow.

Assailed by squall or shower
Or wafted by the gentle gales,
Let's not lose the favoring hour
But drink success into the sails.

—Writer unknown (Lettering on an old, cracked bowl, Haugesund Museum)

Skudeneshavn Days Festival came along, and Einar had an old coastguard cutter tied up there. He was a member of an organization which fixed up the old vessels and financed the repairs by taking people or groups out for trips or parties in the summer. Would we like a ride back to Kopervik, he asked. Casting aside memories of the worst trip of my life aboard the Skudeneshavn ferry two months before, I stepped aboard. We gently nuzzled out of a harbor crammed with the largest group of restored wooden boats that had ever come to Skudenshavn. Tall-masted ships lined the quay which seethed with crowds. Ropes, knots, carved bows, and wrapped sails spoke the pride of work of the early 1900s. No factories turned out these vessels; rather they were the heritage of individuals—men who had cut, chiseled, and crafted every piece.

Our vessel's history and wood trim set me wondering about the men who watched it leave the harbor decades before. The Haugesund welders on Mike's gas processing module shared the same pride about their ocean-bound concrete and steel creation. To them it was a living thing. It had been part of their lives; the designing and constructing, welding and painting. As it floated away, a man might wipe away a tear, knowing it may last longer than he himself. Norwegians respected and had a passion for boats. One modern-day rig builder harkened back with fondness to his birthright, asking wistfully, "Can we build a boat next time?" Einar's boat had come into the world that same way years before and I felt honored to be on board.

Einar and two friends captained us out and surprisingly swung the boat southwest not north, and we leapt in heavy waves. I tried to look calm. Mike braced his legs, Viking-like, up front, holding on to nothing. The vessel tried to turn against the strong cross tide, and all there was between me and the water was a swinging rope.

As we pitched side to side, frighteningly close to jagged rocks, I regretted my impetuousness in taking this way home. After a seeming eternity we straightened out and turned south then east until finally passing the southern tip of the island, heading for the smooth waters of the Karmsund.

Einar produced a vacuum flask of coffee. Mike finally unlocked his legs and sat down with me. Our friend poured the unfiltered black liquid into white china cups. The grounds hung thickly, and I waited for them to sink half an inch. Sipping carefully, I shunted them around my back teeth with my tongue. I was not too lily-livered to drink Einar's ship's coffee.

We faced off oil tankers and container ships heading south, and we passed like neighbors with a grudge. No one waved on ships like that. Still one man in a sleek, shiny-hulled wooden boat waved leisurely from the distance, leaning out from beneath his sail, and Einar and his friends returned the acknowledgment. Everyone knew everyone on the small boats, and this was just a nautical version of taking a weekend stroll around town.

"He built that boat himself, took him five years in his spare time. He used his own oven to heat the metal and made all the metal pieces himself," Einar explained. The man in question was a picture of ease in the distance, steering his masterpiece across the waters looking as carefree and relaxed as a man in his favorite easy chair. Maybe once his rite of passage would have led him to a full-time career on the water which he so evidently loved. Now, however, he pursued his dream on the weekends. But he was an inheritor of the island spirit—a seaman from the *viks* or the small coves, giving him the right to the name *viking*.

We were doing about five knots, and Einar explained that knot speed calculations derived from dragging a knotted rope in the water. Despite the convivial conversation we touched on a favorite complaint among Karmøyans—Norway's big shipping company owners, the country's elite class. Some felt the magnates cared little about Norwegian pride of ship ownership and just wanted to make money. This day however we heard about a shipping owner who once made a certain captain and his crew change their vessel's distinctive neat black and white colors to pink. "Pink!" Einar growled. "They said it would make it easier for the ships to be seen. Companies were doing studies about colors. One company used dark red on their ships and found out they were having more psychiatric disorders than usual with the crew. They related this problem to the ship's colors, so all the companies were looking at these effects on the people on the ships and changing colors."

Sipping his coffee, he stared into the distance. "When they wanted our colors changed, I was mad, you know. All we had done over the years to take care of the ship and the good advertising all over the world was recognized, and it was for nothing! Just thrown overboard! I sent them a letter with my opinion in the form of a poem about it and got a rather sore letter back from them saying we couldn't keep doing things in the old ways! And they weren't the only ones sore at me. So was my Else!"

Possessing a vessel you are proud of makes a Norwegian happy and others happy for him. A newspaper had reported that a ship owner had given the king a sleek, high-tech yacht, and our friend's face glowed with pleasure as we talked about it. "That's fine with me if he wants to give a beautiful boat to the king!"

An hour and a half later my husband's staunch-looking sea legs failed, and we waved our friend goodbye at Kopervik. The coastguard cutter curled away, trailing a fishing boat. Far too vulnerable-looking for the deep, wide waters, it had safely gotten us home, because of the men who cut and nailed the planks. And because we had the best captain in the world, our good friend Einar.

Kopervik's windowsills fluttered with lace curtains and smiled with potted plants. Many shops occupied the street-level quarters of white, wood houses on the main street. Their fortunate location below people's living rooms imbued them with a personal, cozy ambiance which softened cold commerce. Although the Norwegian word for such a shop is *butikk*, the little businesses would hardly qualify for the trendy title "boutique" in modern American shopping centers. Old-fashioned storefronts of one or two plate glass windows invited you to view a small scale world close enough to touch. Since the business day finished by four-thirty or five o'clock, you could window-shop without interference along *gågaten* (the pedestrian part of the main street) on foot or bicycle, taking as long as you liked. The town's two dozen shops invited you to contemplate a pretty outfit, stationery, tablecloths, a vase, hair products, toys, earrings, men's shirts, or a new leather purse, *bunad* silver, blue plastic snow sled, red Hula Hoop, cosmetics, sturdy axe, toaster, an oil painting— or fish.

Until I had passed through town several dozen times, I had not really noticed the fish shop. It was so low-key as to be a front for a secret government operation—nothing to see, no fish smell, nothing. Across the seas British fishmongers' windows were often giddy with extravagant portions of fresh, shining fish of many shapes, sizes, and colors and festooned with sea-type accouterments such as cute streamers of smiling cardboard fish, ceramic mermaids, and bright, green plastic parsley hedgerows. Houston fish departments mixed the artistic and appetizing—and an unnerving array of imprisoned monster-faced lobsters.

Our local fish shop eschewed any frivolity. In fact, the only visual clues to the country's number one industry were in places far from the shop, and then in their dried state. We had seen racks of fish maturing in stiff breezes over the Lofoten Islands, preparing for their Italian and African soupy destinies. Others hung over garage entrances in Åkrehamn or dangled over a Finnmark patio. *Lutefisk,* dried, treated cod, remained a national delicacy. Drying the ocean's bounty seemed a national pastime for Norwegians with no restrictions on how and where.

On a side street in Skår and in a backyard in Skudeneshavn the local catch hung undisturbed by sea gulls, sharing a clothesline with flapping hand towels and socks. Other than in the famous Bergen Fish Market I had seen little evidence of fresh fish, and our modest little outlet in Kopervik conspired to keep it that way. I saw none in the window. In fact, all that existed there was a bowl of plastic fruit. You want fish? You know where we are. I feared that an advertising man would starve if he had to survive on the fishmonger's account—and would probably be too poor even to buy fish.

What brought the place to my attention at all was a threatening group of wrenches hanging high up on the wall inside, which somehow implied that the local fish were extraordinarily large with complicated parts to dismantle before becoming benign filets. Visions of fish the size of whales, with gaping jaws and snapping teeth and tails thrashing on top of wet decks of tiny fishing boats, filled me with new respect for the fishermen who dared to bring them in. Fortunately, after several bike rides past the shop and craning my neck, I saw the reality. The wrenches were for loosening nuts and bolts on cartons and crates, but they added some life to the place and, after that, I did not write it off as the most boring shop in the world.

One Christmas the fish shop surprised me when its one concession to the season appeared overnight. Their dreary, brown fishing net window sparkled with a collection of red and gold gift-wrapped packages with festive bows, and the plastic fruit was gone. Nothing else had changed, and I wondered whose idea it had been to switch out the regular window display.

"Why?" was the million dollar question. Was it to attract more customers or to encourage people to buy fish for Christmas presents? The fish shop's burst of optimism and confidence in its product forced me to review the fish issue. Norwegians loved it, along with their boiled potatoes, yet I failed to do anything very creative with it. The real, scary gourmet world of living and happily-swimming-until-a-moment-ago-and-now-you-are-eating-me fish still took away some of my appetite. It was easier to cast my line across the anonymous strips of iced white fillets in the supermarket freezer. I wanted to eat fish without feeling sorry for them, so I passed up any with eyes, mouths, tails, or scales.

Once I inadvertently offended Einar, slighting his favorite food with a suggestion he cook it in milk and onions to remove the fishy taste. It was the worst thing to say. "I *like* that taste," he answered, looking hurt.

Einar was big on fish and on fishing. He would await the fish shop's call as eagerly as Mike waited a response from a bookstore about a special title he wanted. On the whole, though, our friend preferred taking his boat out and catching his own. One lunchtime I walked in on him as he devoured a fried fish which looked like mostly bones to my uneducated eye. But the way he leaned protectively over his plate, looking wary as I neared the kitchen table, gave him the air of a man prepared to fight for it. Einar had the grace to admit that not everyone was as partial to fish as he, however.

"When I was a captain, I thought the crew weren't eating enough of it and ordered one lunch and one dinner of fish prepared per week. You know, soon I heard all these complaints. They were grumbling to each other, 'We have this captain from the West Coast and he keeps making us eat fish every day!'" Their mutinous dietary attitude still bothered him, and Einar reiterated that it was *only two meals* each week! I never doubted his word, but had his memory colored the events? Perhaps it was more like fish for lunch and dinner every other day?

Mike played an innocent role in Einar and Karl's friendly fishing rivalry one season. After Einar and Mike returned after half a day with no fish, Karl swung into action.

"They didn't catch anything?" he questioned me later, eyes glinting with astonishment.

"Listen," he continued, lowering his voice conspiratorially, "if Mike wants to go fishing, he can come with me on Thursday, okay?" His voice took on an urgent tone, "You tell him to call me, all right?"

I sensed more was at stake than just fishing. Karl wanted to prove that it should be darned near impossible to go out and come back empty.

Mike agreed to go, adding ruefully that he'd be leaving around daybreak. Several hours later the reluctant fisherman, no longer half-hearted, rather half frozen, returned carrying several kilo of fish. Karl looked triumphant when I bumped into him later.

"We had a good time fishing! You liked those fish? You know, I still can't understand it—how he went out before with Einar and didn't catch *anything*."

I never told him that only after a little heaving, and a long, lie down did my husband get his land legs back. But we did enjoy the fish filets!

The fish shop's decoration intrigued me. Was it the ultimate gift in Kopervik to receive a kilo or two of freshly caught *torsk* in a colorful gift box? Had the fishmonger recently subscribed to a business magazine which preached maximizing his seasonal market potential? Indeed, if one neighborhood boy was anyone to go by, business looked rosy.

"What's your favorite food in the whole world?" I inquired of the lad. After thoughtful concentration, his eyes lit up. "*Torsk!* That's my favorite!"

"Cod, the fish, right?" I double-checked.

"Yes!" Few American children would have shared his passion yet evidently some Kopervik youngsters inherited a taste and appreciation for fish, and their trimness as adults verified it.

Still my survey was incomplete. "What about you?" I asked his young brother. "Is cod your favorite too?

He could barely contain himself. "No!" he exclaimed, placing his vote squarely on another more land-bound food, "Pizza is! I love pizza!"

Thrifty Pea Soup

Putt en ert i en stor panne vann. Kok opp.
Hvis altfor strek, to bort erten!

Put a pea in a large pot of water. Bring to a boil.
If the soup is too thick, throw away the pea!

——From *Velkommen inn in våre kjøkkener,*
Editor, *Fru Hagny Thorsen.*

12

Letters from Home

As independent as we were from America, we still looked
forward to the mail. The mail provided a spiritual nourishment.
You read to get the news but also to keep connected to a former
life.

I rarely missed hearing the mail lady's little red car pull up.
Anyone who thinks mail carriers' lots are solitary ones as they
purvey the boxes, lighting on each like a bee, then winging off in
search of the next bush, is wrong. Our yards and gardens,
windows and terraces are filled with eyes, watching, waiting. Each
morning everyone's hopes rose and fell in time with the squeak-
ing symphony of the mailbox lids. Finally the gentle varoom as
she sped away sent us, ever so casually, over to see what she had
left us. "Give us this day our daily bread ... and our daily mail."

Mail was the daily surprise and big chance for good
news. It had the power to infuriate, make you groan or feign

disinterest, but getting stood up by the communicating world was sometimes worse. Like the lottery, it demanded a fatalistic attitude. Oh well, maybe next time?

Norway's residents, like America's, received their Reader's Digest Sweepstakes accompanied by exciting letters about their special good fortune to have been already selected for some list of potential millionaires. In Norway I still entered even when I couldn't decipher the message. Maybe being one of 4.5 million instead of 250 million would improve my chances.

Mostly our green mailbox was a cache for advertisements, flyers, and catalogues, community messages and package delivery notices. Advertising bulletins illuminated the Norwegian character. They were not known to brag; therefore, it was odd to me that, in print, ads for a product or service were frequently touted *Verdens Beste!* The World's Best! Companies abandoned corporate humility in their print ads. Perhaps because nothing could actually be the world's best, *Verdens Beste* was used for holiday tours, pen knives, hot dogs, and radios.

One afternoon I stared at an advertisement almost willing myself to find the magic phrase. A pack of cheery-looking condom men, cute little cartoon creatures, creatively named to emphasize their own special qualities scampered across the page. I admired the ad writer's restraint but was disappointed too because he could have made my day. If he had added *Verdens Beste!* who would have dared asked for proof?

Interestingly American copywriters rarely relied on international comparisons and never referenced other nations or their strengths at all. Consumers were expected to need state and city references only. "Texas's highest rated swimming pools! Mississippi's oldest paddle steamer. San Francisco's jumbo bagels!" Perhaps self-sufficiency was the reason. Separated from the rest of the world by two giant moats, the Atlantic and Pacific Oceans, America played its products like footballers. "World's Best" might count in the Olympic Games, but not for hot dogs.

If my Norwegian mail was skimpy, my corporate-processed mail from the United States weighed as much as some small animals. Starting out at Conoco's offices in Houston, it had developed its own life, cherished by its handlers at many stages who recognized what it was and where it was supposed to go. I felt sure it would still come on automatic pilot even when we had left. In winter I lugged it home over slick sidewalks, counting each step as a building block of character.

During cold, icy spells moms often hauled children through town on small plastic sleds. When a lady used hers to haul kitty litter, it gave me an idea; I'd drag the mail on a sled. Unfortunately the ice cleared before I could try it.

Magazines were what nearly gave me a hernia. Many appeared which I could not seem to cancel, and those just newly subscribed to worried for early renewals. Subscriptions became more permanent than some marriages which, once entered into, defied the best divorce lawyers to untangle. Moving across continents may not free you, but crying poverty might.

To my consternation, someone had misdirected a brochure touting, "For Size 14 and over" and it bore my name for the world to see. Had U.S. clothiers been spying on me? But … but … hey, guys! I was the one receiving the *Petites* catalogue, remember?

Cookie crumbs lay next to my coffee mug as a testament to their detective work. Brushing them guiltily into the trash, I threw the offending brochure after them. Maybe something decent would come—tomorrow?

A Thanksgiving Portrait

A pleasant purposelessness invaded the warm atmosphere. My ideas built up like impressive clouds which floated away as I tried to harness them. I missed the tangibility and form of winter with all its hard edges and contrasts, the source of much of my creative energy. Neighbors began returning to work and children at school meant a too-quiet lane. Einar reported a highly successful fishing trip, sans his unlucky partner, Mike. Going out alone, Einar had regained his luck. "This morning I used different kinds of lines and caught some really big fish. I can't think of their name in English, but they were this big!" His outstretched arms indicated fish at least two feet long—hinting at three—proving that, in fishing, Texas-style exaggeration was perfectly acceptable.

"Else and I sat outside the house and filleted them, and we had over ten kilos of fillets!" He looked forward to sharing the catch with his relatives, but Elsa had had enough filleting. "My wife said no more fishing for awhile!"

I was glad when Mari, one of the neighborhood young-sters, asked me if she could come over and practice reading in English to me. I felt useful at least. She stumbled over the peren-nial bugbear v's and w's despite her excellence in everything else. "That is werry nice!" read the twelve-year-old who had three years of English language. I corrected her, saying she should pro-nounce it exactly the same as the Norwegian word for "very," *veldig*. Both words began with the same sound. She thought for a moment, then her eyes locked on to mine as though I had asked a trick question.

"Yes. *Veldig, veldig,*" she repeated with confidence.

"Sure! *Veldig,*" I agreed. I asked her to repeat, *veldig, veldig,* very. She frowned and concentrated hard.

"*Veldig, veldig. . .w-w-w. . . .*" My ferocious look scared her into compliance. . . "V-ery!"

"Good, Mari!" I praised. My young friend continued resolutely as though it was the hardest thing in the world to remember . . . "*very*-e-r-y, very!" Why the "vee" sound was okay for veldig but not for "very" I had no idea. We rested from our "vee" labors and practiced ordinary reading, questions, and answers until I threw in another chance for her to prove she had mastered the "vee" sound. What was this word, I asked, pointing to "very" in a paragraph. "Werry?" she inquired and only another frown forced her to correct it. "Very?" It was hopeless. All around me were wegetables and werries and maybe I should not *worry* about them for the moment!

One afternoon Liv-Marit appeared solo at the door on the pretext of coming to see Rudy and Calypso. We had already lost our lovely Nicky to ill health, and she missed him as much as I did. Unusually quiet, she went straight into the television room and returned with the Checkers game. "Pleeeze, *skal vi spille en gang?*" Just one game of Checkers was all she wanted, and her blue eyes challenged me to say no.

"*Nei! Jeg er opptatt med datamaskin,*" I said, pointing resolutely at my computer as though she didn't know it were there.

"Pleeeze?" she repeated. I gave up, turning off the machine. Children were more important. My writing could wait awhile. Besides Checkers needed two people, so what choice did I have? "Okay! GOOD!!" she triumphed, peeling off the box lid and stacking the red and black buttons in the right places.

I let her win the first game as we had only recently taught her to play. At the end I knew that refusing another game was pointless. "Now this time, it will be hard," I threatened, but she beat me although I tried to win.

The phone ringing gave me an escape. A newly arrived oil company spouse called to let off steam about moving to Norway. "All the women I meet tell me how hard it is for them to adjust," she said, "just like it was for you." (Although there were a few male spouses around, they seemed to be less vocal.) The litany of "whys" sounded familiar—leaving a rewarding career, missing work colleagues and sense of fulfillment "back home." Filling one's days productively while a husband worked long hours on a high-pressure project drove some to distraction. The added hurdle of being unable to communicate in the local language or meld into the new culture made for some very frustrated people. The days she talked about were over for me and, after dispensing some wisdom, I hung up feeling like a victor in Norway. Life felt good—except when a child beat me at Checkers, that is, and when I didn't dwell on the fact that I was coasting along, going nowhere.

Liv-Marit appeared regularly for the next week, finally explaining that her mother was in the hospital awaiting her new baby. Afternoons consisted of playing games, drawing, dangling on my ballet barre, or just hanging around looking listless. We baked cookies and made dessert concoctions she took with her when her father came home from his job. Once she idled her time away by sectioning my newly curled hair into a style she liked. Miles-away looks told me she was worried about her mother and any possible complications. Keeping Liv-Marit busy and happy was my goal and watching her no sacrifice at all for I *wanted* to participate more fully in community life.

When summer comes so late then lingers, it is hard to say goodbye, even harder to know when it is really over. September flirted like a gorgeous stranger who showed up just as the party was ending, insisting he was single and looking for a girl like me. Somehow he didn't really seem available, but his words and smile promised an exquisite future. I wanted him to stay around forever. He was sleek in burnished ambers and yellow, and we trysted in the balmy breeze off the waters outside my windows. Sweet, soft languid days delayed decisions to part and any subtle hints of change were so natural and gentle, they drew no alarm. Purple heather faded down to rosy-brown, and thick tufts of tall grass in the bumpy fields turned from green to yellow-orange. Everyone said that September had been the most beautiful in memory and I believed them. Our love affair continued until October first.

A roar of a heavy truck going to Liv's house and an hour of logs crashing onto her driveway brought it to an end. The mountain of fuel lay in silent testament to their experience with Karmøy winters. They were expecting the worst, and they would have work to do first since the wood needed cutting to manageable lengths. I mentally divided it into fireplacefuls. Many dozen cold evenings lay ahead. I turned to bid the handsome stranger of summer goodbye and he slouched off with a wink, enticing me to follow. I turned my gaze back to the hundreds of logs, then back to him, ready to follow. But by then he had gone.

Indian summer days became a little wetter and overcast. Torches of glowing yellow-leafed trees replaced sunlight. When leaves scraped the road behind me, I looked over my shoulder, half expecting a face, but no one was there. I hoped it could even be Nicky. My beloved dog still seemed to be with me, just out of sight.

After the time change, we raced evening's darkening without success. Coming earlier and earlier, at seven-thirty, then seven, then six forty-five, it inevitably won the daylight war. We could only attain the best of the day if we started everything earlier. Our neighbors attacked the log pile like foresters, electric saws buzzing over several nights. A truck delivered heating oil across the road. I pulled out heavier sweaters and ordered logs for us.

Scandinavia cooled as the world's axis tilted, the light changed, and by midmonth winter left its own love letter of things to come by coating our car windshield with a glinting layer of overnight frost. In case we missed the message, two days later a second early snowstorm blew across the island, concluding summer. The locals called it a fluke, but these were the people who said Karmøy didn't get snow anyway. To me, snow was snow. A fall sun shone gloriously across Håvik at ten o'clock one morning on its new, almost horizontal path across the horizon. One morning a week later a deep, voluptuous peach sunrise scored with deep purple blue transformed the sky into a soft-looking pile of draped velour I felt I could run my hands over.

In the backyard chirping birds pried worms from the softening lawn, and my answering machine blinked with an invitation to Elise's for coffee. A good start to the day although first Rudy and I had a trip to the veterinarian. His age showed more and more, but I pushed the upsetting thoughts away.

As the year slipped into its winter season, evenings darkened by six, foliage turned browner, and a farmer drove through, selling apples from his station wagon. Roses burst out in final glory, and tiny birds foraged in a half-denuded bush and on food scraps. Two flew inside my kitchen and had to be shooed out again. Per-Rune and buddy Erik got our garage three-quarters cleared and swept out so that at least one car could fit inside. Mike scheduled having snow tires put back on his car, a requirement in Norway in winter.

Countdown to year's end continued, but those who equate November with gloom in Norway should have seen the month's first sunrise. It lit the sky to a burnished red-gold and gave us a day of pleasant thirty-seven degrees Fahrenheit. The previous night's full moon lingered in the west, and cirrus clouds scattered across a fresh blue sky. By eight-thirty early sunlight had softened thin layers of ice. Nubbly fields of turnips lined the hill, sheep munched grass delivered by trailer, and a sweet beery smell floated from the cow barn. Gray-white frost encrusted the neighborhood sand pit, and a bench seat glinted half red, half white. Icy frosting transformed the ordinary into the beautiful.

Outside the world changed, and indoors I did too. I cherished my two remaining animals. Living in our house on the water, watching the white turn to green, green leaves turn yellow, then brown, then fall away and be covered in white again, fine-tuned my perception of the circle of life. In Houston the world outside was often hidden behind another person's house or a massive billboard on the freeway, at the end of a private road, across a dangerous part of town, or far away at the end of a two-hour drive. There I had been ungrounded, so distracted that I missed the song and rhythm of the seasons and nature. In Norway I was safe, and in Håvik life was simply for living.

From our den which looked out across the water like Skudeneshavn's old lighthouse, I could listen to the outside world if I chose. If I didn't want those worries, all I had to do was click off the television and watch the sun glint across the Karmsund, and nothing else mattered.

Despite my hope that summer would draw forth some spurt of writing success, publishers rejected my few article proposals. My surge of appreciation for my creative environment and flurry of work for some reason was not translating into winning proposals. I felt out of things and out of sorts. The only thing that had given me any satisfaction, my language class, was over, and I wondered if there was some way to get back into a more structured situation, keep speaking Norwegian, and make more friends.

When the paper advertised evening classes, that seemed the answer. Pauline nudged me to check out one on portrait drawing while she signed up for *bunad* embroidery. Drawing had been a favorite activity earlier in my life, so I jumped on it. I had to do something to get out and meet people. Way at the back of my mind the Oslo restaurateur's words held out a promise. If I learned to understand the people around me, I would get to know "their soul." Maybe the drawing class would move me in the right direction.

The first evening went well, and Mike actually recognized the subjects of my portraits. "Yes. That's Sean Connery ... and, oh, Tina Turner," he confirmed. I was ecstatic. Learning, camaraderie, and being with people who all shared a common interest provided that familiar feeling of belonging that had bound me to my Norwegian class. Laura, our instructor, spoke several languages, including English, and gave me all the help I needed. As I lost myself in my sketches, little did I know all the good things and wonderful people art would bring into my life.

Sigrun was the first. My occasional seat mate at the drawing class was particularly friendly and nice and surprised me with an invitation to visit her. Had I known she had no intention of speaking English to me that day, I would have been nervous. But after two hours over *kaffe og kake* I left feeling proud that I had struggled through it, Berlitz pocket dictionary in hand. Sigrun was a whiz with languages, especially English and French, and understood the importance of practicing what you had learned. She and I alternated locations and languages for the remainder of my time in Norway. I was luckier than an American woman in Oslo whose poignant advertisement asked some local resident to please meet her for coffee and Norwegian language practice.

Under instructor Laura's guidance my drawing evolved into a deeply satisfying process. She urged me to study shadow, light, details, and contrast. "Can you see it? Can you *see* it?" she probed as I evaluated a photograph or object, and her question rang in my head, even at home. When Laura's six-week course finished, I was hooked. Now where could I go? The place was right under my nose.

In the Radio 102 building opposite the bus stop a sign appeared for "Karmøy Kunstskole," art school. I worried, though, that if they were real artists, they probably wouldn't let me join. And if none of them spoke English, then what?

Several weeks later I made sure I had Mike along for support as I went to see them. We scrambled up the dark stairs, kicking snow off our boots, and dusting off our parkas and reflective vests. In the room half a dozen painters worked at their easels, and two spoke English perfectly. Apart from looks of mild surprise on their faces, they listened politely to my little inquiry. They would get back to me in a week or so. How amazing! A studio had appeared within walking distance of our house, and the artists seemed to like me. I hugged Mike as we crunched through thick snowdrifts. Without his solid, supportive presence, I would never have been brave enough even to go in the door of the art school.

Two weeks later I was accepted and I joined the group. After the first evening I felt I was moving forward again, maintaining the momentum of my new love affair with drawing. Our regular art group consisted of five women: Cecilie, Lillian, Margit, Brita, and myself, and occasionally Eli-Bente, who came on a small motorcycle. Since she drove it herself, I guessed she could not claim to be an *exsos-rype* which seemed to mean "exhaust bird"—a rather delightful term a local motorcyclist's wife had given herself in *Ditt Distrikt* telephone book. Cecilie was proficient in English, extroverted and, like the others, had a great sense of humor. Brita did not speak any English at all but understood it, and Lillian would speak it but often had to be cajoled into doing so. Once when I called her at work, she sounded flustered. "Wait," she said, only to return giggling after she had closed her office door. "I don't want anyone here to hear me speaking English!" Margit and I talked often in English, but she had periods when, out of the blue, she would speak only Norwegian.

Our art evenings followed a winter routine—coming in out of the cold, getting our boots off, shaking off any snow, and generally unbundling ourselves before taking possession of our own little areas. We brought thermos flasks of hot drinks and snacks for our breaks. My colleagues all worked on easels, looking like real artists, staring intently at their color palettes as they mixed and chose their oil or acrylics and directed their brushes to their canvasses. I, on the other hand, claimed a wobbly old desk next to a wall, leaning over my sketchbook, and warm enough in thick clothes and warm socks. Small floor heaters did what they could to help keep our blood moving. Conversation and kidding around only burst forth after everyone had been at their work for awhile and needed to unwind. The rest of the time we worked in contented concentration. It was clear that they cherished their time in our ramshackle studio in the middle of winter.

One evening giggling broke out behind me. As the racket got louder and more boisterous, I turned to see someone's pink hip partly exposed a few yards away. In the spirit of cooperation with a colleague, one of the group had obliging tugged down a modest section of her navy tights and was posing to assist Lillian make the finishing touches to a painting of a rearview nude. Such unexpected ingenuity and nerve sent them, and the rest of us, into hysterics. Only when Lillian's nameless benefactor had completed her considerable sacrifice to art in our chilly studio and restored her portions of clothing did we all settle down.

"Å, jeg visste ikke at Karmøy hadde så dårlige damer." I didn't know Karmøy had such wayward ladies on it, I commented with mock seriousness. They laughed even more. Their artistic talents, they insisted, made up for their bad ways! Feigning naughtiness kept us amused and warm until the two perpetrators returned to their paintings, chuckling with satisfaction. Light moments were treasured. In the silence of our studio each one temporarily blotted out the daily situations and stresses of family life and found a refuge as an individual—not someone's mother or wife or widow or daughter—to work for a few precious hours to create something which gave her pleasure and challenged her to do better.

Cecilie was the most outgoing and forceful in the group, giving me helpful hints and suggestions as we were mostly a teacher-less class. She rarely held her feelings back on anything important and complained about my irregular attendance. "I *missed* you!" she cried one Wednesday. "Why weren't you here last night?" No one seemed to have missed me in a long time and I felt quite touched. Maybe I had found another friend, a woman friend to talk to, to share things with.

Cecilie's directness and open, delightful personality cemented our destiny as friends. Nothing was too much trouble for her. She loaned me her reading glasses when I forgot mine, invited me to stop in anytime, loved to tease my husband, and encouraged me to draw and learn new techniques. Mostly she cared about me and forgave my stubbornness. New at art, I worked painstakingly slowly, afraid to make mistakes. Cecilie would wander over, evaluate my progress, and offer a few suggestions. Most seemed too much of a leap for me then, so I kept doing what I thought I was capable of, nothing too risky. She refused to be offended.

We met at a restaurant one day and one of her friends stopped by our table, complimenting Cecilie on her command of English. *Flink!* I heard the lady say. The magic compliment was usually mine, yet here was my new friend earning it through speaking English! Our lunch lasted a pleasant forever, and I loved Cecilie's vivacious personality. It seemed a lifetime since I had enjoyed such a wonderful get-together with someone. Two hours flew by and we prepared to part company, regretfully, still buoyant with the excitement of a new friendship which could merit two or three more hours of talk. "I liked you right away," she announced, looking me in the eye with a satisfied smile. "And although I don't think I speak English very well, I feel I can relax and speak it with you." She let me in on a surprising secret. "You know, I asked God to please find me a friend I can speak English with!"

Astonished beyond belief, I wished she could have known it was not so one-sided. She was an answer to my prayers! She was giving me a chance to contribute—something I wanted to do. My secret sorrow was never being asked to help or do something for somebody on Karmøy. I always felt locked out because everyone had their own friends, families, and activities and never needed me for anything. Now I could actually do something useful! Cecilie needed to practice English, true, but I needed to practice Norwegian. It would be a perfect situation.

Her smile faded with the news that I would be gone for a couple of weeks to the States but returned when I promised to call her the moment I came back. We made plans for our next meeting. For the first time someone Norwegian would be waiting for me when I returned. My batteries recharged, I zoomed home, thrilled to have acquired yet another friend, all due to taking the evening art class. First Sigrun, then Cecilie. My cup was again full—I was rich with friends!

Joining the art class turned out to be a major step in my assimilation. In the course of just a few more months I added a dozen new friends to my address book and stretched myself creatively. The intensity of drawing paralleled writing and brought it into sharper focus. I became obsessed with shadows. We see them and don't see them everyday. Shadows, even those we don't like, identify our faces precisely. We are recognized. Without them we are baby-faced robots. With them, we share and earn our life experiences with others.

Concentrating on lights, shadows, curves, and angles on my still lifes revealed that people's lives, personalities, and behaviors too involved shades of light and dark, positive and negative, warmth and cold. As a one-dimensional sketch might almost be a caricature, a hastily written paragraph might only touch on part of what composed a whole person. By applying what I had learned about portrait drawing I realized I could improve my writer's profiles.

When Lillian asked me to exhibit at their upcoming art show, I said "yes" first and brainstormed later. Before long I had four still life sets arranged and was drawing full-time, five days a week, in order to meet the deadline. The exhibit was a hit, and when Pauline generously bought one of my drawings, I felt like a real artist. After that I bravely called to enter another show. I stumbled through my request in Norwegian and heard a delighted, *"Ja! Det er greit!"* It was at that show that I met Alison, an American-born islander. "That must be Patti Morgan. I read about her in the paper!" a voice rang out as Mike and I carried things into the building. Our language made us friends immediately.

Subsequent trips to Bergen and Stavanger to arts and crafts shows followed and, if our wallets never swelled much for all our efforts, the fun made up for it. I sold three prints to the Helly Hansen Corporation and dozens of pictures and note cards to complete strangers. My new passion replaced writing for six wonderful months and provided the kind of gratification my writing had failed to do since my arrival.

Mike took on a special, unpaid, role. He became adept at setting up display boards; hanging pictures; dusting off tables; applying hammer, nail, or pliers to whatever we needed; and disappearing into kitchens to find us food. If I was the Karmøy arts and crafts group's token American, Mike was their token general helper. He seemed pleased with his rewards: invitations to coffee, even home-cooked meals, and he basked in the sunshine of his association with a bunch of creative, some would say offbeat, women. It was a step or two down from his day job, but it didn't hurt. Heidrun *was* big and important, but so were our dreams also.

Winter was approaching, with reduced chances to see people, and I wanted to beef up our social relationships. Since Thanksgiving with its family connotations was imminent, Mike and I discussed inviting our neighbors in for a special meal. It seemed a perfect answer to a touch of homesickness and would feel like a family occasion.

Elise Eriksen sounded thrilled when we invited her and Karl to join us for a real Thanksgiving dinner. "Ooh, turkey! Good! Stuffing too?" she anticipated. I silently thanked my mother-in-law in San Antonio for sending me some of the instant variety. "Yes, definitely, we'll have stuffing and some other things that are coming over. It will be a typical American Thanksgiving meal," I promised.

One cold November afternoon our dinner guests arrived: Elise and Karl Eriksen, Einar and Else Henriksen, and Lone, one-half of the Danish couple we had become friends with. High tension had gripped me for hours before they arrived, but at four o'clock it was all systems go. The largest turkey we could find, five and a half kilos, sat breast brown and glistening on the table, candied sweet potatoes shimmered, jellied cranberry lurched slightly sideways in its bowl, rolls were retrieved after a heat-up in the oven, gravy pale but tasty swam in a tureen, steamed broccoli clung to its dish, and seven individual salads perched aside dinner plates. Mike had taped his contribution to the season, a cardboard Hallmark turkey, to our china cabinet. Oh, Lord, was everything ready? Had I forgotten anything? I checked the microwave and refrigerator where I often found food I had meant to serve but forgot. Nothing was missing.

The bell rang. DING DONG! "Oh, hello! So glad you're here. Oh, the flowers are beautiful, thank you. Come on in!"

Seven sat for dinner at Thanksgiving, five looking at their dinner plates a little mystified. Elise, with a fondness for stuffing, eyed the lonesome mound on an otherwise empty plate. It hadn't quite met my expectations, and I felt it would benefit from companions. "Elise, let me give you some turkey and gravy to eat with that!" I said, a little panicked.

"Oh, you must tell me how we should eat all these different things!" she replied.

"Put it all on your plate together," I said, knowing that once everything was piled on the plate, American style, no one would have to worry about not liking any one particular item. Soon bowls and platters were being handed around the table, and I realized I had to remember that food was not only different in other countries but sometimes eaten differently too.

Our guests glanced at Mike and me, watching to see what we did first, exactly as I did when I was around Norwegians. Once everyone had some of everything, serious eating started. Elise's eyes lit up when she saw and smelled the candied sweet potatoes. "I haven't had them since I was in America," she told us. Einar tasted the salad appreciatively, and Betty Crocker and I felt pleased. Her recipe of grated carrot, crushed pineapple, raisin, and salad dressing salad on a bed of lettuce, all items I could obtain in Norway, was delicious.

The *skinke,* a large holiday sized ham, was a hit. That we even had it was thanks to Bjørg, a former occasional language tutor. She had taken me to a well-regarded Haugesund butcher (*slakter,* a word which reminded me of "slaughter") who had patiently listened to my request for a suitable ham. After his first cutting he returned with what seemed half of a pig in his arms.

"*Nei! Ikke så … big!*" I exclaimed. Cupping my hands about ten inches apart, I tried to clarify.

"*Å,*" he nodded and stepped back to his electric saw, still cutting an enormous portion for me. Bjørg and I tried "Wait!" and "*Vent litt!*" but they were mere whispers against the buzz of his saw, and a few noisy minutes later he held out a large pink ham as proudly as a mother shows off her babe in arms.

"Um, *hvor mye vekt?* How much does it weigh?" I inquired, thinking it must weigh ten pounds at least but resigned to buy it, no matter the cost at that point. It tipped the scale at two kilos, four and a quarter pounds, and a bright ninety-five glowed from the dial. Ninety-five *kroner* seemed like a good price, and the ham, although larger than I had planned on, looked pretty and wonderfully fresh. I was very pleased with it until the bill came. Ninety-five was the cost per kilo, so my ham set me back about thirty-two dollars!

Not a ham eater myself and with no experience in cooking it, I needed instructions. Patiently the butcher laid out the process. First you salted the meat or smoked it, then cooked it for about two hours, he said, or until the meat thermometer, which he happened to sell as well, registered eighty degrees, for well done. The three-way discussion took several minutes, but I hoped I could figure it all out eventually at home. But he had one last wonderful thing to say.

" *Men, jeg kan koke for deg!*"

"YOU can cook it for me?" I responded with relief.

"*Ja,*" he nodded politely. If I could have run around the counter and kissed him, I would have, but I did the next best thing. "*Jeg elsker deg!*" I declared passionately and he looked quite delighted to be loved, even briefly, in front of his amused regulars. He noted the order and delivery date.

Bjørg and I left his shop in high spirits and even she had enjoyed herself. My ham was as good as on the table, hurrah! A little bit of Norwegian, a friend's help, and a good-natured butcher made it a successful transaction. Now I could make a special dinner for neighbors who had been so friendly and nice.

Mike collected the ham on the allotted day. He was to keep it in his office refrigerator, then bring it home. Ever the worrier, I called him to check that he had it under control. "Yes, I picked it up and don't worry," he replied, whereupon I immediately did. "I left it in the coldest place around here—in my car, next to the North Sea Hall. It's freezing in there!" Visions of salmonella, and guests being rushed to the hospital swept into my mind. "Why did you do that? It needed to be refrigerated!" I exclaimed in horror. Barely thirty degrees that morning, plus wind chill off the ocean meant that his car was ice cold but ... Sometimes I wondered about men—especially husbands who were supposed to be on your side yet could almost wreck a whole dinner party.

Reservations aside, the ham was beautiful to look at and tasted good because a second platter disappeared promptly. Our American dessert was pies—pumpkin and pecan, which everyone loved. Einar however contributed the most memorable highlight when he offered a traditional Norwegian *takk for maten* (thanks for the food) toast. He rose to his feet, clearing his throat, and proclaimed the meal wonderful and that everyone was glad to be invited. Mike and I were welcome neighbors, he went on, especially since we had just fitted in with them and the life of the community. Their special American Thanksgiving dinner would go into their memories as a once-in-a-lifetime event. Being toasted like this was a first for us, and Mike and I felt truly accepted. We had much to be thankful for.

"Einar, you said just what I wanted to," Elise added, " just exactly the right words!" Einar sat down, attacking his dessert with a chuckle. "Elise, I have known you all these years and when I see that look in your eyes, my heart just picks it up!"

That evening we got to know one another even more as we exchanged stories. Karl talked about his time, long ago, in Brooklyn. "My father took us there before the Depression, then when it got so bad, we all came back here. Then after Elise and I married, *she* was the one who wanted to go back over there!"

"Well, I was born there," she responded playfully. "I am an American and two of our children were born in America." They returned to Norway after a few years, however. "Family was the main reason," Karl explained. "Things were changing in Brooklyn where we lived. Our Norwegian people were going out of the community, marrying non-Norwegians, and we weren't used to that. So with family things and our parents back here, well, we decided to come back."

The evening would not have been complete without Einar treating us to a seafaring tale. "I was in Houston one time," he explained. "I had brought a ship into Louisiana, and I knew my oldest boy was working in Houston that weekend. I called him and he said, 'Daddy, fly over here and we'll have dinner and a great time.'

"*Vel,* I flew to Houston and went to this big hotel where he was staying and found out they had this fancy limousine that could take us wherever we wanted for dinner. Six o'clock, seven o'clock went by, and my son was still busy, not ready to leave for dinner yet. Eight o'clock and nine o'clock passed and I reminded him. 'Yes, we'll go in a short while,' he told me. Ten o'clock rolled around and I said, was he ready, hadn't we planned to go out and have a good dinner while I was there that night? Wasn't he ready to go yet?

"'Oh, yes, sorry, Dad,' he told me, 'we'll go now.' Off we went and tried to find a restaurant open. By then it was almost eleven-fifteen. All the ones we pulled up to were closed.

"My son said, 'I don't understand why this town has all these beautiful restaurants, but they're all closed!'

"'They're closed because it's too late. People will not be going out to dinner at this hour!' I told him. At last we were about to give up when we saw the big M sign in the distance. McDonald's—and it was open!"

Einar laughed as he told of their dinner at the fast-food place, but he wasn't amused at the time. "Next morning I left the hotel, went to the airport, flew back to Louisiana and my ship," he concluded. "Tell you the truth, I was mad!"

The final touch to the meal was another imported delicacy, Hershey's Kisses. Afterwards people finally patted their tummies and assured us they could eat no more. In the hallway Karl pumped our hands with thanks for the meal and evening. "You know, that was wonderful. It was the first Thanksgiving dinner we've had since 1956!"

Elise agreed, "And it was the first real American one."

"But you lived in Brooklyn," I responded, puzzled.

"Yeeess," she said, with a delighted giggle, "but we always had it with *Norwegians!*"

Rules for Friendship

Use equal amounts of generosity and thoughtfulness.

Add a dozen smiles, followed by a few friendly words.

Flavor with a little fun.

Blend well with a spirit of love,

Lastly, sprinkle with good humor.

—From "Velkommen inn i våre kjøkkener."
By Norheim Church Group's *Kirkeringen*
Translation courtesy of Milli and Lori

14

The Blue Bell Saga

The joyous mood lingered. Our neighbors made it easy for us by speaking English, and we felt very much at home. Back at the start of our sojourn, in Oslo, we probably stood out like sore thumbs. Mike began by practicing *takk,* thank you, around his new office. When he progressed to the effusive *tusen takk,* a thousand thanks, a colleague finally spoke up. "That's funny," he commented, tongue planted firmly in cheek. "I don't see a thousand ceilings up there!" Mispronunciation of the vowel had created ceilings instead of thanks. A secretary gently pulled his leg. "Actually, I thought someone from Texas would say, *'T-o-o-s-e-r-n t-a-a-ahk!'*" she drawled playfully.

All was well in the thank-you department except during the remaining fifteen hours in a day when a little more was required of a new immigrant. The first problem was shopping and remained so for a very long time. Although 100 kroner was exchanging at about 15 to 16 dollars then, I couldn't avoid thinking of 100 dollars when I saw 100 kroner notes. I felt that they invited theft. Yet since a two-pound chicken took care of half of one of my 100 kroner notes, the hundreds were a necessary evil.

In supermarkets I clutched the culinary bible of the English-speaking community, Melody Favish's *Trolldom in the Kitchen*, consulting it as ardently for the word for oat bran (*havrekli*) as a poet scans Thoreau. Periodically I would linger in a corner to try to calculate how much I had spent so far. The process tied my stomach in knots. Were the numbers on the label the price or the price per kilo? Let me see, what was a kilo again—2.2 pounds? Never mind that the word *kilo* registered with no one until I pronounced it as "cheelo." I dreaded having to return things to the shelves or arrive at the checkout short of cash.

While awaiting a Norwegian bank debit card and checking privileges, my worries forced me into unnatural frugality. For months we ate only sale-priced cheese stamped *tilbud*, special offer. As a result, my poor husband came to believe that this was the product's actual name—that "cheese" translated as *tilbud*. The word was *ost*, but he had happily consumed *tilbud* for so long that it required the combined efforts of several people to convince him otherwise.

Once I slipped and slithered down to a small grocery store for just three items, one of which was sugar. A package bearing an unhelpful picture but words hinting at sugar contents was all I could find. "This is sugar, isn't it?" I blurted out and the shop owner shot me a terrified look.

"*Nei!*" he answered.

"Well, what is it?" I persisted, hoping he was mistaken.

"I don't know," he said looking stressed, unable to explain it in English.

Our situation was generating a frenzy of mental activity in the lengthening checkout line. "Uh, um it's . . . um . . ." one customer began, rubbing his chin. "*Ah. Hva heter?*" What's it called? added another. A waving hand indicated a lady with the answer, but her idea was voted down. My auditory system was whirring like satellite dishes trying to pick up the words. All six faces were soon deep in thoughtful concentration, and the straining team seemed on the verge of supplying the word. It was just like the television game show Jeopardy! Alex Trebek should have been there, and a buzzer should have been timing the contestants as the minutes ticked painfully by. The owner looked trapped. No one could get checked out until the logjam cleared, and I was the cause.

After several tries a lady came up with the right answer. "It's something they give to . . . babies! It's. . .ah. . . ."

"Cream of wheat?" I queried.

"YES! *Ja!* Cream of wheat!" came a chorus of relieved affirmations and reshuffling of feet as they all began inching forward. I handed back the cream of wheat and gave up on the sugar. The customers were impatient, and I wanted out. Apologizing, and thanking everyone, I slunk home. Grocery shopping required a certain amount of nerve and stamina, and all mine had gone.

Another time I was searching for pine disinfectant, reading labels and sniffing contents. Potent fumes from concentrated household ammonia roared past my sinuses and targeted my brain. Dizzy, with streaming eyes, I blinked through my tears for the exit.

Shopping in Houston had been so easy. I could fill a Randall's supermarket basket in thirty minutes with dozens of products and not damage myself. In retrospect, the effort seemed worthy of a college credit or two.

On yet another trip to a store, I had found some silver-cleaning polish whose instructions were naturally in Norwegian. "Hello!" I greeted the man at the cash register, giving him forewarning I was English-speaking. "Could you please tell me what it says I must do?" I asked, pointing at the instructions on the back of the bottle.

"Mmm. Yes," he nodded, sitting back on his chair. Slowly and clearly he began reading it, line by line in Norwegian.

"In *engelsk*, please?"

He looked worried and carried it off to get another clerk's help. Quickly a voice called out from behind us.

"Do you want that translated into English?" A tall, blonde woman carrying a grocery bag and a bicycle helmet came to the rescue. In addition to translating my bottle instructions, she shared the name of one of her favorite brass-cleaning products. All I had to do was mix it with soapy dishwashing water for great results. I thanked her and, as we walked out together, she explained she had just returned from a trip to Spain and knew what it was like not to understand the language for she neither read nor spoke Spanish.

Most of the time I believed I was the only one struggling with another language for I lived it every time I walked out the door. But Norwegians had their rocky moments with English. A friend had shown me a built-in wardrobe her husband had installed. "It's beautiful," I commented. "You're lucky that your husband is so talented at this kind of thing."

"Yes, I am," she responded, looking proud. "He is very hand ... hand ... handsome."

My puzzled expression made her tut-tut at her own mistake. "No! I mean han-dy, handy!"

Her husband preferred the original version. "No! She is right. I am handsome!" he insisted, laughing.

One word has a dozen definitions and picking the right one can be tricky. A British friend chose a seemingly appropriate Norwegian word only to be told politely that it meant something to do with going to the bathroom. Another time she was on the receiving end as she inquired about the status of her husband's Norwegian drivers' license application and found it had not yet been approved. "Sorry, but you'll have to wait two more weeks," the clerk told her. "We have to check to see if he is a vandal." Her husband, Steve, was one of the least vandal-like of men so it gave us great pleasure to accuse him, after that, of being one. And, judging by his smile, it was not an altogether unpleasant alter ego for him to adopt temporarily.

Another light moment came in a park in Bekkestua. A gentleman stopped to puff on his dying pipe as we happened along. What was the time, the man asked, and Mike valiantly managed to answer in Norwegian. *"Å, du snakker norsk?"* the man queried, looking suitably impressed.

"Ja," Mike replied with a modest chuckle. *Jeg snakker litt norsk.*

Maintaining a deadpan expression, the man puffed thoughtfully for a couple of seconds.

"Å, jeg snakker mye norsk!" (I speak a lot of Norwegian), he volunteered.

They chuckled happily at their repartee, and I knew, right then, that as long as Norwegians showed such healthy senses of humor, the chances for us having fun during our stay there were excellent.

Oslo, in fact, did offer some amusing and strange memories. Being "patted down" for drugs at the airport was one. My heart skipped a beat as I visualized the agent's reaction if she found my little plastic bag of whitish powder. On trips I always carried low-fat coffee creamer with me, but it could look suspicious. Would she believe that was all it was? Fortunately I made it on board. Then there was the visit to a doctor who announced that her children had broken her only thermometer that morning. She would be happy to take my temperature, but only if I agreed to climb up on the table so she could use her rectal thermometer.

In another situation, I sat in a waiting room, waiting supposedly to see a gynecologist a Norwegian art friend had referred me to. A steady stream of gray-haired ladies checked at the service hatch, then went off happily. Was Norway doling out enormous amounts of hormone replacement to grandmothers? Finally the woman in the office called me in and pointed to a chair. She prodded, poked and took blood without asking a single question. How did she know what I wanted? Or, worse, had she confused me with someone else and was prepping me for their procedures? Exhausting my ideas and knowing I could always yell, "STOP!" If things got complicated, I decided she "just knew" what women of a certain age came there for. To my relief, another door opened and a doctor introduced herself. She was a doctor all right, but not a gynecologist. Finally, though, I had someone who wanted to talk to me and see what I needed.

I fared not too well with things electrical in Oslo. The disconnected cable television incident was the first. The next was my inordinate amount of lint build-up in my "foreign" dryer. The appliance's booklet, even translated, hadn't mentioned the lint trap. "My goodness!" an American friend remarked as she removed enough lint to weave a sweater, "You're lucky you didn't have a fire!"

The most embarrassing incident was the out-of-control washing machine, which refused to stop filling, spinning, and emptying. Mike's socks went round and round like prisoners in a space capsule. Nothing I pressed, pulled, or clicked turned the machine off or opened the latch. The company's maintenance man had left for the day, so, desperate, I went outside and waved down two nice Norwegian ladies. Amazingly they followed me upstairs, clucked unconcernedly around the machine, stopped it, and opened the door so I could rescue the socks. That machine terrified me from then on.

My only success story in Oslo concerned ice cream, a Texas brand, at that. I had been in the States on a brief trip and wanted to try bringing a gallon of Blue Bell ice-cream, Cookies 'n Cream, back to Norway to surprise Mike on his birthday, but how? "You can buy a lot of dry ice and pack it all around the ice cream," a dry ice supplier in San Antonio told me, "but the problem is that it uses up the cabin's oxygen on the plane." Suffocating the passengers, me included, seemed a very undesirable side effect of merely transporting ice cream. "Or you can always just ask the cabin attendants for a few packets once in a while," he added.

With this thought, I began my trip back to Norway, hard-frozen Blue Bell tucked in a special cooler bag. After several departure delays I quietly asked a stewardess for a couple of packages of dry ice, explaining my dilemma. To my embarrassment she shared my secret with everyone. "I need some drah aahce!" she yelled down to the galley. "This lady is trying to take some Blue Bell aahce cream to Norway for her husband's birthday!" I shrank into my seat.

Nevertheless I begged little bags of dry ice all the way across the Atlantic, slipping them deep into my cooler, eventually provoking the suspicion of my final, Swedish seat mate. "What do you have in there?" he asked, sounding annoyed. He clearly knew it must be illicit or explosive.

"Blue Bell ice cream, from Texas, for my husband's birthday party in Oslo!"

He looked startled. "Pssh! That won't work! It will all be melted by the time you get there!"

When we landed he rushed off quickly, glad to be clear of the peculiar lady and her alleged birthday surprise, and I rushed off to disprove his statement. The cooler bag and the dry ice held up as well as they could, and while Blue Bell's sales manager would have rejected the mushed-down ice cream by then, my husband and his birthday party guests a week later weren't in the least bit critical—they enjoyed every creamy spoonful at the only place in Oslo that served Blue Bell.

"If you will cling to Nature, to the simple in Nature, to the little things that hardly anyone sees, and that can so unexpectedly become big and beyond measuring; if you have love of inconsiderable things ... then everything will become easier, more coherent, and somehow conciliatory for you, not in your intellect, perhaps, which lags marveling behind, but in your inmost consciousness, waking and cognizance."

——From *Letters to a Young Poet* by Rainer Maria Rilke

Olympic Ideals: Sports & Peace

Christmas clues started appearing so I went shopping in search of Nordic elves, *julenisser*, to give as gifts. The shop owner wrapped them up, looking preoccupied, then pointed at the highway, sharing some apparently vital information. After a couple of tries I caught the word "Olympic." Was the Olympic flame coming now? I asked.

"Ja, ja!" he answered, rushing off to get a good view. By chance I was in the right place to see the flame being carried up the island on its way to Lillehammer for the Winter Olympics. I should have known it was happening but because I never could follow the radio properly, I was not ready and waiting like everyone else.

The parking lot overflowed with people staring south so I drove back toward Kopervik looking for a parking place. People sprang up along the Skudeneshavn to Haugesund highway like flowers. A blue flashing police car light in my rearview mirror signaled that I should get out of their way. Pedestrians stared at me with impatient curiosity, itching to cheer. I was cheating them out of their reward, but my emotions responded to the spotlight. So few people do anything that warrants public cheering that it was powerful medicine even to imagine it.

Down the way I joined a man craning his neck for a sign of the flame. *"Det er ikke i Åkrehamn ennå,"* I advised, so he knew it was a way off yet. Our *norsk-engelsk* bogged down just as a familiar figure appeared. It was Brita, my art class friend. Official Olympic vehicles and police cars filed toward us. The flame was almost here! It happened so quickly. Runners in white Olympic jogging suits ran by, one holding the flame aloft, eyes ahead. "Hey, Hurraaa ...y, Hurraay!!" we yelled. The Olympic motorcade slowly moved on. Making quick calculations that I could drive home, get my video camera, and film the runners as they passed my own neighborhood if the procession detoured through Kopervik, I jumped in my car and followed behind.

The Norwegians were going all out to support the Olympic dream, and I marveled at their fervent, yet conservative, show of pride. Certainly competition was almost alien to Norwegians, certainly between individuals. Social equality was the prize. They didn't even approve of mild bragging. I would never forget a friend's expression when she caught herself talking with maternal pride about her children. Her bright eyes turned dark, and she looked uncomfortable.

Olympic enthusiasm was acceptable though. Patriotism was contagious, and I yelled for Norway as hard as anyone else.

Once the runners had passed, a mother took her young child's hand and searched for a break in the stream of traffic. A man stood waiting too, someone who one day could tell his grandchild, "I saw the Olympic flame carried through Karmøy years ago! I stood right over there, next to the Shell station, and watched everything!" Whole families milled around, not ready to say that it was all over.

I paid no ticket to be there. I would not attend the Olympics in Lillehammer, yet I was part of the whole thing—even driving, sort of, in the parade itself. For awhile an American who had never been near an Olympic event in her own land participated in another country's. I blessed my good fortune. On my tiny Norwegian island I had played a part in something wonderful and good. Ordinary people filled with a joy for great purpose, just for that moment, made them a near-invincible army for peace in every corner of the world.

Later, with my video camera, I waited again for the runners. With darkness came penetrating cold. We juggled cold cameras and warm gloves. People materialized from the lane— Liv-Marit on her bike with her dog wound around it as usual, her brother Per-Rune standing close by. Children lit torches from each other, their faces bathed in yellow light. Our ebullient young paperboy raised his arm, cheering. With a wide smile spread across strong features and a shock of blond hair no one could mistake him for anyone other than a young, happy Norwegian thirteen-year-old. He acknowledged me with a quick smile and a word. The flames carried my wishes upwards, like a prayer; let life be good for him and all the country's children, all the world's children.

Finally the runners arrived, a man and a woman, slowing to allow a man in a suit to keep up. Fortunately it was our enterprising Radio 102 representative trying to get a few words from them. Then they were off again, running north to Avaldsnes, Haugesund, Stord, where other runners would maintain the relay. The flame streaked off into the coal black night, up and down hills. It would circle Norway for two months, even going out onto an offshore rig, until finally being carried into Lillehammer to open the 1994 Winter Olympic Games.

When it was over, families melted back into the darkness, and shadows against the few street lamps were soon all I could see.

Gudrun had said a few words into my video camera earlier. She saw I was chilled to the bone. "Come home with us," she insisted, taking pity on me, "and have some food and coffee to warm you up!" In her cozy kitchen we were soon eating Paul's favorite apple, almonds, and raisin applecake while savoring the drama of the evening. Gudrun watched me nibbling and day-dreaming and brought over the coffee pot. When I shook my head, she scolded me. "You can't be a good Norwegian if you don't drink lots of coffee!" That night I felt pretty close to being a Norwegian, and it pleased me that she might perhaps like me to be one. I wanted to say, "But, Gudrun, you know I can't be one. I have to go back to America," but was afraid to. Totally immersed in my new life, I couldn't bear thinking about, let alone put into words, anything which pointed to it ending one day.

From the **Coffee Song**
(kaffevise)

What would life be like without coffee?
Good friends, answer me that.
How can we enjoy ourselves, laughing,
If there's no coffee to be had?
Therefore its praise I'll keep on singing,
because for our humor's sake,
nothing cheers us quite as much
as a pleasant coffee break.

Kva er livet uten kaffi?
Gode venner gje meg svar.
Kan ei festlag stund oss skaffa,
når ein ingen kaffi haar?
Difor til hans pris me syngja,
han gjer livet ljost og lett.
Druknaar kvaar ei sorg som tyngjaa,
i ein herleg kaffiskvett.

With thanks to Milli Meyer, Karmøy.

The family's Christmas star hung benevolently in the kitchen window. It looked so beautiful from our living room window, I said. "Oh! It's so old!" she said with an apologetic laugh, "but our oldest boy won't let me get rid of it! I have repaired and repaired it. I told him I must stop putting it up, but he says, 'No, Mother, we have always had it at Christmas. You must put it up again!'"

Back home I looked up again at Gudrun's Christmas star in the window. I already missed its close up comfort and my friends. Before closing the blinds, I took a final look at the star, knowing that watching from the outside symbolized reality. While my heart ached with the sad knowing that we couldn't stay, how I wished that we could stay in the house at Håvik forever.

Feeling at home at Christmas made all the difference, and so it was with our second Christmas in Norway. We returned from a quick trip to Texas to be greeted by Paul and his youngest daughter, who brought us a Christmas tree tagged with a cheery card. Einar rang to welcome us back and inquire how we enjoyed our visit to America. Toralf, of the powerful vocal chords, froze in shy silence as he and Hanna's boy pressed a wad of damp advertising flyers from our mail box into our hands, and a card from the Eriksens. Merry Christmas and welcome back home, they wrote, and home was how it felt because of our neighbors.

The newspaper called it a "dream Christmas" and everyone agreed. Hilde, my friend in the grocery store, pointed out that on December 24 Håvik looked just like a Christmas card. The wind lulled and all was quiet, she said. *"Så stille, så fint!"* she added, smiling. Peaceful and beautiful it certainly was.

Olivia brought her new boyfriend, Jan, to visit and updated us on school. At first students had not been very friendly to the young woman and she felt hurt and confused. Somehow, however, she had the courage to keep on track toward a normal academic life. Jan had helped her. Her year ended on a high note. Even though her father was away at sea, she and her mother had enjoyed themselves. "Last year we didn't know anybody. We visited people, including local relatives, but felt out of place because no one really sat with us and talked. It was horrible! But this year when people invited us over, we got to really know each other. It was much, much better!" she told us, her optimistic smile returning.

For immigrants, in particular, holidays can be lonely. A Karmøy man, Erik D. Hillesland, who emigrated to America, wrote on January 4, 1882, to relatives back home: "I should tell you we had a bit of a 'Norwegian' Christmas going from one to the other and having fun. Last year it wasn't much fun since I did not know many people, but now there are so many newcomers from Skudenes that we have had a merry Christmas."

On New Year's Eve Lone and Torben invited us over. Lone had prepared a feast: tender, whole baked salmon; creamy sauce; boiled potatoes; lemon mousse; two kinds of wine, plus champagne. She had artistically arranged thick red candles on brass trays where they glowed amongst pine cone centerpieces. With Torben's persistence, match, paper, and wood combinations finally worked, and the fire spluttered into life. The atmosphere seduced us with log and pipe smoke.

Conversation focused on family and hobbies, work, our first full year in the neighborhood. Lone burst out with something she had evidently been saving for the right moment. "Do you remember what you asked me when you moved here? You asked me if it was safe?" her eyes danced with amusement as she continued. "I was so surprised at the time that I don't think I answered but ..." She looked around and waved in the direction of our little community. "You know now, of course it's safe!" We all laughed because if anything were true, that was. We lived with a sense of total safety. "Håvik is a very special place," she added as solemnly as if they were words from the Bible.

Over the months I had heard "special" used about Karmøy in general and our neighborhood in particular, always in near-hallowed terms. To me, God's presence was close—reflected in the water, mountains, wind, circle of seasons, and in the silence which promoted contemplation. The island flourished under divine protection, and the tiny little place of Håvik seemed to enjoy an extra special blessing. Our friends spoke of their grown children and their foster son who, although troubled, was making some small steps of progress in their home. I hoped the handsome young boy's life story would have a happy ending for he was too young for it to be otherwise.

Out in the bay, ships set off red emergency flares which arched downward as spooky, slow-motion, fluorescent dots. In a science fiction movie they might start wending their ghostly way towards us making weird, high-pitched whirring noises. Someone recalled a story about a couple's boat which capsized on a holiday evening and everyone ignored the flares. Across the cove fireworks dazzled against the water. Rockets swooped and boomed into the cold, starry night, disintegrating into plumes of yellow and red—bright exclamations greeting the New Year. The dog, startled, ran to the deck, barking.

In the midst of the grand display I knew we would never experience such a thing again. For fleeting moments we experienced an enthralling night, warming our hands around our wine glasses, stamping our feet. We were two Danes and two Americans, and a dog, four people from two lands and living in still another.

What would the new year bring? Later Mike and I walked home arm in arm home, past windows glowing electric candles left on all night. The four non-Norwegians had once again paired up for a special occasion, and I was grateful to our friends for taking us under their wing.

It took me until January 4 to pronounce *Godt Nyttår* properly. Spitting out a couple of *"t"* sounds in quick succession without worrying that one's tongue might become a pinched casualty wasn't easy. I repeated my "Good (Happy) New Year" well into the month, just for practice. One sunny afternoon I slithered over to the post office with a little gift of American brownie mix for Britt, the post office clerk. Always friendly, patient with my Norwegian, and a minor art fan, she made my trips to the post office special events.

I eased off the main road and onto a footpath so that Einar wouldn't catch me. He had pulled alongside the day before. "What are you doing walking on these dangerous, slippery roads? Yesterday the radio said fifty people in Rogaland have fallen and broken arms or legs since the icy conditions began. Jump in. You come to town with me."

Britt's colleague was on duty, so I left my package and walked home. When Liv saw me out with Rudy before dinner, she called *hei* and something else.

"*Lufter du hunden?*" she called, nodding at my dog. Since *luft* meant "air," I saw no connection between it and "dog" in the same sentence. She liked teasing me, and it took awhile before she relented and explained her little greeting. Literally it meant, "Are you airing your dog?" she laughed, but she really meant was I walking it. She added that you could use the expression in another way. "*Lufter du mannen din?*" Are you airing your husband? Liv had a great sense of humor. I just wished she would go back to speaking English to me. I would catch on to jokes a lot faster.

Temperatures held at thirty degrees, allowing a slight daytime thaw to ease the skating rink conditions, and trucks graveled the roads. Nature had no qualms about dropping into the mid-twenties overnight, however, to recrisp the sidewalks. Åkrehamn beach lay winter white and eerie, and even wind surfers stayed away. Snowy sand crunched beneath our boots chasing away memories of July when the place looked as inviting and tropical as a tropical island, minus the palm trees.

In addition to hosting the 1994 Winter Olympics, Norway brokered the groundbreaking Oslo Peace Accord between Israel's Prime Minister Yitzhak Rabin and Palestinian leader, Yasser Arafat. Tragically the leader of the negotiations, Johan Jørgen Holst, died soon after, and I couldn't help but assume that the strain of months of intense and difficult diplomacy had contributed to his unexpected death. Gudrun agreed, saying that on television his face looked gray from fatigue. The endless meetings had robbed him of sleep, but the goal was so important, he said, that he had to keep going. In the end his legacy was the peace agreement and dignitaries worldwide attended his televised funeral. To my amazement one of my Norwegian friends countered my praise of the statesman with criticism. "Perhaps he was too big for little Norway," he said, his expression indicating that the deceased minister was earning too much attention in his passing.

But look what he did, getting a peace agreement between Israel and the Palestinians, I insisted. No one else had managed to do it. How can you criticize brilliance! My friend looked surprised. "I'm not. It's just that some people say that—that he was too big for little Norway." Too big for his own boots, is that what you want to say? I almost added, disappointed with my friend's small-minded attitude. When someone accomplished something of heroic proportions, why withhold wholehearted praise?

Traditionally, seeming too big, or too anything, as an individual was frowned on where we lived. Improvement or elevation in one's social status could be viewed as undesirable, snooty, or worse, deliberate sabotage of the social balance. Some were outright critical of people who had done a bit better for themselves. No matter that it was due to the jobs they had chosen and career decisions they had made, others could view the matter as a bit of an affront which somehow made them feel less satisfied with their own success.

One person remarked, "Yes, well, people do criticize. I think it has to do with his career in the past. He received his education overseas and worked abroad for many years. When he returned, there was criticism." Perhaps it was the overseas reputation which went against the modest way Norwegians are supposed to have? "Yes, I think so. The *janteloven*, the basic tenet for this society, still survives, reminding each one that he is no better than anyone else and that no one else deserves any special admiration either," he said.

JANTELOVEN (The Law of keeping things even)

You shall not think you are special
You shall not believe that you are more intelligent than others
You shall not believe that you are wiser than others.
You shall not behave as though you are better than others.
You shall not believe that you know more than others.
You shall not believe that you can fix things better than others.
You shall not laugh at others.
You shall not believe that others care about you.
You shall not believe that you can teach others anything.

It struck me that Norwegians and Americans were miles apart in this area, for Manifest Destiny remains the core of our drive for individualism and personal success. Such good, honorable, *desirable* goals sparked the American spirit. Interestingly many immigrants have no problem adapting to this very work and lifestyle while they live in America but revert to their old ways when they return home and need to fit into a different society.

Sometimes an attitude change is all it takes. A Norwegian couldn't get his teammates to make a decision, so his American colleague made a suggestion. "Here," he said, chuckling, handing the man a baseball cap. "Maybe this will help. Put it on and pretend you're an American for awhile." The man snatched it up and put it on. "Right! Now I'm going to kick butt!"

Forced social restraint appears to be a powerful tranquilizer as well as a prime breeding ground for jealousy. "Jealousy is a natural disease in Norway," someone admitted. "A person may think, 'Who do they think they are, being that way or having that thing!' It can happen when people accomplish a degree of fame or accomplishment. They sense others feel jealous of them when they are doing well. It makes people behave differently toward them because of it." Even on a minor level, jealousy can replace goodwill. When one couple began expanding their home, they drew their neighbors' criticism. Certainly, the improvement was very nice—quite fine, in fact—but maybe the homeowners thought themselves pretty fine folks themselves to need such luxury!

People disliked making a fuss about material wealth, even real-estate agents. Unlike Houston agents who talk up a house, Haugesund's are more stingy with sales points or compliments. "I suppose you get a lot of wind here?" is all one could manage after inspecting our custom-designed, rented hillside home.

Norway's reputation for fairness—sometimes taken to extremes, an American might say—results in a nation of peaceful, fairly satisfied, happy people who enjoy a standard of living many would envy. There seem to be no ghettoes and pockets of poverty, and everyone can live decently. All mothers receive children's allowances, and daycare is available and affordable. Even the long-term unemployed appear to live comfortably. A nationalized health system protects everyone.

Class distinctions aren't easy to define. A truck driver might live next door to a bank officer. I once asked a friend who worked for a large company how she would address her company's chairman. "Hansen," she answered. 'Not Mr.—*Herr* Hansen?" I double checked. "No!" she insisted, looking bemused that anyone would be so concerned about this unimportant issue of title. Equality means too that you carry your own bags in Norwegian hotels and carry your own groceries to the car.

That Norway was capable of creating a national son of the high moral stature of a Johan Jørgen Holst reflected well that her society was doing many things right, although Americans might chafe under some of her methods. He had hosted warring leaders in a farmhouse where they talked peace. And while the statesman's little boy played at their feet, how could they have done otherwise?

Norway's magnificent, unspoiled landscape promoted peaceful thought. In the Hardanger valley, for example, people quietly tended fruit trees, and the sun seemed in no hurry to rise from behind enormous mountains to light crevices and shadowed fields. Nature, order, and religion blended as a church spire reached up from the center of a diagonally planted orchard. A tractor puttered up and down the rows, yet I could barely hear it. The air hung like a held breath. Only when a bird splashed into the water, or a tree jiggled while being pruned did the scene look real. An elderly man surveyed a bus stop sign uncertainly. Behind a small cottage a cat stared at me through a wood fence, and the family's underwear flapped briskly against a splendid horizon. Life moved in slow motion.

At nine o'clock one morning two motorboats strained across the fjord like leashed dogs, shattering the calm. Excited hotel guests chatted, waving at the boats. They were ready to leave, but why?

Silence contributed the greatest part of the natural harmony. Subconsciously you waited for an interruption, a bird's cry, an engine noise, a shout, so you could measure the quiet against it. Norway's Edvard Grieg composed some of the world's most beautiful music in Ullensvang. Years later international concert pianist Leif Ove Andsnes revealed how his native land affects artistic creativity. "In Norway, even in the cities," he told

me at his parents' home on Karmøy, "you always have the
opportunity to get outside and discover nature and its silence.
And, as a musician, I feel that it is essential to experience that
silence because of its importance to my music. To me, in fact, the
most beautiful music is the silence between the notes."

The poet's words, "You are nearer God's heart in a
garden than anywhere else on earth," came to mind as I watched
the workers tend their trees in the silence of Hardanger.

Ullensvang was as solemn as a cathedral and grand as a
palace. It drew my eyes upwards, searching for something just out
of reach—a reason for being, perhaps, when my imperfections
and inadequacies glared in the light of total perfection. Surely I
could have contributed something of consequence in this world
by now?

It was the opposite of staring at the stars. They tended to
dissipate my urgent concerns to nothings under the perspective
of eons of time passed and to come. Nothing I did would matter
in the end. But Hardanger was quite different because the peaks,
though monumental, were touchable, suggesting your own
capabilities were greater than you thought they were, and that
you had been freewheeling thus far through life. The mighty
presence of valley, mountain, skies, and water made me want
more of myself.

"Go into yourself and test the deeps in which your life takes
rise; at its source you will find the answer to the question ...
For the creator must be a world for himself and find everything in himself and in Nature ..."
    —From *Letters to a Young Poet* by Rainer Maria Rilke

SKALLER (?)   Patti Jones Morgan

16

Easter in Samiland

Norway's scenic grandeur extended north into the Arctic Circle, home of many of the country's indigenous Sami people who were formerly known as Lapps. How did they survive way up at the top of the world? I wondered if their native lifestyles and traditions compared with those of the American Navajos, people we had lived near in New Mexico? Certainly the exotic place names alone, the Navajo's Land of the Double Rainbows and the Sami's Land of the Midnight Sun, mixed a potent cocktail for my imagination.

But how could we actually see them? I visualized them as nomadic, still reindeer herders. I had no idea if the modern, urban world was knocking at their door. Mike and I pored over the atlas until we found their self-proclaimed capital, Kautokeino, northeast of Tromsø. Our guidebooks showed it as gathering place for Samis during the Easter holidays, *påskeferie*; the red carpet was out for tourists too. Finnmark's remote arctic plain, or *vidda*, beckoned, and we fancied ourselves explorers ready for a completely new and thrilling experience. We would go!

Talking about the trip was part of it. "We're going to Kautokeino for *påskeferie!*" we told the neighbors. They responded with a series of dubious *A-a-hs,* followed by *"Kautokeino? Hmm ..."* Still, seeing how seduced we were by the mystery and novelty of it, they upgraded their reactions to a sort of bemused interest reserved for the sadly confused or for foreigners—we hoped the latter was our excuse.

The rainbow of travel brochures from Kautokeino usurped tablecloths and dishes from our kitchen table for weeks. Easter week festivities looked fantastic. Once winter's semi-twilight, *mørketid,* had passed Finnmark sprang to life. Colorfully costumed Samis reveled in a dazzling white playground, entertainers drummed, children tumbled about on reindeer-drawn sleds. Despite the town's shared latitude with shivery-sounding places like Siberia, Greenland, and Alaska, everyone smiled with high-power warmth. Over the phone our hotel manager guaranteed us sun but not heat, and we packed parkas, thermal underwear, warm sweaters, and sunglasses.

For a few days we would experience life in what many considered a hostile environment and, more importantly, see the land's indigenous people. No one we knew had ever been to Finnmark, and all we knew was what the brochures told us, but our imaginations assured us it would be very different from anywhere else we knew. There was a niggling feeling that it was too far to go, it would be cold, maybe we would find nothing interesting there after all, it was costing us a fortune, and, if it was so interesting, why hadn't any Norwegians we knew gone there? These reservations were a hint of how the trip would affect my senses. Already the polar magnetism was creating a push-pull sensation. Kautokeino, with its location at the top of Scandinavia's landmass, seemed the very essence of northerliness and remoteness, and how its native people managed to live there bombarded us with questions that needed answers.

Norwegians in the south consider it more normal to fly to the Canary Islands, Norway's offshore sun capital, or any place south and warm at Easter. We Americans demonstrated our contrary ways and headed north toward the Arctic Circle.

Easter week found us jetting north far above blinding white mountains climbing out of deep, coastal fjords far below. Our plane cut through blue skies at 32,000 feet, bathed in brilliant sun, but the impression was deceptive. Weather reports from the flight deck confirmed steadily decreasing ground temperatures ahead. As long as the sun streamed down, cold outside or not, I felt positive. Already the trip felt exciting and different because we were further north than we had ever been. In Kautokeino we would come face to face with a minority people hardly known within their own country, let alone on the world stage. One who particularly interested me was Sami singer Mari Boine, the featured artist in a live concert over the holiday weekend.

We circled down to Tromsø over ribbons of mountain roads which snaked downtown. On our brief stopover, dogs barked unhappily from the hold and a young, serious-looking South American man dressed in black and wearing a large, straight-brimmed black hat disembarked. What brought him so far north? Cabin attendants descended angrily on a passenger they caught illegally puffing in the rest room; then a short while later we were up and off, winging inland.

Alta was the end of the line for the flight, and we straggled off. In front, a lovely young Norwegian woman flowed along like a princess in an ankle-length embroidered black skirt, long-sleeved white blouse and decorated, red bodice. She was alone in her elegance in the tawdry Alta airport. Bringing up the rear, our flight's last passengers, two freed, happy retrievers, dragged their owner toward the lobby at breakneck speed.

The dogs had it wrong. None of us had to hurry. While we all exited our flight in the driven, anticipatory manner that continuing travelers do, we were in for a long wait. Coffee, food, and magazines helped keep eyes off the clock. In the restaurant adolescent soldiers smoked, ate, and joked inanely as harmless and beard-free as teenage newspaper boys. One hugged a long, bulging package of Cheez Doodles snacks to his khaki chest as though it were a teddy bear. Before glasnost, Norwegian-Russian border duties were serious business, but now national service focused more on military training. Recalling my earlier chat with a young man from Haugesund, I realized that this was probably their first time away from home. Their mothers were worrying about them. But they didn't need to; I would look after their boys if a war broke out in the next thirty minutes.

In the lounge the beautiful *bunad* girl sat at a table, transformed, a scruffy, brown leather bomber jacket emblazoned with "Hard Rock Cafe" across her shoulders. She sat stiffly one leg crossed over the other, jiggling her foot impatiently from beneath the skirt and fiddling with her cigarette packet. Smoking killed tedious lengths of waiting time, and she produced her own personal cloud. For awhile she had been the bright star in a crowd of jeans and jacketed, travel-weary passengers, but now she hid in their grayness, and far too successfully. She had changed, but by accident?

Already the touches of oddness nagged at me. After the talk down south I had expected the remote airport to be practically empty, but it was packed. Then there were the baby-faced soldiers, a Scandinavian poster girl who suddenly wasn't, the mysterious Latin man in black we left in Tromsø. Here things just were not exactly what I had imagined. The local newspapers amplified the feeling. Norwegian and Sami readers read about ritzy BMW autos or holiday packages to Bulgaria. Bulgaria? Later I learned that Bulgaria was to Finnmarkers what Miami was to New Englanders in winter. One article addressed the perils of nibbling one's way through the long, dark nights and pointed to an upcoming weight control lecture by an expert coming up from the University of Oslo. Offsetting her mission and flaunting the country's tradition for businesses closures over the national holiday, Alta's Chinese restaurant emphasized its extended hours over the weekend. Contradiction and the unexpected were everywhere, including in the restroom. One of my doggy co-passengers from the airplane greeted me with a genial smile, red tongue dripping between slurps of water from the sink faucet.

Well, flying dehydrated us all, four-legged friends included.

At four o'clock a noisy but welcome bus appeared, "Kautokeino" barely distinguishable on the front. With a scant dozen passengers on board we swung out of the airport lot onto roads crowded down to single lanes by snowy embankments. Wood-trimmed houses solemnly guarded the route, roofs bulging with snow. Thin, sparse trees reached skyward, branches lacy against the white backdrop. At another stop a passenger puffed aboard in Norwegian style, *"Uff, uff,"* as he manhandled an awkward bag down the aisle.

The snowscape played with my eyes and imagination, provoking contrast and questions. Would Björn's driving school clients have to cancel lessons now that a snow wall blocked his *Trafikkskole?* And what of the "Laguna" idling in a white, palm-tree-less desert next to six inches of a bus stop sign poking out of a snowdrift? The coach was empty, and I wondered if some poor frozen soul would be unearthed during the summer thaw. An eerily marooned office building which looked like a prefabricated box anchored *sentrum,* downtown, adding to the starkness. Downtown Alta had the film set picturesqueness of a one-street Colorado mining town. Unexpected luxury glowed from a rooftop logo. Mercedes Benz, one of the world's most expensive automobiles, evidently had a foothold in this economically austere land and had the horizon to itself.

Rocked by the bus's rhythm, I snuggled against my dozing husband, hoping to feel warm and safe. But the cold world outside unsettled me. Only a thin pane of glass separated us from a strange and lightly populated land. We were miles north of everywhere, and snow blew heavily against the window. Only our driver knew how to get us where we needed to go, and the road was slick. I hoped he could get us there safely.

We left Alta on Route 93 South. Two girls rode along leisurely on thick, arch-necked, golden *fjording* horses, and a lone jogger puffed clouds of breath. Farther on, an orange car lay buried up to its roof. Snow added a mysterious dimension to the landscape, eliminating the comfort of definitions, obscuring the frozen river, trees, and land under a harmless-looking white coverlet. Tantalizing glimpses of the Arctic world evoked questions, but we had no time to linger for answers. As the minutes passed, I wondered more and more about the Samis and how on earth they lived in such a land.

On the way a teenage boy waved us down on an icy stretch. His mother helped him up, then drove away. Later a cheery, yellow wooden sun sprouted from a five-foot snowdrift in front of Alta River Camping, and we passed a half-finished wooden house. Our bus maneuvered along the center line of the slippery road. Boulders threatened, tenuously attached to steep mountainsides. Glistening high walls of curved ice on switchback mountain corners turned me into an unwilling luge contestant as we slid through them. A thin row of short trees crowned distant mountain ranges with tonsorial cuts. We stopped to drop off an older lady. She slipped a cheery pink snowsuit over her street clothes, then disappeared, ghostlike, into a world of white nothingness, ski poles in hand. In America abandoning someone in a blizzard in the middle of nowhere would be a punishable offense, but not in Norway. Here grandma crocheted, but she also cross-country skied.

In the town of Masi I saw my first Sami family. The husband's ornate, flared, hip-length jacket of red, blue, and green, embellished with silver studs, topping dark pants, belonged to a character in an Elizabethan play, yet he was probably a reindeer herder. He led his family across snowdrifts, his thin legs stretching out in the deep snow like a daddy longlegs. He and his wife, hands linked, became a moving cutout decoration on a fantasy Christmas card landscape. An elderly Sami lady gingerly negotiated the icy road, leaning over a *spark*, kick sled. Her old-fashioned bonnet the shape of a tall loaf of cottage bread perched on her head, asking for the wind to blow it off. A snowmobile rider followed alongside the bus, on the embankment, then raced full out across a white expanse so flat I guessed it must be a wide stretch of frozen river.

At last, something familiar—tepees. But not covered. Rather just long wood poles propped together. Animal skins and fish tacked up to porches and balconies showed that people still needed nature's harvest. A man stood smoking fish over his house chimney. His neighbor's house boasted a satellite dish. Wood-trimmed houses, the only color in an otherwise monotone landscape, clustered like friends on the curve of the river, reassuring me that there would be someone there if I were suddenly stranded.

Kautokeino stayed light well into the late evening, entrancing us with a blue and gold sky.   Our tourist hotel, some guest houses, and *kro*—small roadside inns which offered food— a few shops and offices and a stream of through traffic were all there was, and that wasn't much. The modest metropolis was a vulnerable outcropping of humanity in the midst of relentless plain. How did people find what they needed to live a lifetime here? A slender church steeple glinted like an upraised beatific baton above the vast panorama. The lonely Navajo reservation or the Sami's *vidda,* or plain, both revealed the same sense of native endurance and peace.

A Sami couple strolled downtown, the woman's top few inches of tall bonnet moving just above a snow hedge. When they emerged, her brightly colored clothes contrasted with our own practical darks. Her full, red and blue, knife-pleated skirt bounced cheerfully with her steps, unexpectedly feminine and summery-looking. Lavish silver neck jewelry sparkled in the sun. If she had been wearing velvet and turquoise, she could have been a Navajo lady at Shiprock Fair. She seemed to wear no especially warm leg coverings, and her boots were reindeer skin moccasins, *skaller,* allegedly stuffed with grass. My feet were cold in my lined boots, and my legs could have done with another layer of pants. I wondered how her impractical clothes could possibly keep her warm.

On a freezing, sunny morning two thousand Samis went about their work, many tending reindeer while, far away, Navajos tended sheep and goats. The Samis, facing blizzards or mosquitoes, working in small pockets of industry, had learned to live with the rhythm of the seasons and the weather. They had survived wartime occupation. Many families were forced to hide or live in caves when their homes were burned down. Historical artifacts were lost, leaving a hole in much of the Samis' history.

Past discrimination from the south's homogeneous society had fostered feelings of inferiority which still remain, a Sami told me. For a long time the Sami language was abandoned in favor of Norwegian in the schools. A Navajo had told me much the same story. Anglo teachers had drummed negative messages into his head at his Indian boarding school. "Being an Indian is bad! Your religion and language are no good. Do it our way, the right way. And stop speaking Navajo!" Twenty tough years later he still found it hard to walk two paths, the Navajo's and the White Man's. Fortunately, not all teachers were as harsh. Some created beautifully handmade books depicting native legends and stories and had the students illustrate them, restoring the children's sense of tribal culture.

In Kautokeino expectations and reality collided. Snow-mobiles outpaced cars at the Texaco gasoline station; a local bank officer moonlighted as a taxi driver; the corner convenience store groaned with two walls for videos and just one for food. Peaceful day-to-day routines belied the sometimes wild-and-woolly life of Arctic climes where cold and dark combine to send some indoors for a little extra sustenance. A business's Santa Fe-style roof line changed its mind and abruptly curved into a Chinese pagoda which housed some of the most expensive oriental rugs and hand-crafted silver jewelry I had ever seen.

We attended the Sami Grand Prix and found it was an evening of traditional Sami *joik*, musical chants. Because of its pre-Christian roots and past connection with bouts of drinking, *joik* is still controversial. Sami artist Nils-Aslak Valkeapää opened the Lillehammer Winter Olympic Games with a *joik*, however, and singer Mari Boine incorporates it, with drumming, into her music. Not all Samis approve of her style. "She sounds too . . . Indian," commented a young Sami selling me one of the singer's compact discs. Fortunately Boine's Easter concert in Kautokeino, quite unforgettable, solved another of our trip's mysteries. The young man in black we had seen on the plane stood behind her on stage, playing flute.

Reindeer conjure up cozy images of Rudolph to Americans, but to Finnmark's Sami they are their livelihood. But even serious animal husbandry has a holiday when Samis go to the races—reindeer races, *reinkappkjøring*. Drivers on sleds try to guide their animals as the creatures run full out yet reluctantly in an awkward long-legged gallop as announcers call the race over loudspeakers. We watched them at the finish line, hyped up and pulling against the reins, occasionally breaking free for a relaxing trot through the crowd. More than ancient skill and prowess was at stake. The prize was 50,000 kroner, or about 7,000 dollars, for the owner whose reindeer won over three successive years.

Påskeferie is the social event of the year for Samis catching up with relatives and friends after the extended winter. Mingling and chatting happily in their slightly breathy voices and short-syllabled style reminiscent of the Navajo way of speaking, they perhaps discussed the season's upcoming weddings and confirmations. Their colorful figures formed a living multicolored afghan spread across the white ground. Sami women sold reindeer skins and leather goods. Friends photographed one another. Others lined up for hot dogs, not the fried bread tacos Navajos might serve. We were cooling our feet at a very northern powwow, indeed, with dances coming later. In the foreground another oddity appeared in our Finnmark experience: a forty-foot crane reached up into the clear blue sky, belching forth Arctic bungee jumpers.

The sun dazzled against the snow, but to stay warm I had to keep moving. My toes became casualties when slush soaked my winter boots. Vendors offered many things—socks included. Wool and made in Ireland, my pair cost me ten dollars and came with a ready-made hole. I balanced on one leg behind a caravan with my bare foot hovering above snow, glad enough to peel off my saturated sock in favor of anything dry, holey or not, even if it cost ten dollars.

In the crowd we overheard American voices and met a Californian and her daughter. "My husband's an accountant and at tax season he hardly knows we're around, so we decided to visit Europe and Scandinavia and have Easter weekend up here in Kautokeino," the woman said with a note of "I'll show him!" in her voice. A minority group of four, we laughed about the fact that, in the swarms of local residents in one of the most remote communities in the world, we somehow found ourselves standing next to other Americans watching the strange and amazing Sami reindeer races.

Photographing or videotaping the exotically dressed residents as they walked by was frowned on. A young girl, sleekly imposing in a thick, cream-colored fur skirt and skin jacket shook her head firmly, "No," when I asked permission and fled behind a canvas booth. A family of three agreed but posed self-consciously. I felt very much an onlooker, tolerated with patience. But the picture I wanted, and got, was that of an old man whose heavily lined face and aquiline nose gave him the regal look of an ancient American Indian chief. However, he had just dismounted a shiny new snowmobile, not a pony. Hesitating before approving my request, he nodded solemnly only once, a trace of pleasure warming his enigmatic features. He would do something memorable for this nervous tourist lady. Thanking him, I clicked hurriedly and left him resting against his red, high-powered machine.

Snowmobiles are the only way, and the fastest, to get around in winter in Kautokeino, and we signed up for a motorized safari across the Arctic tundra to a Sami tent, *lavvu,* where we would be rewarded with a traditional Sami meal. Thick, polar-insulated jumpsuits and gloves with gauntlets up to our elbows were necessary, and we waddled up to Kurt's Safari headquarters. I hoped for an expert snowmobile driver and found him close by. It would be my husband or me, Kurt said, smiling at my horrified reaction.

Mike swung courageously onto the seat, received thorough driving instruction in sixty seconds, and with a lurch we were off with six or seven others in the team, across roads and sidewalks, out onto the plain, up and down hills, one snowmobile trailing a sled. Treetop branches stuck out of the snow and Arctic wind cut into our cheeks. On steep hills we regularly toppled off the snowmobile, then scrambled back on our feet like lumbering Michelin men, amazingly undamaged from our spills on the thick, soft mattress of snow. We had become the group's unofficial entertainment. Many prayers later, after my husband discovered the thrill of accelerating across a frozen river, we spied a distant, welcome cluster of Sami *lavvu* in the midst of uninhabited wilderness.

A log fire blazed inside lunch headquarters, and we squeezed through the tent flap to meet the rest of our safari contingent. A fellow traveler exposed my wimpiness: a ten-month-old baby whom Daddy unpeeled from under his jacket to feed baby food. Our smiling Sami hostess fed us reindeer steak, steaming hot cups of bone marrow soup, black coffee, bread and waffles. Lack of space forced me to dine horizontally, head in the triangle where tent and skins met cold ground, my enormous boots—the only size the excursion company had left—sticking up into my husband's face. Time disappeared into a warm blur as we practically swooned in swirling black clouds of smoke. Swaddled as thickly as the baby, I was fading away when a cold blast of air and open tent flap announced Kurt's return. "Ready to go back?" he challenged, delighting in our woebegone expressions at having to leave the heat.

We flew back across the snow, my arms aching from hanging on so hard, then stumped like robots past a frozen pond marked by holes and flags from the morning's fishing event. The elements had taken their toll on me. Wind-lashed and smoked, my face had not been privy to a mirror for hours. But surviving the experience, feeling what Samis must in their own tents in winter, and not breaking anything made the day a success.

Just as I was visualizing a long, hot bath, I met Mari Boine exiting the hotel's back stairs, suitcase in hand. In this unlikely situation I managed to engage her in some conversation and ask for an interview.

When I met with her that summer in Karasjok, she admitted that she felt particularly nervous when she returned to Finnmark to sing. "Before my performance in Kautokeino I had to work harder to prepare myself. I know my people are proud of me, but they can't show it the way they would like to. People hold on to their feelings a lot."

Reared in a deeply religious family, Boine was separated from her Sami culture and heritage for many years and went on to become a teacher. However, when the Alta Dam project was proposed by the government, she joined many who opposed it and began feeling her way back to her own Sami roots. Singing expressed her feelings, and her music, like her sociopolitical opinions, didn't please everyone. Yet she drew on this very tension and adversity for strength at the outset of a performance.

"When I have all those feelings just before I am going to sing, I pretend that I'm on the very top of a mountain with barely enough ground beneath my feet to stand. Then, as I start to sing, I take my wings and fly!"

That summer she would sing from her *Ørnebror,* Eagle Brother album, in Albuquerque, New Mexico, she said, providing for me yet another connection between the peoples of the Land of the Double Rainbows and those of the Land of the Midnight Sun. She would feel at home in the Southwest, I felt, among other native people who have honored their ethnic identity and heritage with unique creative expression. I wished I could have heard her there among the pink mesas singing her powerful songs.

THE SAAMI ANTHEM

Far to the north, beneath the Great Bear
Sápmi reveals its mystery:
Never-ending mountain crests,
Ever-lasting lakes and tarns;
Crag, fell and moorland heights
Reaching out to the firmament;
Gushing rivers, sighing forests;
Steel-grey headlands
Rearing over roaring seas.

In the eye of wintry storms
In the teeth of howling blizzards
Saami kinship spreads its warm embrace;
Moonlight guides the wayfarer
Under flows of flashing Northern Lights;
Forests, frozen, creak
Echoing to the grunting reindeer;
Over lake and fell a low persistent roar,
As through the snow sleds, swooshing, go.

Summer sunshine gilds
Forest, ocean and shore;
In golden light fishermen row
On sea and tarn.
Gold-like sea birds sparkling;
Silver-like rivers shimmering;
Glinting oars, glistening punt-poles,
Singing boatmen mastering
Raging rapids and deep-moving rivers.

Sápmi, land of Sami kinsfolk;
Ever-vigilant, never-yielding
To murderous raiders, malevolent
traders
Or sly, deceitful tax collectors!
Hail! Indominatable kinsfolk!
Hail! Bedrock of peace!
No waging of war,
No shedding of brothers' blood-
Peaceful Sami kinsfolk!

Our forefathers of old,
Achieved victory over adversity,
Kinsfolk! Let us confound our
adversaries
With our patience and stamina.
Indefatigable sons of the Sun-Father!
Repressors cannot triumph
If we cherish our golden language.
Treasure the words of our forebears:
Sápmi for the Sami!

—By Isak Saba, 1906
Trans. by Martin Pope, Karasjok

EAGLE BROTHER

Eagle brother
eagle brother
when will you let me
fly with you again

Far up north
under the Great Bear
I saw your brothers soar
I saw them lose themselves
under the endless sky

They said
go ask
go ask who
who tied your wings
so tightly

Eagle brother
eagle brother
when
will you let me
fly with you
again

©Mari Boine
(English version)

GOASKINVIELLJA

Goaskinviellja
goaskinviellja
goas
goas
goas beasan
duinna fas girddait

Guhkkin davvin
dávggáid vuolde
oidnen mun
oidnen mun
oidnen
du vieljaid
girdimin

oidnen
sin
balvvaid vuol'
luoitimin

Goh o jearrat
goh o jearrat
geat
geat
atne du soajáid
nie avgadit
atne du soajáid
nie avgadit

Goh o jearrat
goh o jearrat
geat
geat
atne du soajáid
nie avgadit

Goaskinviellj
goaskinviellja
goas
goas
goas beasan
duinna
fas girddait

©Mari Boine (Sami version)

ØRNEBROR

Ørnebror
ørnebror
når
når får jeg fly
med deg igjen

Oppe hos oss
under nordlige stjerner
så jeg
så jeg dine brødre
fly
så jeg dem
slippe seg
under skyene

De ba meg spørre
de ba meg spørre hvem
hvem
buntet dine vinger
buntet dine vinger
så hardt

Ørnebror
ørnebror
når
når får jeg
fly
med deg igjen

©Mari Boine
(Norwegian version)

Easter Sunday dawned sunny and bright, a single church bell tolling insistently out across the town for what seemed an hour. No buses meant that our chauffeur back to Alta airport was a young, fair-haired waitress driving the hotel's pick-up truck. I remembered snippets of conversations of our weekend. One of Mari's band members had called out as I left a restaurant.

"Where are you from?"

"Houston—Texas," I replied.

"Hmm. I know someone in the States. He lives in Hollywood, I think," the musician recalled. "Have you been there?" Glitz 'n glitter Hollywood seemed the last possible topic during a sunny, crisp Finnmark morning far from the mecca of moviedom, but it was another example of the oddities of Samiland. Norway, Kautokeino, Navajos, Samis. Now Hollywood. Interestingly the young man assumed something all travelers do—that anyone from another land is almost sure to know its every corner.

Our young driver manipulated the hotel's four-wheel drive expertly across the plains, soothing herself with skinny, self-rolled cigarettes. We passed a golden-orange fox in the snow, motionless and perfect, looking like a photograph from *National Geographic*. He stared at our truck and we at him and he did not even quiver. Our driver warmed up to my writer's questions after we had been squeezed together in the front seat for an hour. "When I was young, some Canadians came to stay with our family for a year, making a film about us herding our reindeer. Maybe you could see it?" Yet another Finnmark illusion vanished. This remote spot was new to me, unknown to most, yet evidently drew a thin but steady flow of people who were curious about it.

We talked in *norsk* and English, and I learned that her parents had given her her own *joik*, or personal chant, and that she would do the same for her own children. I played with the idea of somebody giving me one. If it were so individualized, what would it say to me or about me? But a *joik* was like a *bunad*. Only those who were Norwegian born could legitimately possess them.

We touched on Sami politics, schools, and employment.

She and her husband raised reindeer which roamed the mountains and the national parks. I asked naively how many they
owned. She scolded me politely. "Would I ask how much money
you have?" Embarrassed, I shook my head. "Well, it's the same
for us, that question. Our reindeer are our wealth."

The moment passed and we went on to discuss reindeer
racing. Did her husband ever race theirs? He did not, and she was
glad because she disapproved of it. Running in harness didn't
come naturally, and the training was rigorous. The whole process
was difficult. Having watched the creatures lunging to shake off
their sleds, anxious to get free, I felt she was right. "I have two
reindeer of my own at home and they are like pets. I love them
too much to race them," she added.

After almost two hours the atmosphere in the cab was so
relaxed, we could have driven forever. Had she seen the foreign
guest pouring uncooked pancake mix instead of yogurt over his
cereal during breakfast at the hotel earlier? I had been dying to
ask. "Oh, yes! I watched you try to stop him," she laughed. At the
airport Mike and I begged her to rest before the long drive back,
and we found a coffee shop and shared our lives over food and
hot drinks. She had not heard about Houston but wanted to visit
the United States one day. When she smiled, she looked very
familiar and I finally realized why. She was almost the twin of my
friend Cindy back in the States, dimple and all, and I wished I had
taken her photograph.

She scooted off across the snowy parking lot, hugging
herself in her thin, white cotton blouse and dark skirt uniform. At
twenty-three, the wife of a reindeer herder, mother of three tots,
and part-time hotel waitress knew Finnmark's winter cold and
clothes better than anyone, yet in her hurry to get us to Alta to
our plane, she forgot to bring a sweater or jacket.

Why was she cold and we warm? The Polar circle tricked
you and your expectations. My preconceptions of Finnmark were
of a cold, barren, lonely place, but its silent, wild, expansive
wilderness touched the heart and its wanderlust. The Samis were
right for that land: survivors—colorful people in their colorful

clothes, quite a variety. Kurt was about six feet tall with dark hair; he was Sami. The waitress was petite with Scandinavian pale skin and blonde looks—Sami too. A short, broad-faced lady at the restaurant was Sami as were two black-haired girls. Then there were other indigenous circumpolar natives who had come to Norway for the celebration: a round-faced lady who sang with a high-pitched monotone, Japanese-style. Another singer was large and round and looked Hawaiian.

Landing back on Karmøy, we shared some of our impressions with our young cab driver, in particular our snowmobile safari to a Sami *lavvu*. Had he ever been up to Finnmark, around the Sami people? Somewhat grudgingly, he said no he had never been nor had he ridden a snowmobile. Were politics, religion, culture, or prejudice clouding his attitude, I wondered. We were soon left in no doubt as to the problem. "The thing is, we can't have them here—snowmobiles, I mean. They're fun, but we're not allowed to have them in the south. Only the Samis are permitted to use them!" His youthful envy of the Sami's snowmobile culture made me smile behind my scarf. Not politics or social issues at all! Why should I have expected a predictable answer? The Arctic loved her game of opposites and topsy-turvy.

We and the neighbors exchanged reports. They had returned from their mountain cabins or from the continent where they had relaxed, got tanned. And us? How did it go in Kautokeino? "Oh, it was great! Wonderful. We ate bone marrow soup and rode on a snowmobile, watched reindeer races, all in bright sunshine!" we enthused, hoping for a mood change. Our vacation pitch failed to budge them. They limited their reactions to noncommittal smiles, nods, and perhaps a few more questioning *hmmms*? We gave up, reconciled to the fact that Samiland held no special mystery for many in southern Norway.

But for me everything to do with the Sami's world stretched the imagination. The old and the ultra new shared ancient territory in contrasting pairings: reindeer and snowmobiles; skins and satellite dishes; two languages, Sami and Norwegian; *joik* tapes sold alongside rock music, assimilation versus separate identity. I went north as far as I had ever been and found cold plains but warm people, isolation but not loneliness, an ancient cultural heritage at the heart of an evolving society. Who could forget Kurt, face wreathed in a smile, calling for a backup snowmobile via a cellular telephone stuffed inside his fur-lined jacket hood, or the pretty waitress who loved her own pet reindeer and feared the divisiveness of a Sami flag, the lady in her smoky *lavvu* ladling us soup from bowls licked by open flames? And always the disturbing, addictive sound of their chants, wailing and wolflike, on the tapes I had tucked away in my purse. For me Samiland would always be a memory of real people with real faces who made us welcome. They were no longer unknown and beyond my caring. When I closed my eyes and listened to the *joik*, joining in, my spirit flew back to the vast and remote land which had caught me up in its spell.

"If you are fortunate enough to live in a place where you feel you belong you will know the landscape of the place has several layers of meaning. As well as its geographical features it becomes an image of a private world where a certain harmony within oneself is experienced as in no other place."

—From *The Winter Fens* by Edward Storey

A KARMØY ALBUM

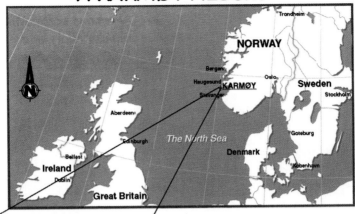

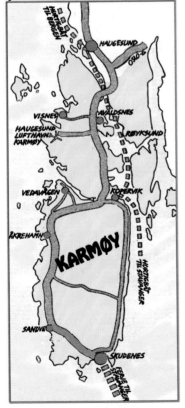

KARMØY (The Saga Island) lies off the southwest coast of Norway, across the sound (Karmsundet). Farming, fishing and tourism are mainstays of life on the island, which is linked to the mainland by bridge, ferries and high-speed catamarans.

Maps adapted from materials used by permission of Karmøy Kommune. Photos by Patti Jones Morgan.

Åkrehamn beach: Mike walking Nicky on a blustery spring day.

Mike sees the completion of the Heidrun gas processing module at HMV's shipyard, Haugesund.

Below: Kopervik Sunday morning. A new papa chats with a friend.

A cookie-making session with "our" neighborhood girls.

Below: Fair at Skudeneshavn Sentrum.

Spring lambs greet the sunshine in a Karmøy pasture.

Samis enjoying Easter Festival in Finnmark.

*May 17:
Norwegian National
Day—bright with
celebration, flowers,
and beautiful
bunader (costumes).*

EDVART SK
TORA SKE

17

Goodbyes & Green Ties

Back in the neighborhood, spring and young men's fancies were in the air. A new boyfriend was visiting Rebekka, who had upgraded her suitor qualifications for the new season. Last year's young man's transportation was two-wheel; this one's, four. These four wheels stood in their immense ridged glory, two large and two small attached to a red, earth-caked tractor, dwarfing Egil's station wagon and Liv's elderly green car which were reduced to bookends in a giant's library. I hoped our friends weren't totally outmatched by the young man indoors.

In the name of love, coupled with the fact he evidently was not yet old enough to hold a full driver's license, Rebekka's admirer had to hotfoot his love machine three or four miles from Avaldsnes on date evenings. This took courage for he risked sour looks from impatient drivers stuck behind him. Maybe they would have forgiven him if they had known his real mission. This farmer's son had no plans for ploughing, but spring had sprung and with it, perhaps, abstract concepts that had a lot to do with a lovely eighteen-year-old brunette with long hair, large eyes, and pouty lips.

Mike waged a personal vendetta against dandelions which, like every green thing, grew almost around the clock. At ten o'clock at night he would tear up a patch, only to find a new cluster awaiting him the next day. "I can't believe it!" he muttered over breakfast, taking their appearance very personally. "A whole flock of them there again!" Like birds they appeared out of nowhere. According to folk mythology, a monk brought them to the island, considering them flowers. Mike and the monk would not have agreed.

In most senses our sojourn had evolved into a sense of permanence: I wanted it to continue. Couldn't we buy our own house, one that we would not have to love and leave at the company's command? I studied house photographs or descriptions in the newspaper, rating their ocean views, and mentally converted kroner prices into dollars. In town I read property descriptions and wondered how you went about buying a house in Norway. I called Egil and asked for a recommendation of an *eiendom*, real estate, company. After that, it was just a step to sharing my idea with Mike, who, I just knew, would require an enormous amount of convincing.

Hanna had gotten wind of my plan. "I hear you want to buy a house here. We'll help you find one!" She showed me a house nearby and I drove by it regularly, afraid to call the owner. Surprisingly Mike agreed to go look at one down the coast in Stangeland. We parked alongside the road and peered at it; the view was good, the house not so, so we passed. The idea of buying a house fermented like ginger beer, however, until Torben and Lone spoke up. "It's a wonderful idea and, you know, you can always rent a house out and we'll manage it for you! It would be no problem to take care of it while you're gone," they assured us. Gone? If we couldn't live there then, when could we? What were the implications of such a drastic change? Would my husband ever, truly, want to work only in Norway? Or if we had to wait until he retired, the whole beautiful idea of having a house on the water and walking the fields seemed irrelevant. Life was now, and five, ten, or fifteen years from then we would be different, certainly older.

Matters took on urgency when Mike announced that he had filled out our "repatriation papers" for returning to the States the following year. It sounded so cold, like a military transfer. "I don't want to leave!" I wanted to yell. At that moment I hated the company for destroying the wonderful life I had found far, far away from Houston. Storming around downstairs, I fiddled with things on our bedroom dresser, dusted, rearranged all the knickknacks, and thought about each one. My body had accepted that everything would be torn apart once again, but my mind still hadn't.

To make matters worse, the company hinted that they wanted us in Stavanger, a major seaport to the south. The town would have offered the companionship of other international residents and expatriates who spoke English most of the time and, its business being oil, it had earned sister-city designation to Houston. But those benefits did not tempt me; in fact, I feared living there would separate me from the Norwegian culture which I preferred to experience at a rural pace with no distractions. My little island offered me all I needed, both as writer and person— one who had begun considering where people fit in their societies and how their choices and limitations, even religious beliefs, grow out of their culture; the importance of nature and spiritual nourishment; the barrier, or open gate, of language.

We couldn't move there, not now, I pleaded with Mike. I have friends, my art shows. I'm writing; I love this place. I can't give it all up and start all over again.

Somehow, the powers that be spared us. We didn't have to move to Stavanger after all, but our landlords were returning so we did have to move to another rental house. Fortunately it was just six or seven minutes away in Kopervik, half a mile from the sea. We were glad to get it, and it was handsome, but it would never replace my house on the water and the wild garden, and the sea practically at my doorstep which had meant every-thing to me.

I still couldn't shake the house-buying idea. I never dared

ask my husband in so many words if he would give up everything and live in Norway because I knew the answer. I felt that the most he might agree to was to buy something we could *visit* on vacation. For days all I could think about was how to make moving our lives to Karmøy work, but in the background there were so many reasons it wouldn't. Our entrepreneurial, independent ways were against us as were the society's more restrictive social parameters. Having no children to bring the culture to us didn't help. And, most important of all, could we ever be totally happy in a place where everyone else spoke another language?

Inevitably the answer was no. Even our work visa prohibited buying property, Mike told me, and we knew that immigration was highly restricted. So that was that; all the angst was for nothing. We would be returning to America in another year and could not buy a house on the island after all. It felt like a relief, in the end, to know that. Yet would I ever find happiness again in America that could even come close to the joy of living on Karmøy? I just couldn't imagine it.

As the date closed in for our short move to Kopervik, I felt drained. Rain drizzled for hours, and the Karmsund sulked, gray and lifeless. In the garden our little forsythia bush, weakened from its annual pecking assaults, barely managed a few new leaves. Beech branches scraped against the window like claws scratching open a wound. Our house was more than a home: it had become a beloved friend and ally and my heart was breaking at having to leave it.

My mourning was interrupted by the doorbell. The children trooped in. "We have something for you and Mike," they said, handing me a large bouquet of wildflowers, mostly yellow. The usually happy faces looked so solemn. I thanked them over and over again. They fidgeted. "You know we are moving to a house in Kopervik on Thursday? I wish we didn't have to go. We just love it here," I explained for their sakes and mine, "but the other family is coming back, you see."

They nodded. "Yes, we know. And—we liked you being

here too," one said, generating concurring mumbles.

"I'm going to miss you all," I said, deeply moved.

From his spot behind the couch the oldest, tallest, biggest one of the group, twelve-year-old, dear Per-Rune added plaintively, "We'll miss *you* too!" as though he were really feeling the loss already. And from small-boned buddy Anders, one who had never been inside our house before although his sister often had came an equally sincere, "Yes, ... we'll miss you!" followed by a sort of disconsolate *tut*. That sad snap of the tongue behind the top teeth said it all. We all hated having change thrust on us when everything had been so perfect.

"But you *are* going to come over on your bikes and visit?" I asked, trying to lift their spirits. Yes, they were definitely coming over to the new house. "How about pizza and ice cream?" Prospects of pizza did wonders for morale and for awhile the room buzzed with their voices although we knew it would never be the same.

The room fell quiet once the little delegation had gone, and I tenderly examined the bouquet. Perhaps the girls gathered the flowers and greenery and Per-Rune did the rest, all fingers and thumbs, wrestling with the bouquet until everything was perfect, finally wrapping it in silver paper and tying it with a large ribbon.

There were no words for such a precious gift. How lucky we were to know these children. At home in my house and my heart, they drew me out into their world, and somewhere along the way I began to believe I could manage in their country after all.

A House on the Water

What more could I want
than a house on the water,
high up on a cliff,
in Norway's cold country.

What more could I want
than a mountainous place,
a waterfall roaring,
birds calling and wheeling.

What more could I want
than a green and blue land
with boats and wood houses,
good neighbors to talk to.

What more could I want
than a fresh, morning breeze,
laughing voices of children,
our dogs to fuss over.

I have what I want
in each season with you,
Joy, work and laughter,
. . . surely any house will do.

But in the house on the water
Northern Lights far above,
grew daydreams of paradise,
in a landscape of love.

—Patti Jones Morgan, 1994.

I left my house on the water on a beautiful, sunny day. I left my picture window view behind as though I had walked out of a theater, leaving an ongoing film rolling across the screen. The expanse of water ringed by trees and mountains and spread across with blue skies would remain, but I would not be the one to see it. The breathtaking setting etched itself forever in my heart and with a loving goodbye I left for our new home in Kopervik, sad but not adrift. Time in that house had healed me in many ways. The island provided the refuge, and the house, a haven. I was leaving as a stronger person.

Over the eighteen months in Håvik, or Austevik as the old name was, we had lived in a separate world, physically and by lifestyle. It was tucked off the highway, with no through traffic, and the only shop was Hilde's near Vorråveien. An invisible wall protected us from everything and everyone else. You could always tell who the strangers were for they drove in fast, peered around, then u-turned back toward the highway. Others just passed through to the union hall for a meeting or a wedding reception, and once soldiers camped on the hill below our house and used the hall for training. I loved Håvik for many reasons, but mostly because, for the first time in years, I felt safe.

People kept themselves to themselves which was both good and bad. We could have done with more interaction, but if we met up away from the neighborhood, they made a beeline for us. At airports or up in the mountains, at the post office, or even shopping in Haugesund, they greeted us like long-lost friends. I was sure it had to do with our little secret. We all came from such a small place that we clustered for comfort together in the outside world, relieved to see a familiar face.

My concerns that there would be no children around our new house quickly vanished. The bush telegraph snapped into action and produced a new army of unofficial little Norwegian language tutors trooping in and out of our house on Nornesvegen. Two brothers across the street broke the ice on move-in day after twirling around the moving truck on their bikes watching all the lifting and sliding, uncrating and rearranging with fascination. Did we have any daughters? The cat and dog I offered didn't seem the same thing at all. Over the next month a little red-haired girl with a round, freckled face and a missing upper tooth began showing up, a little blonde friend with her. They hung around so long on the doorstep with toothy and toothless smiles that their curiosity was disarming. *"Skal du komme inne?"* I invited. *"Ja!"* they chorused and marched in for an inspection. The little brother and sister next door paid a call and did a little drawing and playing with toys.

Jacqueline from across the street quickly became, like Liv-Marit, another special child. Surprisingly mature for her seven years or so, and tall, she acted like a big sister to the other children. Jacqueline's nurturing ways extended to offering you a bite of whatever morsels she had in her pocket. She may have been from Chile, but how long her family had lived in Norway we had no idea and didn't understand how she had learned so much English. Her favorite task was walking Rudy; my little dog was becoming more fuddled as his eyesight and hearing were getting worse by the day, but Jacqueline watched over him solicitously. When other children began competing for the job, she insisted I let her reserve Rudy's walk for her for the next day, and always asked one day ahead. Thus she became his chief walker.

She wore her heart on her sleeve, and her sensitivity guaranteed a few hurts. When one of the scrappier boys pushed her one afternoon, her large brown eyes filled with a sea of tears and I had to give her a comforting hug. I consoled her in the best *norsk* I could, *"Han er bare en liten gutt, gutter er gutter, du må ikke føle triste om det,"* saying he was just a little boy and that boys will be boys. She was not to feel sad about it. Somehow my explanation made sense and she sniffed, dried her eyes, and bravely ran back to the group with upset forgiven if not forgotten.

Soon our Håvik children came over to see the new house. Pizza and ice cream and much thundering up and down three stories to test the acoustics made the events loud and fun. They brought little gifts and flowers and surprised Mike with something he treasures to this day—a loud, green, multiprint tie. He examined the gift with pleasure, however. "Very nice," he commented, and Anders, the bearer of the gift, who was not tall, visibly grew an inch or two with pride. "And, Mike! It only cost five kroner!" he confided, pleased with his bargain at the local cash and carry, we gathered. My husband held up the tie appreciatively and made one of the kindest remarks anyone could have. "Really? It looks like it cost much more!" Anders beamed as the others huddled around admiring the present they had chosen.

Afterwards their attention returned to pizza. I had not yet figured out the dials on my oven, but the children were polite about the condition of one of their pizzas. "This was pretty nice, but the one with brown bits didn't taste so good," Anders remarked as he helped me clear away the party debris. In horror I rechecked the oven settings. I had broiled one of the pizzas!

After they biked off home, I shared my thoughts about the awful green tie, kindly given, of course, with Mike. He leapt to its defense. "Nonsense! It's great. I'm going to wear it to the project completion party!" And to my amazement, he did. And not just then. He wore it on many occasions in Norway and later in Houston without the least amount of shame. Anders would be proud.

Our new neighborhood was termed *barnevennlig*, which literally translated as "child friendly." Dozens of youngsters amused themselves in the community playgrounds all Norwegian neighborhood's have, or clambered up and down rocky embankments, gathered wildflowers and berries or tore about on bikes, heads encased in helmets. Even boys pick bouquets; little Mads brought me one and as usual I was amazed.

On rainy days the center of activity in front of our house was The Puddle, which provided endless hours of entertainment

for the little boys. A few hours of rain filled the parking lot
pothole nicely and, judging by the intense gazing into its four or
five inch depths, one could be forgiven for thinking there were
fish or other creatures swimming in it. But there were not. It was
simply a fascinating puddle which expanded to thirty inches after
a good rain of which we had our share. It drew the boys like a
magnet, and they crouched in it, feet in rubber boots, buckets in
hand, then formed busy little processions to slosh water back and
forth to all manner of rocks nearby. They leaned over the water
lost in deep discussion of heaven only knows what. The puddle
was for splashing and jumping, floating toys, and dragging stuff
through. The boys made a wonderful sight, and I sneaked out to
take a photograph. Before I could click, they scattered and no
amount of " … just go back to the way you were before" in my
inadequate Norwegian could convince them to do it.

My *norsk* didn't do quite as well with my *Nornesvegen
barna* as it had with my Håvik ones. One little fellow behaved very
oddly when I asked him something. He kept lowering his voice. I
asked the question again and he lowered his voice even more.
Finally he was saying something so quietly I had to bend double
to catch it. In the end I discovered that my question was not
coming across properly. He just thought I was asking him to
whisper.

Cool, wet, or windy weather was no excuse to cosset
Karmøy children, and they played outside in adverse conditions
and fair, a tradition that went back to infancy when their parents
pushed them around in baby carriages, rain or shine. Even on
blustery days mothers tucked their children inside little plastic
enclosures which hooked onto baby carriages. Fall and winter
brought about a sort of indoor incubation for children. When
milder weather appeared, they cast off the all-in-one zippered
suits and stepped out into the sunshine about five inches taller
than before.

A thunderous rumble accompanied by shrieks and
laughter drew me to the kitchen window one afternoon. Six little

boys had custody of an old-fashioned-looking wooden cart. Equipped with a small steering wheel, it boasted a Volvo logo on the front which hinted at the idea of a motor, although it seemed to have no mechanical means of propulsion. Delightfully controllable, it was perfect for the boys. One stood, shoulders back, at the wheel looking like a steam engine driver from the Old West sans the handlebar moustache while the others hopped on and off, alternately pushing and riding, depending if they were going downhill or up. They used their yells as brakes and clustered so tightly together, one would think they were hiding something. One small boy was the last pusher as the green cart gathered speed. His little heels pumped the air as he was forced to take larger and faster steps to stay up as the green machine flew off down a gentle hill, weighed down in the front by five others. He was sprinting, holding on by his fingertips, determined not to let go because he was part of the army. He reboarded when it slowed down at the end of the incline, looking winded. I caught sight of a little girl's face in the midst of the boys as they changed their places. Someone's little sister was squeezed in the middle, like a rosebush in the middle of a copse of trees. She just enjoyed the ride as she sucked a popsicle, ears ringing with the boys' wild exuberance.

When I saw her next, she was sedately pushing her doll carriage a bit later, practicing for her future role as a mother. Since real baby carriages are often not the neat collapsible ones American women use, this was not an issue of training to take lightly. Norwegians prefer enormous, Cadillac versions which are great for clearing pedestrians off the sidewalk. Mothers push through crowds, indoors and out, scraping innocent knees and compressing toes as they go. Mothers load up the carriages with groceries as well as other less practical items. Once I observed a customer at the state liquor store slip her purchase under her baby's blankets. Off she went, past the church, pushing everything home oh so innocently.

The first time I saw a Norwegian manipulate her baby carriage onto a bus, it seemed an impossibility for she was loaded with groceries too. The process inconvenienced all the passengers near the doors, and the bus driver and a passenger heaved the whole thing on board. Children learned that nothing stood in the way of their being outdoors. Mothers pressed forward along the street confidently. "I am Norwegian. I have a baby, and it is supposed to be out. If my baby carriage is in your way, you'll just have to move."

I still recalled the sight of a young woman out with her baby one January afternoon. She appeared out of a snow cloud and should have been accompanied by the theme from *Dr. Zhivago*. Only a neat, high pile of linens, blankets, and coverlet protruded above the carriage, offering a hint of a baby's presence many layers below. She slowly pushed her infant through a park as though it were a Sunday in June. The saying that *barna har det bra*, or children have it good, was true in Norway and, although their transportation slowed down my progress sometimes, I envied their lucky and luxurious starts in life. They were happy, healthy children, with fair skins and pink cheeks, doted on by family and strangers alike, and they thrived on being outdoors, no matter what.

Women Who Wait

The change in our residence coincided with a change in Mike's work routine. He would *pendle* (the word reminded me of "pendulum" and meant "commute") between Karmøy and Stavanger on a *fjorten dager ut, fjorten dager hjemme,* schedule while the Heidrun project went into its final phase. Two-weeks on, two-weeks off was a way of life for families around us. *Ut* usually referred to the North Sea, but in my husband's case it was the Stavanger fjord.

Commuting by boat in all weathers took a strong constitution or the ability to close one's eyes and doze mercifully when wind and tides had the boat climbing the waves. Mike tried the latter to overcome seasickness. His life would have improved considerably had we moved to Stavanger during his watch as hook-up and commissioning superintendent, so I deeply appreciated his sacrifice. Rides were smoother on the double-deck catamarans such as the *Draupner,* but the smaller *Sunnhordland* or the newer *Tjelden* often served the Stavanger-Haugesund route, guaranteeing a bumpier ride in rough weather. On those days my husband always arrived at Kopervik after a fifty-minute trip home, looking gray.

Sunday afternoons around one o'clock things got busy at Kopervik's boat terminal when offshore workers waited for the Stavanger boat. Loaded with rucksacks, they smoked, chatted with friends, or waited in cars out of the wind with their families. From Stavanger many helicoptered out to rigs for two-or three-week work shifts. To break the tension of waiting, people paced the harbor wall, peering at the horizon.

Taxis spun down the hill, timing their trips to the minute. Our old neighbor, Liv, cut it close one time though, Egil related. "She watched from our window until she saw the boat coming from Haugesund—then jumped in the car and beat it to Kopervik!" he said, smiling rather proudly. Passengers needing taxis had already ordered them from the boat and had only to provide their assigned number to commandeer a waiting vehicle.

The expert operation of a fast boat coming in or leaving was a work of art, and nothing delayed its schedule. I once saw a young man who was a little worse for wear unloaded to a quay where he simply lay down and fell asleep. Watching the ship's crew look back at him as the boat accelerated off, I got the feeling they were old hands at dealing with him, and did so quite compassionately.

One Sunday the *Tjelden* swirled in after blasting her horn twice at two small boats, then negotiated a tight turn in frothing water to position herself correctly for the ramp to be set down. Like clockwork, a uniformed crew member appeared at the stern, grasping a thick rope to lasso a yellow mooring post. Another man set the switch to allow the metal gangway to growl its noisy descent. A dozen passengers, including Mike, shuffled into a straggling vee, jackets billowing in the breeze. Within moments the crowd handed over their boarding passes, stowed their bags, and disappeared inside the boat. My husband did this every fourth Sunday.

I clung to the sight of the *Tjelden* as she made her u-turn
and sped away, churning back the waters on her sprint south.
Mike was gone and I already missed him. For two weeks I would
be an oil platform widow. Nothing had changed about life for the
women of Karmøy in that regard. The sea always carried their
men off—to ships, on ships, now to oil platforms. People left for
two or three weeks, three months, even six months. To China, to
Holland, to the North Sea. Olivia's father worked six-week
shifts—year in, year out—as did a Kopervik neighbor aboard a
North Sea supply boat. I had joined the modern-day ranks of
Karmøy women with a most respectable calling. I had become
one of the women who wait.

Karmøy-born Marit Synnøve Vea knew all about waiting:
"The history of the coastal people of Norway, and this island, is
not just the history of the fishermen and sailors. It's also the
history of the women and children back home waiting for their
husbands and fathers to come back," she told me. "When I was a
child, my father worked in America, fishing, nearly all year, coming
home to Ferkingstad for about three months. And he was just
one of the many men from Karmøy who looked across the sea
and decided that America would offer better opportunities for
fishing. For us the ocean has always been a path, not a barrier.
    The fishermen would come home in December, and my
mother and I and a lot of other people would take the ferry to
Stavanger to meet the boats from the United States which
brought our parents home. When the *Stavangerfjord* or the
Bergenfjord would come into the harbor, we'd all wave and shout
excitedly when we saw our fathers on deck. 'Look! There's my
father! There's Daddy!' None of the children had seen their
fathers for nine months! Sometimes we ate a meal on the boat
and, you know, it was there I had my first bacon. I had never
eaten bacon before although we had heard of that meal—bacon
and eggs.
    "The day your father arrived was very important because
you got him home again after he had been away so long—and

he brought you so many presents! We looked forward to opening his big 'America Trunk' crammed full of wonderful things he had bought us, things we could not buy in Norway. My first doll was American, and my mother and I would find lovely dresses, the boys would get cowboy boots, and there were American records—the music became very influential in our area. Oh, and we got Juicy Fruit chewing gum! At Christmas, around Åkrehamn all the fishermen's houses would be decorated with American Christmas lights! People today still use them and they say jokingly that we are part cowboy, part Viking in that area known as 'Little America.' Many people bought homes and stayed in America. I am a typical Karmøy girl and my great-grandfather, grandfather, and my father all worked in America. My grand-mother was the only daughter in a family with eight sons. The boys all went to America, so she luckily inherited the family farm.

"We never used the term 'United States' because to us it was always 'America.' As a child I felt much closer to America because my father worked there, and we would know the names of New York and the cities, towns, and places where he was, and we could find them on the map. Names in our own country of Norway, like Kristiansand or Oslo, sounded more exotic to us because we had never been there or talked about them. So because of our parents, America became our fatherland, but I remember having mixed feelings about that. America still was the culture that had taken our father away from us. In those days we relied on letters from him—we had no telephone—and every ten days I would check at the post office on the way home from school to see if the little airmail envelope with the red and blue stripes was there. If it was, I could take it home to my mother knowing she would be happy, but if the letter did not arrive on time, we would all worry that something had happened to him.

"As children, we always felt that when we had wild storms at Åkrehamn, there would also be the same storms in the Ameri-can seas around Alaska or Seattle or wherever my father was fishing. It was not true, of course, but we believed it and felt afraid. We lived near the sea and tried to muffle the storm's sound by covering our heads with a pillow and going into the kitchen on the other side of the house. Once during a hurricane in America we heard that the *Viking Queen*, the ship my father was on, and another one with the same ownership had gone down and its crew, from Ferkingstad, had all drowned. We were so worried that it was Father. We didn't know what to do or who to contact in those days and had to wait for letters. Fortunately we heard from our father that he was all right. Letters were so important, and I still see the airmail letters in my mind, our only contact.

"When he had been home for about three months, it would be time for him and all the men to leave, and I would watch him begin to pack. As the boats picked the men up on their way along the west coast past Karmøy at Åkrehamn, they would give long, loud blasts with their horns. I still remember the '*Whoo-whooo-whoo!*' as the ships passed, and that they were known as the 'America Boat.'"

Marit's words reminded me how Norwegians had personalized their boat routes: the America Boat, the Karmøy Express, the local *hydrofyken,* and of course the famous Shetland Bus, the name given to the fleet of fishing boats which helped Norway's resistance effort.

She continued, "My father fished king crab and was on the first boat to fish scallop in Alaska. He decided he wanted us all to join him there, and we got our passports ready. But then they felt that it was the wrong thing to do, to interrupt my brother's education, so we stayed home here on the island. It was lonely with him being gone so much, but eventually he came back. This island had a nickname in America—Karten Island. Perhaps it was because people could not quite pronounce it or it was a mixture of *Kormt,* the old name for the island, or even meant *kart,* meaning "map" or "chart." I don't know exactly. But somehow Karmøy has become 'Karten Island' to many Americans. I have had people ask, 'Oh, are you from Karten Island?'"

Marit's explanation reminded me that I had seen Karmen,

once even Carmen island, written on Dutch and Spanish maps from the 1700s, yet I had never seen any word that looked like the island's nickname.

Fielding nonstop telephone calls and greeting drop-ins at her *kommune* office, Marit Synnøve Vea displayed a vivacious personality. Given her deep roots and passion for Karmøy, it came as no surprise to learn that she performed and sang in Viking pageants in Norway and northern England as well as in historical festivals at home. Had she continued the Karmøy tradition of marrying a man who worked on the sea and was gone much of the time? I asked her. An emphatic "No!" followed by a delighted laugh quickly put that idea to rest. "I married a teacher! I promised myself I would never marry a fisherman!"

The eternal quality of the sea drew and consoled me, especially when Mike was gone. My daily patrols around Karmøy in rain, wind, snow, or shine put me in touch with my feelings and the compact, predictable little world I lived in. I studied the jellyfish population beneath the moving bridge and wandered near the quay, hoping the big Newfy dog who lived there would sashay over for some petting.

One afternoon I arrived just as the Stavanger boat pulled in. Mike was not due, but I stayed awhile so as to surprise him with my witchery if he were on it. I waited until one of the last passengers got off, a man who looked like my husband.

The man wore a fluorescent, North Sea safety jacket, and his shoulders sagged with a couple of heavy bags. His wife ran over and gave him a hug, taking one bag so they could lock arms as they walked to the car, heads together. They could have been us. Watching them was like observing Mike and myself from some out-of-body experience people talk about. She was meeting him just as I would meet my husband after his fourteen-day shift. I left and headed home, engulfed by loneliness.

A good dose of bike riding always cheered me up though and later when a small figure with a large hat appeared on the horizon, I felt my heart lift. I was not quite alone. The elderly lady, my unofficial cycling buddy, was out too. We both arrived at a dip in the shallow hill, and she slipped off her bicycle, casting a determined look at me. Maybe she was going to speak?

This was a special event. After almost three years of pedaling past one another we were at last face to face. Her face reminded me of a tiny, delicate cracked teapot covered by a large, wool tea cozy. The wider she smiled, the more cracks appeared. She inquired sociably after me in a stream of indecipherable *norsk,* her darting eyes warm. *"Kan du gjenta?"* I asked. She repeated herself, but too fast for me. I tried "Could you say that again?" just one more time before giving up and moving on to something else. I recalled her limping along, pushing her bike awhile before. Was her leg better now? I drew an air diagram of her leaning on a stick and pointed to her leg. She looked puzzled and gabbled on, her high, thin, voice cutting the words into small, sharp pieces. I caught a word or two. *"Masse av slektninger i USA,"* (lots of relatives in the States), something about speaking Norwegian and English, and something about money. And she said she had visited a friend up the road. Mainly I just snatched juggled words and tried to make sentences. She uttered my favorite word, *flink,* but since she seemed not to understand any of my questions or answers, nor could I tie in her answers with anything I asked, I hardly deserved a *flink*. Perhaps it was for my bicycling habits? However, a *flink* a day kept the doctor away and I felt better already.

The lady with the big hat allowed nothing to stop her daily routine. Perhaps she knew that being outdoors cured a lot of things which festered indoors? Hundreds of drivers passed the hardy little landmark and that day she had cast her light on me. In her effort to communicate and in her warmth, she had lifted my spirits and swept away my loneliness.

I fought against feeling aimless when I was by myself. Even the benefit of not having to cook dinner for two lost its appeal. I looked for ways to bring the outside world in and expected more from the mailbox. Unfortunately letters from home had dwindled to almost zero by then, a result, I guessed, of people considering us out of sight and out of mind. Maybe that was the lot for all people who disappear overseas for extended periods and whose friends imagine their new existence as a mad, social whirl. If that was their reasoning, they couldn't have been more wrong. We lived the most ordinary country life imaginable. At that time the Internet and e-mail were still in the future. Now they are lifelines for expatriates who need to let off steam, share scary experiences or troublesome political turns of events, or just connect with someone on the other side of the world who speaks their language, knows and cares about them.

When time weighed heavily, I would brood about my social and spoken inadequacies; then a spate of good days came along that filled me with happiness and endless joyful reasons for living in Norway.

One Monday was such a day, for it began with success. An Oslo company confirmed that they did indeed distribute the American product I wanted, had the sizes, and would mail the package out that day. What luck! It had not started out smoothly though for one of their employees left a message for me in Norwegian, indicating I ask for "*Guy-er-ull*" when I called back. Despite several playbacks of the message, I could not catch his name. Embarrassed, I called the company, asking for a *"Guy-er-ull,* please?' A helpful receptionist untangled my phonetics and brought a *Geir* to the phone. Obviously he had said *Geir* somebody when he had called but blended them so well that it was impossible for me to figure the two names out.

Tuning into conversational-speed Norwegian was like trying to tune a short-wave radio. Geir, nevertheless, could not have been more helpful and took down my address for the delivery. "You live in *Kopervik?*" he asked, sounding surprised.

"Yes, afraid so!" I joked back, knowing he was a city boy in the nation's capital and would hate living far away in the country. As it happened, I was wrong. "I wish I did!" he replied wistfully.

Later at my mailbox my neighbor and I exchanged pleasantries about my impending bike ride and the beautiful weather. "Come and have coffee later!" Mona invited. I made finger-tapping movements on an imaginary keyboard. "Oh, you're so busy!" she allowed, giving up on me. Waving her goodbye, I decided I would pop in the next day. Friends were both luxury and necessity. Mona had been the first on our street to invite me in, and for that I was grateful. In her living room I learned about various Norwegian customs which helped me understand the culture more fully.

The back road was prettier than the main street, so I chose it regularly. I walked or cycled past white waterside cottages with neat gardens and stopped to stroke a lonely little dog who always leapt into a frenzy of happiness when I came along. At the end of the trip success at the post office meant that the obliging clerk helped me obtain some special "maritime theme" stamps. She filled out an order postcard on my behalf in her very neat handwriting, then indicated that all I had to do was add the quantity and mail the card to *Postverket* in Oslo. I was thrilled. She smiled a bit shyly as I blurted out a couple of *mange takks*, then lest I leave empty-handed, awarded me a giant-sized corporate pouch mail envelope to which were strapped two Sunday *Houston Chronicle* newspapers. The tightly banded collection resembled the United States space shuttle with its two solid rocket boosters and looked almost aeronautically sturdy enough to have made it to Norway on its own.

This lady clerk earned my admiration because of her conscientiousness. When she re-taped a package, for example, she was an artist in action, getting every corner. If your package did not arrive at its destination intact, it would be through no fault of hers and no shortage of blue tape. I hoped the post office would promote her to supervisor. I loaded the missile in my

basket and pushed my bike to the grocery store, which after a
two-day hiatus had restocked my lunch staple, cottage cheese.
Success!

At the hardware store I hit bingo for the morning although I had first tried the easy way by inquiring *"Du snakker
engelsk?"* after my request for brown spray paint failed to register.
"Nei!" the lady smiled back. I tried asking for spray paint again *på
norsk* and spray painted some imaginary furniture as I spoke. She
checked through the cans on the shelves but found no brown
paint. Undefeated, she checked her catalogue. We studied the
color blocks together, mumbling in our respective languages, and
concluded that brown was not available in the brand she sold. By
this time she was ready to help me find the paint somehow.

"Har du vært på Bilgummilageret?"

"Beelgummylag-er-et?" I repeated, dumbly, not sure what
she was saying.

"Bygnes ..." she gave me the location. Ah, the auto
supply store, certainly a place which could have some kinds of
automobile touch-up paint.

"AH! Ja!" I cried like someone seeing an oasis. I had
passed the location only a million times but had never been
inside. *"Nei. Jeg har ikke vært der, men, tenker du at de har—*spray?"

Ja, she assured me they did, and certainly in the color I
wanted, brown. But would acrylic paint work on wicker, I wondered. Again, no problem with that, and to prove it she returned
to her display of cans, extracted one, and helpfully read the
instructions aloud, in Norwegian, her finger underlining the rows
of tiny print. She read which surfaces accepted such paint. *"Metall,
TRE!"* she smiled triumphantly. "Wood" was mentioned right
there, on the can. Five minutes had evolved and, thankfully, there
were no other customers in line. Considering our mutual limitations, we were rather pleased with our ourselves. She was spared
speaking English but still helped me track down some paint.

From my perspective, following along with her sentences
and getting the drift of everything eventually inspired me to
bigger and better things. This lady was one of those energetic,

efficient people who viewed difficulties as mere challenges, and I
was the happy beneficiary of her extra effort. I streamed off my
takk for hjelpen! mange takk! and *ha det bra!*—as my way of
thanking her for everything, to which she responded with a
pleasant *like så!*, the same to you. We parted as equal winners in
the conversation with a foreign language speaker that day.
Euphoric, I floated like a little hovercraft out on to the pedestrian
street, then spied my loaded bicycle basket. What was I so smug
about? I still lacked my can of brown spray paint. But what the
heck! I'd had a great conversation and proved I could *cope!*

My weekend streak of good luck continued, strengthen-
ing my ties to Norway by allowing me to contribute something,
not just take. This time it centered around a new assistant in the
nearby convenience store-gasoline station. He was off to study
theater in London, he told me, and liked speaking English to me.
We chatted about young people's prospects for education,
college, and work in Norway. Young Rolf felt the *Storting*, parlia-
ment, was isolated from people like him. "They don't try to find
out what *we* want," he said, voicing a universal complaint. Our
discussion roamed over many areas, and an idea popped into my
head. Would he like to visit my mother when he was in England?
A day out in Berkshire would guarantee him lunch with a local,
and even a chance to compare Kintbury's village church of St.
Mary the Virgin, over a thousand years old, with St. Olav's at
Avaldsnes. Rolf was polite enough not to look horrified at such a
boring idea. However, he seemed quite pleased with his English
practice. I was glad to be useful and stepped off for home, light of
foot and spirit.

Downtown later a friendly lady I had talked with before
waved me over from the bridge. Hearing her call out my name felt
wonderful. I felt like broadcasting, "See, everyone. This lady from
your town knows me! I am not a stranger." By then we had been
in and around Kopervik for a long time and I yearned for that
unattainable thing: that everyone would know me and that I
belonged. We talked until her dog gave up tugging on his leash
and plonked himself on the ground to wait us out.

"What's his name again?" I asked.

"King," she said. Then despite her layers of sturdy clothes she added a light sweep of an arm heavenward combined with a dancer's quarter turn in her practical boots. Her impish smile readied me for the conclusion of the mini-performance. "You know! The KING and I!"

Kopervik Christmas

Just before Christmas Gudrun and Paul invited us over for a party. Dozens of relatives packed the living room, and I felt privileged to be invited to what was really a family affair. Struggling to catch names and make conversation, however, made me feel like the lone American. Having Mike along would have felt better, but he was working. Still I took comfort in knowing that Gudrun and her brother, Thomas, had both actually been born in the States, only moving to Norway when their parents, Karl and Elise, returned. I had wondered, often worried, about how our neighbors had viewed Mike and me. When Hanna volunteered, "It was kind of refreshing to have someone from 'over there' back here," I felt relieved.

Gudrun whisked the youngsters into the kitchen to make Christmas decorations and the guests began sampling cakes and desserts; one particularly delicious cookie melted in my mouth. "They're *fattigkaker*," Thomas said while Hanna reeled off the list of ingredients which included fresh cream, egg yolks, flour, and lots of sugar. In class we had learned that *fattig* had to do with *sulten*—a very serious state of being hungry to the point of starvation. Thomas chuckled at my puzzled expression. "These cookies have a lot of expensive ingredients, so people started calling them poor man's cookies—because it made them poor to bake them!"

FATTIGMANN KAKER
(Poor Man's Cookies)

Ingredients:

5 egg yolks
1 egg white
65 grams (about 1/8 cup) sugar
1/2 dl. (about 1/4 cup) heavy cream
1/2 tsp. grated lemon rind
175 grams (about 3/4 cup) flour
1/8 tsp. cardamom spice

Directions:
Beat egg and sugar together. Blend in the whipping cream and lemon rind. Sift flour and cardamom together and add to the egg mixture. Blend extra lightly, do not let it become too thick (gummy). Sprinkle flour over the dough, cover and chill it overnight. Next, working in a cool place, and using a smooth surface, roll out small amounts at a time using the flour sparingly. Roll out thinly and cut it into diamond shapes. Make a slit at one pointed end and gently draw the other end through the slit. Make all the cookies the same size and place on a floured baking sheet. Do not wait too long before cooking the cookies in a deep fat boiler. The cookies should rise slightly and be a golden color when they are done.

—Translation courtesy of Milli and Lori

Newlyweds Trond and Camille had fallen into a new habit since their engagement days. Then, each spoke independently. Since marriage they had begun piggybacking their answers when responding to, say, a question about a vacation. One spoke for awhile, then abruptly stopped as though struck by instant amnesia. Then a pointed gaze got the other to pick up where the first left off. The narrative ended with a joint response, proof of marital democracy in action.

Grandparents beamed, grandchildren bounced on knees, jubilant voices and laughter emanated from every corner. The intense familiness seemed almost too perfect, too idyllic. A chilling scenario pushed into my mind. Had these people taken their summer trip to Estonia just one year later than they did, they might have been lost in a tragic ferry accident. An enormous gap would have been left in the community, the sorrow never erased, this party never to happen. Today the gathering was a blessing, a testament to life and hope. And a moment for me to remember not to take the precious days of life for granted.

Little Kristine was waiting patiently outside. She was on her way back to northern Norway, where her father's new job was. Wordlessly she handed me a Scandinavian Airlines postcard, pointing at the picture of an airplane. We hugged before I took her picture. I missed Kristine and all the children and our old neighbors. I missed my house with the beautiful view, whose living room lights beguiled me back in. But that part of living in Norway was over. My little neighborhood had nurtured me and only let me go when it looked as though I could cope. Pulling away, I left my special life in the rearview mirror.

Our door bell rang throughout December with children selling us *lodd*, raffle tickets. They cost the equivalent of about twenty-five or thirty cents each and funded various community activities and good causes. Winners were promised impressive prizes, but in that regard our luck equaled our success with

Readers Digest and Publisher's Clearinghouse in the States—
zero, unless you counted a lace tablecloth and a plastic tote bag
donated by a local savings, *spare*, bank. *Spare* meant "save" in
Norwegian, thus "savings bank." It always made me think of
"spare" change, the money you might save. One delightfully
rhythmic expression, *spinke og spare*, sounding like "spinker-o-
spahrer," meant "scrape and save." We alas had little chance to
spinke og spare and after several weeks emptying all our small
change every other night and often buying tickets for the same
cause from many different children, I decided to stop being a
pushover. The first child who marched up to our door each day
could sell us a few tickets. After that, *jeg beklager*, sorry!
    Keeping hard and fast to the new rule was difficult.
Adorable little faces invariably did me in as did nervous children
who had not expected Americans and were shocked or excited to
hear us answer in a combination of *norsk* and English. Then there
were unwilling ones. One afternoon an all-girl *lodd* seller cum
baby-sitting team brought a little toddler along. The red-faced
passenger clung on to her stroller, white-knuckled, as the two
girls thu-bumped her all the way up our sixteen steps. She blamed
me, I could tell, and angry looks from her large, teary eyes told
the story. Guilt-ridden, I coughed up more *kroner* hoping to
guarantee her an easier, safe descent. They thu-bumped the little
victim all the way down and went on their way, pleased as can be.

    Then there was Jeltsin (pronounced Yeltsin in Norwe-
gian) the dog who finagled more money out of me. Fortunately I
loved dogs, and it was no hardship to make the acquaintance of a
second dog named after a political or semipolitical figure. Ollie
had been the first; a frisky little puppy born in Texas during the
Ollie North television spectacular and who bore no resemblance
in personality or bark to Mr. North. Little Jeltsin too was named
after a strong character yet had not the personal demeanor nor
temperament to match. The wiry, alert little fellow accompanied
three clutching telltale plastic lottery ticket bags. When three sets
of eyes locked on me expectantly, Jeltsin's bore the same exact

expression. Eyeing this little salesman, I had the distinct feeling that Jeltsin would not have refused an invitation indoors, a doggy treat, and an investigative sniff around. He wagged his tail while I bought five more lottery tickets.

The girls left smiling and successful, and, after a regretful glance that he had not been allowed in, little Jeltsin scrambled back down the steps. I was certain he paid his way on lottery ticket raids. But any more visits from babies or dogs, and I would have to be promised a prize in advance.

Kitty, a friend's daughter, appeared one evening, face peeking out from behind enormous sheaves of grain. Did we want to buy this, she asked, or seemed to, smile glinting with orthodontic braces. She was selling the *nek* to raise funds for the school band. Wild birds loved the grain in winter and I was always happy to buy some.

After Christmas Day many children returned, disguised with face paint and costumes, to serenade us with carols and songs. Guessing who was who added to the fun, and the children often sang in English, then left with candy. The after-Christmas tradition made sense; by then Christmas candy and chocolates had become dangerously habit forming. Far better the children ate it for their waistlines would spring back afterward while ours would not!

Over Christmas Kopervik's pedestrian way turned into a Victorian postcard scene. Little gnomelike Santa Clauses stood watch outside the shops, each holding a lit lantern. Shops sported more colorful window displays and people popped in and out, tugging their scarves up around their necks. If wishes could have made it so, we would have enjoyed a white Christmas, but the weather had not cooperated. Temperatures held at forty degrees, trees budded, and one bush in our front yard had turned bright red, a sure sign it was in the mood for spring. Over on Gofarnesvegen, a persistent woodpecker drilled away for three weeks, oblivious to my stares. Inland, the white mountains shimmered. December twenty-third, *lille julaften*, signaled the official beginning of the brief Christmas holiday and offices prepared to close. Christmas Eve itself, *julaften*, was the most important day of Christmas. Try to buy a gift at four o'clock that afternoon, and the best you might do is find a wrapped box of chocolates at a convenience store.

Norwegians love to gift-wrap and if you insist they need not bother, it is merely a little something for you and you're quite happy for them to put it in a bag, they can look put out as though you are spoiling their sale. You may as well enjoy the little extra service, even if the item *is* only for you. Wrapping is good psychology. Plastic bags never say that "this is a gift," but a wrapped package looks and feels like a gift and evokes a sense of value.

Doors swung open at the florist's and at *Hilleslands* book and office supply. *Kopervik Herreklær*, the men's clothes shop, sent its customers off with new shirts and warm jackets. *Interoptik*, the opticians, lured people in for new glasses, *Teklan* framers filled last-minute pick-ups of family photographs, and the *frisørsalong* fixed everyone's tired hairdos. A five-and-dime equivalent did a brisk trade as did three ladies' dress shops; grocery store; hardware business; jewelry stores; and stores which sold china and crystal, bicycles, and sportswear. If you were a bargain hunter or a bit short of money, the nicest looking Salvation Army clothes store in existence, *Fretex*, offered fresh, attractive things for all ages. It did so well apparently that it relocated to Oasen shopping mall shortly after we left. After shopping, people revived themselves at *Lundbergs Bakeri* with coffee, rolls, and pastries and watched the townsfolk pass by. Americans frequently limited their stay in respect for their lungs and clothes, however. Perennial puffers owned the small cafes of Norway, where windows remained firmly closed.

Some dog owners huddled together on a corner, exchanging pleasantries while their four-legged companions pulled at their leashes. A *Haugesunds Avis* delivery boy screeched to a halt in front of a candy store, gazing a hole in the window.

He could taste the *sjokolader* in the *kiosk* window, but I enjoyed saying "shockolahder from the chosk" just as much. Children swung and shrieked from the playground, already in high spirits.

Christmas Eve was the time to decorate the tree and enjoy Christmas dinner of perhaps *kalkun*, turkey, with apple dressing or *ribbe*, spareribs, with mushroom and pineapple compote. *Pinnekjøtt*, salted and dried rib of lamb, was a favorite as was baked trout seasoned with *laurbærblad*, bayberry leaf, and *pepperkorn*. Desserts ranged from *multekrem*, which was a delicately sweet concoction of whole cream and cloudberries, to *eplekake,* and pastries. People exchanged handmade gifts such as embroidered table runners, crocheted tree decorations, ginger cookies, *julekake.* We often received handmade Christmas cards from Liv and Hanna and, not surprisingly, the cards were used as fund-raisers for the band.

Though parents complained that their children were beginning to be demanding, Norwegian children generally had modest desires at Christmas. Some wrote up little wish lists for their parents while, in certain parts of Norway, others wrote a note to the big man himself, *julenissen,* hoping the nice bowl of porridge they left out would encourage his generosity. Others seemed quite unconcerned about what they might or might not get for Christmas. On Christmas Day afternoon many people recuperated from the excesses of the previous couple of days or paid social calls to family members. Just as in America young couples avoided family squabbles by dining with each one's family separately over the holiday. Since meals were adequate, not lavish, during the rest of the year, Scandinavians remained slim before, during, and after Christmas. A mild Christmas week meant a rosebush cozied up to a second-story deck, thumbing its pretty nose at anyone who would say it was winter. Electric candelabra lights twinkled from lace-swathed windows and silver-gray satellite dishes nearby reached out to the universe.

A highlight of Christmas Eve was the anticipated visit of Santa Claus to our neighborhood, per a poster in our mailbox. When he hadn't arrived by ten a.m., I blamed my inept reading. Maybe it meant ten p.m.? I called my neighbor across the street. His little son answered.

"*Kan jeg snakke med din pappa?*" Could I speak to his daddy, I carefully enunciated.

"*Ja!*" he said, following with some little-child social talk. He appeared to be in no hurry to get Papa to the phone so I gently repeated my request. A mumble or two later he called out the season's refrain, *God Jul!* and Martin picked up. I wasn't wrong about the time; the *julenisse* was indeed on his way and would visit every house. He would give something to each child, and we were not expected to give anything back. "Last year when we had snow, he had a sledge, but I hear this year he will be on wheels, in a cart," Martin told me before we hung up, bidding one another merry Christmas.

I would have waited for this mythical creature all day long if necessary, just for the joy of having him ring our bell and stand there in all his glory on our doorstep, but I didn't have to. Mike, who was recuperating from his fourteen days away, and home less than sixteen hours, nursing a cold, called out from the kitchen, "He's here, he's here! Quick . . . quick!"

Sure enough, there was Santa, leading a small procession. One girl helper led a gentle black horse while two friends sat up in the cart seat, holding the reins. Santa wore an authentic red outfit, sported a long beard, his feet togged out in designer label running shoes. A tantalizing little hemp sack hung over his shoulder. He paused on our driveway and asked something like "*Har dere unger i huset?*" which I understood to mean was did we have any young ones in the house. "*Nei. Vi er to alene,*" I answered, feeling somewhat like Marlene Dietrich with my "We are two (people) alone"—sort of pitiable-sounding.

"*God Jul!*" he nodded understandingly and waited while we videotaped him. No children meant no candy for us, and I felt just slightly miffed. He set off for the next homes, our Viking

Santa, tall and slender, one who, despite all the *komler, creme fraiche*, hot dogs, and cigarettes he likely enjoyed would probably outlive any jolly Americanized version.

He and a suited helper canvassed the homes, and the low-key event made it more reflective than Christmas with Santa parades, mall photo sessions, and so forth that American children cut their teeth on. Apart from the almost indiscernible clip-clop of his horses, one would hardly know the *julenisse* was there. What struck me as strange, and had all morning, was the total absence of children. It was very noticeable, therefore, when young Stian lunged out into the street, like a cork out of a bottle. He looked as though the suspense was killing him.

He hopped up and down watching the red-suited figure getting closer, twisting himself about in anticipation. A gray wool cap pulled down over his ears and rubber boots up to his knees, he waited until the entourage was within twenty yards, then turned tail and accelerated like a rocket ship back to his house. His jubilant cry, *"Julenissen!"* rang out as he raced inside. Moments later Santa arrived at number six on our street where both children were waiting in the hallway, exactly where they should have been although one was panting hard.

The visit of the red-coated Christmas patron came and went as quietly as a whisper. The dozens of children stayed indoors, except one, and each family played its role, maintaining Christmas customs and comforting rituals. Yet not everything was old-fashioned in the neighborhood. Within minutes of the *julenisse's* departure in his horse and cart, a car swept down the hill with its passenger deep in conversation on a mobile telephone. In the marina a luxurious pleasure cruiser cut out across the icy blue waters. The *julenisse* was already a memory, perhaps by then at home, running shoes off and resting his feet?

Santa's visit was, apparently, civically organized. One neighbor, Annemor, explained that, when he arrived at their home, her youngest son, six-year-old Kristian, was first at the door to greet him. *"Er det noen snille små barn her?"* Are there any good little children here? the man bearing candy inquired. There were three boys indoors and only one felt the need to make a comment. "I am good, but my brother, Simon, isn't," Kristian reported. "He just kicked me in the stomach!"

To Kristian's chagrin the *julenisse* doled out Christmas candy to them all, perpetrator of the kick included. The youngest child got no extra, nor his brother any less, and Kristian thought this most unfair. When the little boy explained to me what happened sometime later, *på norsk*, he tapped himself on the chest to emphasize that he was the injured party. I nodded sympathetically into the little fellow's perplexed blue eyes. Life with big brothers wasn't always fair, and it was evident that Kristian wasn't about to forget his grudge!

To make our last Christmas in Norway memorable, we invited some friends over for a little *romjulsfest*, a house party given between Christmas and New Year's Eve. Each of our Norwegian guests had connections with North America—Long Island, New York; Boulder, Colorado; Fargo, North Dakota; Minnesota; even Calgary, Canada. One friend, Morten, told us of a relative studying in the States who won a major marathon, and with it a Mercedes. Morten and his brothers flew over to pick it up and tour America a little before shipping it to Norway. His English was quite smooth and so was his wife's, but she admitted that she had lain awake worrying about having to speak it at our party. She too had visited America. Only one guest, Andreas, refused to speak any English, as usual, but contentedly chattered all evening to the others in Norwegian.

Our friends had few reasons to speak English on a daily basis, but they were so good with it, I tended to forget. In many ways Mike and I were sounding boards. When I complimented one man on his daughter's excellent English, he looked surprised. "Oh, really?" he responded. "Well, I don't know. We never speak English at home."

Americans always compliment those who have learned

another language proficiently, but Norwegians resist much praise, preferring to believe their English is merely adequate. Speaking English around their colleagues or friends can present a dilemma. English spoken too well may imply superiority, or spoken poorly might make them feel inferior, creating some undercurrents. After having a couple of friends over for coffee, I asked my usually outgoing friend why she had been so quiet. "I felt stupid speaking English around a more educated person," she replied. She could hold her own beautifully with anyone, but she refused to believe it. After that I worried that asking more than one Norwegian over at a time, and expecting them to speak English, put undue pressure on them.

Food was American style, once again due to some special imports via my mother-in-law. A little incident highlighted how certain foods define a nationality. Elaine detected a familiar aroma in the kitchen. "Is that . . . pumpkin pie?" she asked incredulously. For a moment her eyes lit up with an indescribable remembrance of childhood. She was lost in another world, one of a girl growing up in Long Island, school days, friends, holidays, Christmas, the year book, plans … Catching herself, she quickly doused any slight misgivings. Her choice was past tense, and over with. She had turned her back on American life—and its unforgettable pumpkin pies.

On New Year's Eve a torchlight procession encircled the neighborhood and wound past our house on Nornesvegen. The night was moonless and pitch dark, and the wind fierce, but parents and children leaned into the gusts, dogs trailed alongside, mothers pushed baby carriages, arms held flickering torches high. They looked like black scissor cutouts against a gray matte, heads and shoulders haloed in yellow, burnished with gold and red.

Neither dark, cold, or wind prevented them from celebrating their endurance at the end of the old year, beginning of the new. Heads bobbed, torches flared, died, and danced back into flame as the silhouettes passed, their voices lifting to compete with the wind. Together the families threw light up into the black sky to make sure the universe never forgot they were there.

20

Ladders & the Ja Jas

Nationalities are often known for odd behaviors, and Norwegians should claim a special and hair-raising one: ladder acrobatics. Never afraid of scaling a wobbly ladder, they did the impossible on them and lived to talk about it. Perhaps their natural mountaineering ability insured success, but the way they pushed their luck left me aghast.

An Oslo neighbor introduced me to this tendency when he painted his eaves from atop a tall, shaky ladder. He stretched out left and right, paintbrush in hand, while I waited for the scream and crash. My hands grasped the phone as I mentally dialed the ambulance. After twenty tense minutes I dragged myself away from my kitchen window. The man was oblivious to any danger. Over the next few years I discovered that ladder acrobatics were a national characteristic.

I couldn't help staring at people on ladders. They invariably placed them in highly unsuitable spots, like against corners, which would normally guarantee disaster, yet men took off up them as though attached to some heavenly cord. One evening a group of fellows carrying ladders prepared to remove the town's street decorations. I waited for the show to begin.

They were in no rush to get started. One or two bandied jokes, moved ladders around, or carried them like briefcases. Finally the secret signal, the completion of the rolling of a little cigarette, and a word or two from a man I had not seen before, and it was all systems go. They scattered in formations here and there and actually began to do something.

Two wanted to remove the green wreath which stretched across one end of the street. The moment I had been waiting for had arrived, and I pulled my voluminous hood around my head like some spy. One man leaned a ladder against Narvesen's wall at store level where it extended past a flat roof and up into the air near the original structure's high roofline. His pal started up the ladder and, to my surprise, the other one planted a steadying foot on the bottom rung. This safety-first attitude was a new twist. I would be on a wild-goose chase if this were a sign of things to come, but in an instant, the show started and my wait was not to be in vain. Another spectacular Norwegian balancing act, one which flaunted physics and hinted at catastrophe got under way.

The first man gained a few steps on the ladder, then stepped onto the flat roof where he balanced on tiptoe, lunging at the wreath. After a moment he exchanged a word with his buddy and proceeded up the piece of ladder which stuck out above the roof. At the very top rung, the one you were never, ever supposed to stand on, he was facing the wrong way to snatch at the garland so he swiveled around. From there he grabbed for the greenery and began slowly loosening it, flexing his feet and holding himself taut. With the eye of an expert, he went about his task without a concern in the world. Afraid to distract him, I padded back down the street. The men near the *Vin Stua,* wine bar, had finally settled on a starting point. They propped up a very, very long metal ladder against a very, very tall house, then pulled in another shorter ladder, snapped it behind, and created a sort of triangle contraption.

After a little strategy meeting the men grasped the newly manufactured apparatus, made some adjustments, then inched it out into the slush. At some preordained spot they halted, and another man nimbly scaled the shorter ladder which placed him exactly where he could untie the first section of garland. After tugging the decoration loose he climbed back down to wait while the men, in a slow, synchronized shuffle, moved the ladders forward. Nothing fell or slipped out of place as their colleague climbed the ladder again and again like a happy forest troll. They had outdone themselves, and I left them to it.

Walking home, I agonized about my fetish. Had I developed into someone who waited for nasty ladder accidents? Certainly I didn't want to see anyone hurt. If anything, I watched the goings on in disbelief and awe as I would a circus high-wire act.

Whoever coined that old saying, "God takes care of drunks and little children," had never been to Norway. Had he done so, he would have added, "and Norwegians on ladders." Certainly only the Great Ladder Keeper Himself could have protected them for so long. Anything else defied normal explanation.

One winter morning snow swirled through the darkness adding more inches to the four accumulated overnight. Darting white particles, caught by westerly gusts, waved in unison against a street light, flowing in long tendrils like a horse's tail or a sea anemone. Despite my license to drive in all conditions, I preferred the safety of a bus and planned to go to town later. At the unmarked stop I found two men chatting, and one called out a question in *norsk*. Did the bus stop there? I confirmed that it did.

"Do you have the schedule?" came his dubious inquiry in English. I said that I did and that the bus would be along in five minutes, at five after twelve.

"Not five minutes to?" he called back.

"No, five minutes after," I assured him.

Such an efficient little American conversation at noon on the corner of Fridtjof Nansen's snowy *vei* (pronounced *vay* and meaning "road" or "lane") surprised me. The gentleman must have lived in America to pick up the hard *sk* for schedule, and he had detected my American accent. He wandered over after his pal left, a cordial look on his face, and greeted me with a hello.

"Hi!" I said, "You said 'schedule' so well you must have lived in the States sometime."

"Oh, yes! I lived in California. Redondo Beach," he replied as though I would know exactly where it was. The word "beach" mocked our winter white environment, adding an amusing aspect. Briefly he tried waving down a passing car, but to no avail. "There! That's my friend. We used to work together!" he said as it disappeared around the corner. His eyebrows arched up and joined his hat band. "If he were an American, he would have given me a ride!" Shaking his head and sighing in mock hopelessness about his fellow Norwegians, he added, "Different, different!"

We waited for the bus together, bodies subtly performing a winter duet. I pulled my scarf closer around my head while he jiggled open his black umbrella to keep the snow off. I stamped and shuffled my feet and rotated my bags. He engaged in the lost cause of tugging his knitted wool hat down over his ear lobes, something it could not do. I dug for loose kroner in my damp pocket; he buried his cold nose into a handkerchief. Fidgeting helped keep us warm. Along with our external choreography we shared a common fear of driving on snow and ice. His earlier drive to the gas station had convinced him the bus would be safer. "I am going to the dentist," he explained, "and thought it would be better to take the bus."

"Tell me about California," I nudged. He launched into his story in flawless English. He had been assigned to California with Norsk Hydro of Karmøy to work with an associated company. "It was during the Vietnam War," he explained. "The owners were several Jewish brothers from the Ukraine." He nodded admiringly at the deceased partners, now in memory. "They were

good businessmen, had a talent for it," he said, looking my way
for an expected assent. "You know, they hired many veterans who
came back after the war, wounded." His eyebrows dropped and
his forehead crinkled with painful recollections.

Unconsciously he reached over to touch one of his arms
and ran his hand down it, just as though he were one of the
veterans who, missing part of an arm, had worked alongside him
at the plant. He fell silent. The sudden turn of events in our
conversation took me by surprise, and our casual exchange had
turned serious like a black cloud over the sun.

For a moment he was miles away at a place and time he
could never forget. He stared into the distance, still feeling his
arm. Somehow we jerked ourselves back into the promise of the
morning and officially introduced ourselves, peeling off gloves
and shaking hands. His name was Øystein. He remembered his
work friends' reaction to where he had come from. "Before long
they wanted to come here and help us at Hydro," he enthused,
nodding eastward across the harbor towards Hydro's aluminum
plant. Could there be a pocket of transplanted Californians under
my nose, some reverse immigrants? "Did they come?" I shot
back, hoping so. " No," he shook his head, " … only the bosses!
Only the bosses came, and they didn't stay!" I felt quite let down
that none of them had a chance to enjoy living in Norway.

The chatty gentleman was a real find, quite willing to answer
questions. His work had sent him all over the world, for awhile on a
cruise ship. This gave me my chance to ask why all the beautiful
Norwegian cruise ships just worked the Caribbean and weren't in
force along Norway's coast. Some were, he said, but the main
reason was the market. "You know why? The Americans, all they
want is sun and sand!" Before I could defend my countrymen, the
bus pulled up and Øystein got in the last word. "I used to work on
that coastal steamer, the *hurtigruten,* that goes up to Kirkenes. Well!"
he chortled, "it was full of Americans and you know where they
were?" I shook my head, expecting the worst and getting it. "In the
lounge, playing bridge the whole time!"

Despite his American experience and poke at the friend

who had not given him a ride, my ex-Californian reverted to a *nordmann* as we boarded the bus. It hadn't occurred to him that I might welcome a hand with my bag. "Well, if he had been an *American*, he would have offered to take at least one of them for me!" I laughed to myself.

My friend sat next to an old acquaintance, full of conversation with another person in another language. I admired his adaptability. Adjusting back and forth between two languages was easy for him, hard for me, and I brooded about those bridge players too. How could people sit and play cards while Norway's dramatic coastline slid by?

Dolly Parton trilled from the bus radio as we climbed the hill out of town. Along an icy stretch the vehicle seemed to shudder, and all eyes focused on the driver who was frowning and peering into his rearview mirror. Øystein filled me in on the situation. "Did you see what happened?" I had been lost in thought so, no, I had not. "There was another bus coming from Haugesund, and it looked like it was coming over into our lane." He relayed the details of the near-miss, eyes lively and not at all like those of a retiree. Nothing bothered him, including his upcoming dental appointment.

His animated conversation filtered my way and, like all Norwegians, in the parts where an American would interject "Well, hmm," or "ah," Øystein used *ja*. A *ja* can start and end a sentence as in *"Ja, jeg har nettopp vært til advokatens kontor og. ... Ja ... "*Well, I have just been to the lawyer's office and ... ah, I don't really want to go into it. And where an American would say, "I see, hmm," Øystein used the multiple, impatient-sounding *ja ja ja ja ja* lowering his voice ominously on the final *ja*. Sometimes he blurted out the four-seater version, *ja ja ja ja*, which was a little easier to bear, and followed it by a more positively intoned *aKKuraT!* which meant "that's right!" The latter sequence was more to my gentle sensibilities.

Life offered me much food for thought at bus stops. I had had a brief synopsis of a man's experience as a temporary immigrant in America and his work around the world meeting people from many nations. I wondered how his friends in California had managed with his "foreign" sounding name? One man we knew, Leo, found his American friends could barely utter those two syllables, so they called him Lee. Norwegian Anne-Britt was converted to Anne, or Anna, for expediency but she didn't like it. "I am used to it now, but I always prefer to hear my real name," the Texas immigrant had told me. Name changes are part of an immigrant's life changes. You can cast off an old culture and an old name and become a new person with a nicer, more worthy, even sanitized family history. Anglicizing "foreign" names was common in the U.S., and borrowing a movie star's name was popular. East Indian Nayan became "Bobby" after Bobby Ewing on the hit show *Dallas* and young Taiwanese college student, Shao-Chung, took the name "Andy" after a popular singer.

Movie stars, politicians, performers, and international athletes had provided names for children all over the world. Did Grace Kelly know how many little girls would be named Grace in her honor? One Chinese-American Grace assured me that her name, after the actress, almost conformed to an actual Chinese name meaning "Happy Poet." A Mexican woman who moved to America had herself been named Graciela after Grace Kelly. She named her own daughter after an Olympic gymnast, or so she thought. "We have named her Danya. You know, after Danya Comaneci, the gymnast," she said. Then there was pretty high-schooler Nazi whose friends tormented her out of using her native name. She adapted it to Nassa. Immigrants everywhere face these problems, and one woman came to Norway worried about what her own name sounded like phonetically. When she finally disclosed her fears to a female teacher, the lady put her mind at rest and she writes this book free of that concern.

Øystein knew about American ways. He respected those men he had worked for and experienced American openness and generosity firsthand. He had learned that many loved sunshine, and some preferred card games over scenery.

On my way home from the library I was joined by an elderly lady at the bus stop.

"Kommer bussen til Karmøy snart?" she inquired, needing confirmation that the Karmøy bus would be along soon.

"Ja! " I smiled, always rather pleased when people spoke to me as though I were a Norwegian. Under a gentle onslaught of snow I scripted sentences I could say to her about the snowy weather. It was not *dårlig*, bad, just typical winter weather, and I shied away from saying *snø* because I felt I was parodying Peter Seller's Inspector Clouseau. "Zees ees theek snuh my gooda man, do you 'ere me, monsieur? Snuh, eet ees snuhing outside."

Could I manage something about the cold, like *"Det er kaldt?"* The bus rolled up and stole my chance for social niceties and I rode home feeling discouraged. Why couldn't I do better? I could have managed a word about it being cold, *kaldt,* at least—that was an easy word. Long sentences about going to an art show, belting out *utstilling, beskyttelse, erfaringen,* and *utdannelse*—I loved those *ut* words—were no problem, even if ungrammatical, but I fell apart on anecdotes and weather. An American friend in Stavanger had gotten into trouble when she used a little expression that usually fit a multitude of situations. *"Helt fantastisk! "* she cried after listening to her neighbor. The man looked shocked. "Fantastic" was the wrong word. Somehow he managed to clarify that his wife was ill with cancer. Terribly embarrassed, she apologized and rarely uttered, "Fantastic!" after that.

Amusing errors were easier to bear. A Norwegian woman described driving through a downpour in the States. Her comment that it was "a tarantula rainstorm!" conjured up some wonderful pictures. A new Egyptian immigrant friend reported buying a new television and spending his time just sitting around it, snacking the evening away. "Yes," he smiled, confident of the vernacular of the day. "I *have* become a potato couch!" In Norway I feared being in a tarantula rainstorm as much as turning into a potato couch and avoided most ordinary expressions which might place me in one or as one.

Still I pondered Øystein's favorite interjection, wondering if I could practice the innocent *ja ja* word and develop some competency with it? I mouthed variations behind my scarf as I picked my way carefully up the slick hill.

"*Ja.*" I sucked my breath in, trying to duplicate the gasp Norwegians make when using *ja* in the commiserating or agreeing mode. I tried the solicitous *ja haw* which meant "I see. Naturally. Eureka, there it is," or "sure, that's the way it's always been." *Ja haw* had a nice comforting sound to it and I felt relatively safe thinking about using it. I rarely heard triple *jas* so I skipped ambitiously to *ja ja ja ja* and *ja ja ja ja ja ja ja*, trying to count the syllables for authenticity. Making it sound pleasant was a challenge, considering its staccato blasts would offend most people I knew.

I visualized a gum chewing waitress in a 1950s B movie, clearing off the counter in a New York diner. Tired of her male customer's hard luck story, or come-on, she glared at him.

"YEAH YEAH YEAH YEAH YEAH, buster! Ya think I was born *yesterday*, or somethin'? Tell me another one, will ya? Now, get outta here!"

It was hard to look on *ja ja* as serious when such comical or worrisome interpretations cropped up. Puffing up the last stretch home, I decided I would have to find someone to help me get the correct tone and rhythm, but whom to ask? "Excuse me, may I come and practice *ja jas* with you for awhile" seemed ridiculous. Could I try some trial runs and use it unobtrusively, raising my voice, eyebrows, and adding a pleasant nod to diffuse its possible inflammatory power? I practiced a few as I reached our door, adding a little space between the syllables to soften the instrument of destruction. "*Ja, ja, ja, JAAH!*" I tried, adding an elongated acute accent on the last *aah*. Calypso's eyes widened at my novel greeting but luckily, four months of quarantine had turned him into a most flexible cat and he calmly accepted his owner's new vocal peculiarities as part and parcel of all the changes thrust upon him since leaving Houston.

I removed my heavy layers and with them the weight of my word. The test run was a disaster and a hot cup of coffee only a slight consolation. It took no genius to come to yet one more linguistic decision in Norway. I would not be adding the *ja jas* to my vocabulary any time soon.

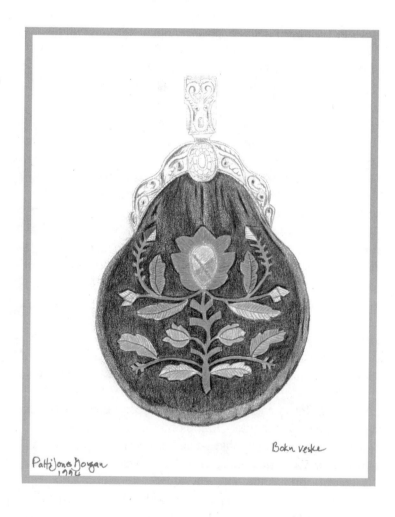

Bokn veske

Patti Jones Morgan
1996

Language Class Revisited

Our final year in Norway began with some difficult changes. My sixteen-year-old Rudy was gone, no longer cuddled up with me on the chair. Years and declining health had caught up with him, and no amount of optimistic thinking or prayers could bring him back to Houston with us. I would be leaving both my beloved pets behind, as it were, with only their memories to comfort me. My birthday, one of those milestones, reminded me that I had no lock on foreverness either. Each day as the sun rose a little earlier over the water, I felt time keenly and tried to come to grips with all the adjustments I had had to make and the ones still ahead.

Winter's drawn-out exit was probably my fault. While several million *nordmenn, nordkvinner og nordbarn*—the latter two my own Norsk neologisms, I hasten to add—had been searching for a touch of sun I had been urging Mother Nature to delay. I wanted to stop the clock, keep winter as it was, and never have to leave Norway.

Winter had been rainy with sleet, and everyone complained *en masse* as though their chorus would force spring to
hurry. Had a vote been taken, unlike the one for European Union
membership, the result would have been a unanimous, "Yes,
please! We vote for spring, for sun! We will pay even more taxes
just to get it!"

A friend, Laura, sometimes met me for coffee in
Haugesund, where we camped at a window table in Hauge and
Lindaas Bakeri to watch the world go by on Haraldsgate. Fashion-
able Haugesund matrons swooped in for lunch encased in stylish
wool coats, silk scarves, and the all-important hat, often fur-
trimmed. A Karmøy friend noted the latter with amusement.
"Haven't you seen the ladies in Haugesund in their big *hats*!" I
had, and my only regret was not owning a hidden camera to
catch the ladies in animated conversation around the tables as
engrossed in affairs as politicians. Their wooden chairs turned
into thrones draped with winter wear, they sized you up ever so
slightly to let you know that they probably knew everything of
significance to the community.

While the venerable women of Haugesund dressed
smartly, their men lagged behind. Predominately gray, green, and
brown, their wardrobe was structured toward utility. Some men
wore ties, but informality was preferred. My husband enjoyed his
tie-free existence. A couple were stashed in his office closet for
emergencies—a visiting company official coming for a meeting—and fortunately the garish green tie he had taken such a
liking to was not one of them. Mike, at least, had not descended
to the level of my British brother-in-law, Richard, who had bought
only one tie in his life and relied on this aging piece of silk hanging dejectedly on his bathroom door for occasional, emergency
service. Since ties were wide, then narrow, wide, then narrow, the
narrow tie was right fifty percent of the time during the twenty-
five years he had owned it.

Laura shook off her snowy coat one lunchtime, nodding disconsolately at the grayness outside and the hunched-over pedestrians struggling against the brisk wind. "I feel so tired of winter. It makes me depressed, like that sort of sickness people have when there's not enough sunlight." For her, and many Norwegians, seasonal affective disorder syndrome made winter joyless, but I enjoyed winter whatever it did, still enchanted with the novelty of cold after living for so long in hot, southern U.S. states. The crisp cold invigorated me, and wintertime seemed perfect for endless introspection about what life was all about.

Sometimes it came as a shock that so much of my time in Norway had already passed. The once important aid, my language class, had faded into memory as something that someone else had done, not me. The woman who, during her first year in Norway, felt incapable of communicating, coping, or even driving, had come a long way. The process seemed unending. You did this, you did that, passed through certain invisible barriers, over hurdles, and then one day you felt you had control of life, and were settled and content in your new environment.

My marked-up *Ny i Norge* still served me well, refreshing my memory with words and phrases. Back in Chapter Ten the text's international slant had introduced us to Argentinean immigrant, Maria. She could not decide whether to stay home and raise her children or take a job in the workplace and use the income to buy domestic appliances. Some Norwegian appliance names amused me. *Norsk* for "microwave oven" was *mikrobølgeovn*, which despite its "bulge" in the middle was pronounced more like "meecro buuriguh-ovnuh." A dishwasher was an *oppvaskmaskin*, up-wash machine, far more frivolous and lively sounding than the drudgy "dishwasher." I especially loved *støvsuger*, dust sucker, which out-visualed the dull vacuum cleaner.

"Excuse me, sweetheart, do you have a minute to run the dust sucker around the room?" or "Wait a second, I need to dust suck under the bed." Chapter Ten was almost child's play in comparison with real life, but it gave us a taste.

I could not help wondering about my old classmates and how they were doing, living in a Norwegian world with dust suckers and up-wash machines. I decided to call Tor and find out. Home from the university that weekend, he admitted he had seen little of his former students, but we exchanged notes. Nadya and her husband had moved to Stavanger; Li and his wife and Hasan and his had both welcomed first babies that year. Young Hamlet, the Icelander, had dropped from view. Mary worked part-time at a local mall, and her daughter, Olivia, was settled in high school, *videregående*.

Videregående's rhythmic syllables always sung themselves to me to the tune of "Where are you going to, my pretty maid," which was a perfect question for young people setting out on the road to their futures. *Videre* meant "additional, go further, wide, or advance" and, given that v's and w's often changed in linguistics, it was easy to see the connection between English "wide" and Norwegian *videre*. *Gående*, pronounced "gaw-enna" was a suffix for "to keep going or walking" and actually sounded a little like the English "going." Norwegian and English shared many common roots in Old Norse, and I spent hours investigating English words beginning with *sk* or *v* in particular and poring over fascinating word histories in etymologist Eric Partridge's thousand-page book, *Origins: A Short* (I had to take issue there) *Etymological Dictionary of Modern English*. Words had always entertained me but no more so than when I lived in the land of the *Vikings*, "the men of the creeks and small bays."

My classmates and I had all been in a variety of transitions during our class, and the eight people had already impacted the new country by providing more babies. The state seemed to encourage babies. Norway's total population of a little over four million was about the same as Houston and Harris County's in Texas. Mothers were awarded generous child allowances, regardless of family circumstances, and whether this was to ensure a steady stream of future, employed, tax-paying citizens or simply to keep the nation's population numbers up, I was never sure. They liked their smallness, the Norwegians, so I wondered if adding too many citizens wouldn't put a crimp in their claim to fame of "only about four and a half million people."

Oddly enough I was once again involved in a language-based group, but the circle had turned and the language was my own. I had responded to a call from a lone American voice in the *Haugesunds Avis* classifieds. "Are you from the States?" she asked, adding a phone number. As a result I met Beth, a new bride of a Norwegian, and fresh from Minneapolis. Our conversation was laced with the familiar and it stimulated me. I had missed the completeness of communication you can enjoy only with some-one who knows the kind of world you are used to. As a result, it seduced me away from my remaining resolve to learn more Norwegian. The truth was that Mike's job and the Heidrun project were almost finished and, like it or not, I had to go back to America. Speaking English, and wanting to, was okay now. I was on the homestretch and in a few months maybe it wouldn't matter anyway.

A dozen phone and fax messages later I met with others like me who missed something important—English language conversa-tion and the comfort of shared cultural experiences. Across the coffee table seven people who had spent a good deal of their lives in America or Britain tentatively shared what had brought them to Norway. Most had come for love. Linda from England met her young *Haugesunder* at a British university. Helen from the States came for love thirty years prior and had raised a family. Long Island-born Elaine returned to her family's ancestral home of Karmøy and married a local man. Her mother, Eva, followed after being widowed. I had come for marital togetherness, the same as love just not as passion-ate. David, a teacher and the only man who came that first evening, proclaimed no such romantic reason. He had come on a teaching job and liked it. He just missed little things like British crossword puzzles and wished he had someone English to discuss poetry with.

We tussled with the visions and issues of starting a British-American club but not before we shared reasons for *not* starting one. "I nearly didn't come. I thought, what's the point of my being here in Norway, speaking Norwegian as much as I can, getting adjusted, only to fall back on English again?" Linda asked. She had a valid point, and it was clear a balance was required in order to strengthen ties with a new culture without totally discarding the old.

However the overwhelming consensus of the group was positive. One woman looked forward just to being able to laugh at jokes. She couldn't catch the subtleties of Norwegian humor, especially delivered at a fast clip in a new language. I empathized. Laboring over a funny anecdote destroyed its potential lift. Almost as though admitting a dark secret, most agreed we could not enjoy the same facility of expression in Norwegian that English gave us. In my heart then I wondered how much harder it had to be in a marriage where each speaks a different mother tongue.

Helen, a grandmother, said wistfully, "I came here and raised a family. This is my home and I'm as Norwegian as you can get, but sometimes I want a little bit of America. I want to just speak American." Eva felt the same. "I have only three people I can speak English to. Even when I teach my small English class, everything starts out fine, then they break away to Norwegian.

Before you know it, it's all Norwegian. It's hopeless!" She reminded me of a substitute teacher in our Norwegian class. The woman had fumed when we reverted to English at the end of class. "Still they speak in English!" she muttered, charging out of the door. What had she expected? Norwegian was a struggle and speaking on our own time, as it were, in English was more comfortable. Another substitute fell afoul of Nadya, our savior. After a tense and depressing first ten minutes with the lady speaking only *norsk,* our classmate spoke for us all when she asked pointedly, "Can't you speak English?" furrowing her famous brows. "Yes, of course," the poor woman said, and to our relief, she did. We had her eating out of our palms for the remaining period.

Now I sympathized with second-language teachers. Their ambitious task was to bring about a complex series of changes which would make automatic what was not. They had to totally reprogram what their students' hands wrote and their lips said all the way back to comprehension and interpretation of feeling, an astonishingly difficult task.

Bilingualism created interesting phenomena. In addition to creating "new" Norwegian words from popular English ones—*vikend* for "weekend," for example, some Norwegian friends frequently switched back and forth between English and Norwegian, customizing their rapport to fit the mood, occasion, and precise subject matter. They had trained their brains to learn two complete languages and had fine-tuned a communications hybrid they all understood. Changing languages back and forth was part of the technique. Calling to a child in Norwegian, answering another in English, throwing an American word into a Norwegian sentence, and reverting to Norwegian while commenting on a television show—the style worked well and facilitated comprehension. This same technique effectively kept strangers out.

Norwegian excelled as a time-saver when what you had to say was not that important. Admittedly the downside was brusqueness. English's strength, however, was nuance, providing dozens of ways to say something exactly the way you wanted.

My friend's living room buzzed with animated conversation, people freed to babble without suffering puzzled looks or disapproval. If I saw them the next day, they might be chatting in Norwegian, using appropriate body language, looking like Norwegians, yet, each had willingly given up his or her own language in order to fit into another society.

A certain self-confidence was required lest you put a foot wrong, so I had donned my cultural slippers carefully for I had not been trained in the dance. If my mistakes made me misinterpret the demands and expectations of those around me, I could crush toes and hurt feelings. I might hear "yes" when the unspoken answer was "no" and find that official agreements were little more than light conversation. Or I might find myself at the right place at the wrong time because I had failed to remember the rule of three: check all big plans three times, for even the obvious assumptions could be wrong.

Just doing ordinary things in a new culture can make you stand out in the wrong way. Years before, I took an American guest to a friend's house in our little English village and cringed as she helped herself far too generously to sandwiches which had been almost mathematically sliced up to provide equal amounts for four people. Sarah came from a country where food was cheap to a country where it was expensive and hadn't known she should restrain her appetite. I wished I could have stopped her or whispered something, but the room was too quiet.

No one taught cultural empathy. You learned by listening, hearing, absorbing—and cultures being different, troubles were just a breath away.

Ultimately our words were all any of us had and needed to be rightly said after weighing their appropriateness to the situation and culture. But those unsaid words had their power too, being in their silence, safe and kind. Most of the time my internal editor guided me patiently in Norway but occasionally flared up in a temper. She would rap my knuckles painfully with her pen like my teacher who tried to teach me math when I was ten. "No!" she admonished. "That'snot right! Aren't you ever going to learn this?"

Karmøy's blustery weather usually excused the inhabitants from any pretensions of glamour and style. In fact, it gave me some perverse pleasure to make a strong anti-fashion statement capable of offending two nations and two international oil companies as I rushed through the showers one day in mismatched clothes. I wore a navy blue baseball jacket emblazoned with the Conoco logo and the battle cry "The Spirit of San Juan," a pair of kneed-out blue jeans, and a baggy red sweater, all topped off by a practical but unlovely plastic sou'wester which advertised both a recent Silda Jazz Festival and Statoil, Norway's state-owned oil company. Such haphazardness in my clothing reflected my current condition; I was mixed up in more ways than one. Extra pounds limited my choice of wardrobe, but harder to explain was my confused mother tongue. When a Norwegian inquired, "What is the English word for that?" my brain went fuzzy. "I just can't, um, think of it right now," I would mumble, like an imbecile.

I arrived secure in one language and, as I was about to leave, insecure in two. Language-wise I had degenerated to the equivalent of a bag lady. Words had long been my visual and mental entertainment; however, in Norway not only was I wandering around daily in a world filled with signs, boards, books, and newspapers in their language, I also had to cope with many peculiar versions of English that turned up. This "English" was usually printed on clothes produced in cheap labor countries where the value placed on English, or need for accuracy, was low. A tee shirt imprinted "Blue Langune," made one think of "languid" and "languorous" or people lying on a desert island beach, and of Brooke Shields in *Blue Lagoon*, the latter obviously the real intention of the manufacturer. A discarded snack cracker box labeled "Diction" lured me to the gutter. Asian-baked, they had been sent to market, I assumed, with a tag sounding phonetically perhaps like "delightful," "tasty," "crispy," or perchance "Ritz"? My imagination went wild. "Are you going to the grocery store, dear? Pick me up some Diction, would you?" Or, "My crackers are stale; how are *your* Diction? You know, those barbecue-flavored Diction really taste great!" The best one I could imagine had to be, "Don't eat any of her crackers; her Diction are terrible."

In Norway advertisements cut a little closer to the bone than American ones, and famous people found themselves targets. During my stay Prince Charles and his soon-to-be-ex, Diana, had loaned their faces unofficially to canned food products. "*Middag for en?*" the ad questioned, showing a pained Charles. His "dinner for one" was a can of pasta. Around the other side of the billboard the lady of his discontent averted her eyes from another one-person canned meal. "Dinner for one?"

Italian blue jeans, *Gaudi,* made me think they were, even if they weren't. The Henry Choice brand, however, was Norway's modest-priced version of Wrangler denim jeans and Lee jeans. HENRY SELDOM TOOK OFF HIS BLUE JEANS, their slogan alleged, yet this rather dubious reputation had never prevented Henry Choice from enjoying a loyal following.

I scanned window displays for the same slogan on his line of Western boots, hoping to read that our Henry seldom took those off either but was denied that pleasure. Perhaps someone at corporate headquarters had finally read between the lines?

Accosted from all directions, my moral acceptance factors descended to new lows in languages wherein I mixed and matched freely, taking handfuls from each as though they were candy or nuts. I took British English, American English, dictionary *Bokmål*; added creative variants; and behold, a mongrel pup, cute usually but undisciplined. A side effect was that my spelling was shot. I regularly misspelled words like "friend," making it "freind" because of the prevalence of *ei* in so many Norwegian words: *stein*, stone or rock, *veien*, road or pathway, *eiendom,* one's property, such as a house. Even playing our Scrabble game got confusing when I mixed up *y*'s and *j*'s due to the Norwegian "yuh" pronunciation of the letter *j*. I admit to once reading "abides" as "aahbeedeys" and foolishly challenging my husband on it. For awhile we considered converting to a bilingual game.

Linguistically I was shell-shocked and unreliable in spelling, which disturbed me. Before Norway you could have placed your bets on me to have *korrect* spelling, but, under such a barrage of the good, the bad, and the ugly, I had become totally *håpløs.*

Under constant attack by foreign words, a person in another land loses the luxury of automatic comprehension. No

longer can one just sit back and let conversation or text drift past
the eyes into the brain to the spot where it settles comfortably
with cookies and milk into little armchairs and takes stock of itself.
Instead these oddly costumed language characters move stiffly,
unsure of their next move. One such little word character is the
Norwegian *fantasi.* To the American ear "fantasy" has a negative
connotation. "That idea of hers is crazy! She must live in a fantasy
world." Yet American royal children and pets, otherwise known as
Disney characters, live happily in the world of fantasy, Fantasia. In
Norway *fantasi* is more closely associated with "Fantasia" for it
means "imagination." These dual-cultured word entities drifted
happily or wandered lost, resisting attempts to herd them into
coherent, grammatical sentences or paragraphs. Wrangling two
languages took a physically fit cowgirl.

Trying to say things properly and failing was not limited
just to me. Norwegians often confused words—English ones, of
course. One problem was the difference between "fun" and
"funny." "We had a funny time," explained Irene talking about a
school band trip. Randi described her new apartment as "funny."
Teenagers used the dreaded *ain't* despite my telling them it was
slang and used more in a joking manner. A few said, "My friends
was going to school " or "I like that very well (instead of very
much)" or "She were saying" or "It was very fun." Even a good
friend whose English was excellent implied dire consequences if I
pursued some train of thought. She wrote, "I must arrest you on
that point."

Then there were daughter-in-love's—a beautiful concept
resulting from mispronouncing the troublesome *w* of "law." And
I loved alliteratives like *barnebarn,* children's-children or grandchildren, *mormor*, grandmother; and the melodious *søskenbarn*, first
cousin, which for some reason had me humming *Edelweis,s* or was
it *Tannenbaum,* under my breath. Words danced like live things
through my vision. They gave me no peace for I was always trying
to decipher their peculiar forms, trying on their amusing and odd
sounds for size, testing their validity.

Norwegians maintained a fierce, if undeserved modesty,

for their skill in speaking English. But given a chance to speak
into a microphone in their own language, they turned into long-
winded, wisecracking, entertaining speakers most of the time.
After careful observation I had decided that, in a perfect world, all
the little Rogaland babies around us would like to be born
equipped with the three necessities for happiness: a pair of skis
like their Oslo cousins, a promise of 365 days of sun overhead,
and their own personal microphone. Genetically microphone-
deprived, they enter the world, fist in a knot, from dreaming in the
womb of clutching a microphone.

   Microphonitis was serious where we lived. Speakers often
brought handfuls of notes to the stage, determined to read every
single thing even if a freak storm blew the roof off the building.
Certainly several hundred people filing out of the room was no
reason to stop. Any Norwegian worth his salt kept talking, bound
by the ancient rule which decrees, "All the pieces of paper have
to be read." Foreigners who think this an exaggeration stand
warned; brief speeches are just warmups as are the jokes. There is
more to come!

   How humans communicate by converting thoughts and
feelings into speech and written language seems improbable. The
eye or heart perceives, then a jumble of electric impulses in your
brain insist on being expressed—tumbling out of your mouth,
through your fingertips to a keyboard, through your conscious
thinking and machinations, or on to paper via your fingers, hand,
and pencil. Somehow, in a millisecond, a coordinated conversion
performed at the speed of light utilizing every piece of information your brain has ever thought it should remember takes place.
Reason, comprehension, curiosity, touch, taste, and hearing
translate and crystallize into yet another form, written or spoken,
sketched, sung, even danced, to be reperceived and compre-
hended by someone else. How can we be so clever?

   It's hardly surprising that when I saw *eple*, apple, followed
by *appelsin*, orange juice, my brain shuffled through the information cards, said, "apple, orange juice," and then tossed a few
down on the table. Use these, discard the rest, it commanded so

fast and so precisely that it astonished me. People see letters in a child's book, spell them into "red apple," then the associations race. I see a red apple—we had red apples at my aunt's house—thick skin, juicy, cold; smooth under my fingers; apple pie; toffee apples; smell of toffee; a bowl of fruit; a painting of apples; red as a velvet red dress I saw in a store; red and green apples; an apple a day keeps the doctor away; an apple for the teacher; indigestion after eating apples; indigestion tablets; drug stores; the last time I was in a drugstore; pharmacists; my friend wants to be a pharmacist. Apple—dress—pharmacist sequences, hundreds of paths leading away, carrying information, and you, the language and comprehension policeman, change the traffic lights, erect barriers, remove barriers, speeding the traffic or slowing it down as it streams along highways. Operating another language in my daily life was like throwing a car into rush-hour traffic and having it bumble haphazardly in the opposite direction. The other drivers adapted and adjusted to avoid frontal collisions. Occasionally the vehicles almost blended, sometimes paralleling one another harmlessly. Or at other times sirens screamed and the fire truck raced in to pick up the wreckage.

A trip to Stavanger clarified much of my torment about English language and communications, whether it was good or bad or if we had too much or too little, I felt we should use it in moderation, like a rich consumable. I did not need to know nor could I synthesize all the neighborhood's, town's, city's, land's, planet's words, pictures, and sounds. I had quite enough to challenge and nourish me with my small neighborhood. But when English speakers walked by shedding little conversation snippets which adhered to me like yellow stick-on notes, I was unwillingly involved. It was like being in Houston; out there clamored to get inside.

People's conversations help you know things, belong, be informed, bind you into the social group, and for the most part were absent in my day-to-day life on Karmøy. This provided me a wonderful quiet place inside my head to think, observe, and reflect with the conversations around me as mere background music. The peace was a blessing in disguise.

While our relationship, often mute from need or choice, had its rough spots, Karmøy and I had arrived at an accommodation of sorts. Only in the silence of *not* understanding everything spoken and written in a Norwegian world did I find freedom of chosen thought. It was a sort of pleasing deafness I learned to cherish.

"The soul has an inherent need for balance. Compelled to do, it desires worldly immersion and enchantment, but the soul also need to know it can just be. This being means occasional retreats from the frontlines of life— retreat into solitude, stillness, and reflection."

—From *The Sanctuary Garden* by Christopher Forrest McDowell and Tricia Clark-McDowell.

22

Evenings on Ice

Invitations out were still scarce enough that I rarely refused one, even when I began hibernating at the onset of winter darkness at four thirty. Such was the case when shortly after her new baby sister arrived, Liv-Marit invited me over. She repeated her invitation earnestly a couple of times, but what could *selskap* and *toopayrvahrer* mean? Her bouncy dog deposited muddy paws on my jacket as I stared into space trying desperately to understand.

"*Kan du sier igjen? Jeg er dum,*" I asked, willing to consider myself stupid if that helped.

"*Nei!*" the little girl said, objecting to my defeatist attitude. "*Du er IKKE dum!*" She continued trying to illuminate me. "*Mamma vil en selskap . . .* toopayrvahrer? *Selskap. Du forstår,* you understand '*selskap*'?"

I pieced the words together. *Selskap* meant "business" or "party" so I tried the latter. "*Ja. Selskap er,* party, right?" She agreed it was, but the word which sounded like *toopayrvahrer* still eluded me. Mouthing the phonetics solved the mystery. "Too-payr-vah-rer—of course, *Tu-pper-ware*! A Tupperware party—your mother *vil ha en* Tupperware Party!" "Yes," Liv-Marit answered, looking relieved. Apparently her mother wanted me to come. Not quite ready to trust me, she reminded me to call her mother and get the exact date, about two weeks hence. She wobbled off homeward on her bike, grappling with her wayward dog which zigzagged in front. Liv-Marit was the most remarkable child I had ever met. She seemed to know instinctively that I needed someone to help me along in my new life. Confident and mature beyond her handful of years, she was my angel flitting about. I dreamed of a golden future for her. She deserved nothing less.

Her mom's surprise invitation, however, struck me as one of those good news-bad news situations. Normally I would have to be beaten unconscious before attending a Tupperware party, but it offered me adult interaction. I would put my money where my mouth was and go to the dreaded event.

As I checked the phone book for Ellen's number I was struck again at the listings. *Ditt Distrikt* let subscribers list their work or special interest on the same line as their name, address, and telephone number. In typical Norwegian understatement it ran in lower case: *tømmermann*, carpenter, *fotterapeut*, foot therapist. The last syllable of the latter was another of my favorites, *peut*, because I liked puffing it out with a semi-kissing lip position. Others were *salgs-innkjøpssjef*, sales/purchasing manager; *husmor*, which shares the same root as "hussy" in English but means "homemaker" or "housewife." *Driftsleder* meant "union leader"; *sveiser*, welder, and *sjåfør* or *drosjesjåfør* was taxi driver. Taxis in Norway are usually beautifully maintained touring cars in which it is easy to feel that you are indeed being chauffeured. Telephone book listings also included *pensjonist*, senior citizen, and not afraid to accept that designation; and *frisør*, hairdresser, one of Mike's favorites since he connected it, unfairly, with the frizzies. Then there were *båtbygger*, boat builder and *sildefisker*, herring fisherman. *Personsøker* fooled me into thinking it meant "detective" but it was merely a beeper. *Jordmor* which literally meant "earth mother" actually translated as "midwife."

Naturally there were many *bonde* listings on the island because so many people were farmers. Occasionally a woman added *fru*, meaning "Mrs." with her name although I never heard anyone ever address or refer to a married woman as *fru*. Our friend Karl, a retired business owner, indicated his hobby *trekkspiller*, accordion player. Then there were professions like *tannlege*, which translated as "tooth doctor" and meant "dentist." A Norwegian expression connected with teeth always struck me as particularly visual—*"tennene løper i vann,"* one's mouth is watering, actually translated as "the teeth are running in water."

Ellen and I were chatting over the new baby a week later when her husband appeared from the garage saying something about sledgehammers. Weren't sledgehammers lethal weapons? I felt anxious and hurried off home, wishing I weren't even going to his wife's party. Fortunately their son, Per-Rune, raced past. "I must go home!" he called out breathlessly. "Sledge Hammer is on the TV." I had to laugh at myself. I could rest easy. The upcoming event might be murder, but not literally.

At the party we were twelve. The *stue* was warm with extra heat provided by a powerful portable heater in the corner, and the family's four or five cats blinked briefly, daring us to even think of displacing them as they snuggled deep into the sofa cushions. Camille, Hanna's eldest daughter, sat next to her mother, and their ages blended, making them twins in their comfortable expressions and matching rested arms. Elise led the familiar sung grace, and afterward Ellen offered us coffee, soft drinks, and open-faced sandwiches. We were more than ready for the Tupperware storage containers representative to get going, but when she did, I was sorry. She discussed and rediscussed the apparent benefits of the same three covered bowls for forty-five minutes, pointing to a long evening ahead. Fortunately Liv-Marit's aunt, Olaug, was sitting next to me. She knew I was fond of her niece and nephew and during respites from the sales pitch we talked about the children.

Ten o'clock couldn't come soon enough and I slipped over to Ellen to pay for my order. She whispered something which had words like the baby's name, "Anne-Lise," "sleep," and "house" in the same sentence.

"*Kan du gjenta?*" I asked apologetically, hoping to catch it on the second time around.

She tried again, and again I could only take a guess. "You want to bring Anne-Lise over to my house to sleep?" I asked, a little shocked.

"*Nei!*" Ellen tried again and I finally put it all together. She was simply trying to thank Mike and me for the baby gift, a sleeping outfit, and all I needed to do was say " it was our pleasure." How could I not understand something so *elementary*. Times like that made me feel I was getting nowhere in Norwegian, and my night wound down on an annoyed and frustrated note.

I had another chance to redeem myself when Margit invited the art group to her home one evening. The roads were icy and I dreaded venturing out, even in someone else's car. Lillian chuckled wickedly as Cecilie, Brita, and I waited for her to get her car out, stamping our feet to keep warm. My two previously kind and considerate friends scrambled past and crowded into the back seat. "*Du sitter foran!*" Brita insisted, pointing at the front seat. "*Vi er redde*—scared!" she added, exploding into laughter. Cecilie chimed in, "*Ja, vi er redde!*" from the blackness. "You sit in front!" Cecilie also felt it her moral duty to explain something to the designated front-seat passenger, but it needed no English translation. I knew "she drives too fast" when I heard it.

Riding shotgun, I strapped myself in, hoping to survive the night with my life. I secretly decided that, had I been Norwegian, they would not have taken advantage of me so. Lillian shocked the engine into life and, as we swung down the whitened narrow lane on the way to Margit's, Cecilie's urgent request rang out from the back seat, "Telephone to heaven, telephone to heaven! Help us, Jesus!"

In Norway in winter, if you have control over two vocabulary words, let them be *vanskelig* and *glatt*. Everyone understands and is sorry about "difficult," and everyone knows "slippery." That evening my personal quota of *vanskeligs* had been exhausted, and some *glatts* were going begging, but not for long, because when my three companions all stopped laughing in the middle of a conversation, lowered their voices, and muttered *glatt*, they seemed ready for a disaster. Since one was our trusty driver, I felt for a grab bar.

My worries about being the main glass-smithereen collector for the evening were interrupted by a baby's high-pitched wail erupting spookily from the back. For some unknown reason Cecilie thought the tension in the car not adequate enough and had chosen that time to introduce us, as it were, to the newest member of her family.

"What was *that?*" I gasped. She held out a plastic square from which came the scary cry over and over again. It was a type of mini tape player that new parents could send to their friends.

"My grandchild!" she boasted happily. "And he is coming to me tomorrow!" The cries pierced our eardrums, and I wondered if tomorrow would ever come if Lillian crashed the car. Lillian, however, just kept chewing her gum, a new cigarette substitute, eyes ahead. Brita and I pleaded with Cecilie to turn the little ghost off for now, that we would love to hear her again later. The silence afterward was almost as bad for we could hear one another's sharp inhalations punctuating our grumbles and gasps as Lillian swung us around corners.

On really slick stretches Lillian slowed down a couple of kilometers an hour, and I had the sensation of being on a motorized sled. But we were not dead yet. I unclenched my fists. With any luck we would get to Margit's in one piece—by car, not ambulance—but coming home would be worse as temperatures were dropping by the minute. Margit's house at the end of the harrowing journey was a heartwarming vision. Lillian began backing down the steep, slippery driveway. I attempted an escape but not even a gazelle would have been fleet of foot enough to get out. She tried accelerating up again, failed twice, and looked quite satisfied. We had arrived.

Our hostess's warm smile drew us all inside, a roomy, big windowed home almost overhanging the Karmsund's eastern shore. She graciously accepted our gifts of flowers and choco-lates, and we all slipped out of our boots and jackets. Her cozy living room was lined with pictures. We settled around the large coffee table to do justice to the banquet she had prepared while I wished, once again, I could get the hang of what condition one's stomach should be in for an invitation to a Norwegian's home at seven. This had happened once before—in Oslo—when Mike and I wound up eating two meals one evening. We had eaten lightly at six, then gone to our new friend's expecting perhaps some wine and open-faced rolls, only to find instead a candlelight meal of reindeer, cranberry-like dressing, potatoes, vegetables, and all the trimmings. Another couple, dressed up more than we were, rounded out our party of six. We enjoyed a lovely evening, eating heartily, and Mike especially so for he managed seconds.

Gazing at Margit's dishes, I saw that empty should have been the correct gastronomic state because her table was loaded with cold meats, crisp and soft fresh bread rolls, jams, jellies, and a rainbow of fresh fruits—kiwi, grapes, mandarin oranges, and pineapple—artfully prepared to show off the colors There were giant slabs of brown goat's cheese—my newest addiction—and two other slab cheeses as well as a plate of cream cheese. Elsewhere, scrambled eggs paired up with strips of pink salmon decorated with parsley sprigs, sliced hard-boiled eggs, tomato and cucumber slices, ham, and more—and more. Our friend poured coffee as we admired her best floral china with gold trim and traced the delicate work on her lacy tablecloth. "Vær så god!" she invited us. Pushing aside memories of my earlier "just in case" supper, I began to eat.

Eating cold foods in Norway requires a little more restraint than in America. Bread rolls are buttered; cold meats, sliced cheese, etc. added; then they are polished off, rather delicately, and slowly, by using a knife and fork. Oddly, though, no similar rule applies to cakes and waffles which are eaten in little bite-sized pieces, using one's fingers or a tiny coffee spoon. This spoon is also used as a knife and as a jam or fresh cream spreader. Since sometimes no napkin is offered, a private supply of clean tissues and some discreet finger licking after this seems to offend no one.

A lull ensued as we attacked the meal. Lillian broke the silence. *"Egg licha icha!"* she spluttered in dialect, crumpling her face and sticking out her tongue as she replaced her teacup. We all stopped in midbite, wondering what she "didn't like." Normally we were all so polite. Whatever would Margit say? Sheepishly our hostess tested a bowl's contents with a damp fingertip. "Salt! I put SALT in the sugar bowl by mistake!" she laughed, looking a bit confused. Both her expression and Lillian's had us all in fits of laughter as we returned to our mission to do justice to the sumptuous meal.

Our conversation covered Canadian summer visitors, gynecologists, home ownership and taxes, social benefits, and the prospect of the art group, or individuals, visiting me in America. Brita's eyes lit up. "Oooooh, *Texas!*" she exclaimed, reminding me how people often viewed someone else's home-land as exciting, when the people who lived there focused on its problems, including me. I felt quite guilty at my lack of patriotism of late. She was right; America was pretty wonderful after all. While we ate, I wondered where I felt happiest, and which suited me most: Norway or America?

Eventually came the passing around of the photographs, an integral part of most family reunions or get-togethers. Norwe-gians value photographs and love to share them. Each picture is gazed upon, then passed over to the visitor along with an expla-nation of the who and the where. We all saw photographs of Margit's son's recent wedding in town, and I learned that, in Norway as in the United States, the bride's parents pay for the reception. Someone else produced wallet photos of a friend's two adopted Sri-Lankan children who would grow up saying *uff* and the *ja jas* quite naturally.

The day's media event was worth touching on, and I inquired if anyone had seen the CNN report about a missile accidently fired from Norway's mainland and landing near Spitsbergen. CNN said that the launch had surprised the Russians, causing an alert in their defense system. Brita heard it differently. *"Nei, det er feil."* She continued in Norwegian to the effect that the radio reported it was nothing. I countered that CNN usually got their facts right.

She shook her head firmly as I tried arguing my side, both in English and Norwegian. We were both firm and logical about what we knew from our own national sources but were unable to explain it fully to each other. Wisely we dropped the subject.

Later I realized that Brita may not actually have been denying the existence of a rocket, but rather denying the strong Russian reaction to the incident. And her conclusion may have been correct. Further newspaper and television reports contradicted the statements of both Norwegians and their Russian counterparts, so who said what and why remained unclear.

Brita, Lillian, Margit, and Cecilie enjoyed pantomiming word meanings to me if I could not figure something out, which was often. When a light passed the window indicating a boat, Brita called it the *hydrofyken*. She demonstrated by flapping her arms and laughing. I got the picture. The commuter fast boats had a local nickname, *hydrofyken*, which Brita insisted meant "water bird." I thought it should have been *fugl* for bird. When I checked the dictionary *fyk, fyken* was a horse-drawn hay rake. *Fyket* could be "drifting, whirling snow or spray." Rake marks and dust flying up did compare with a water wake though, and if such an ancient tool had loaned itself to high-speed water travel, I was impressed. But Brita had flapped her arms, and only a bird did that.

Despite my confusion I later showed off my knowledge of the water-rake-bird to a Norwegian from Stavanger. *"Ja! Hydrofyken!"* he repeated, nudging his wife, a former Karmøy girl, into commenting on how *flink* I was in Norwegian. The cherished *flink* was beginning to lose a little of its power, but I still needed my regular *flink* fix.

The evening at Margit's was in full swing, and I prodded my coffee-guzzling friends to supply more idioms with which I could impress people. Conversations led to people going east or west, and I learned *gå rett vest* was the equivalent of the American "gone south." Lillian's example was *"Mine penger og min kone har gått rett vest."* My money and my wife have gone straight west.

Eli-Bente's late appearance prompted another expansion of my vocabulary. She rubbed her hands together and mentioned some work that had kept her busy. *"Vaske-kjerring!"* she chuckled. What could that mean? They eagerly explained it had something to do with cleaning lady, washerwoman, or housewife. *Kjerring* was the funny part. If your husband referred to you as his *kjerring*, his tone of voice made the difference. Endearing was okay whereas *kjerring* accompanied by a derisive retort was not. My friends chorused correct and politically incorrect voice inflected versions of *kjerring* for my edification. This homely piece of vocabulary needed a balance, and they offered another word, *gubben*, and a demonstration.

Gubben referred to a *kjerring's* husband and, to demonstrate this gentleman precisely, Brita opened an imaginary newspaper and pretended to read it, looking as stuffy as possible. She brought Andy Capp of comic strip fame to life, at least as perceived by his long-suffering wife. *Gubben min* was, like *kjerring*, either an endearment or criticism between long-married couples in the Karmøy area. We giggled in a female conspiracy of understanding. We knew our menfolk in both stages—and knew exactly what *gubbe* was.

I performed my *pièce de résistance* toward the end, a not-quite-spitting, guttural, explosive rendition of "receipt," *kvEET-erghinggg*. I had developed this pronunciation to a fine art, thanks to the clerks at the post office. Pronouncing it correctly became a challenge I never tired of. A tricky word like that won me many bonus points in the community.

The real purpose for the get-together was finally completed: the doling out of any refunds due after the recent art

286 Patti Jones Morgan

show. Occasionally Cecilie's grandchild shrieked from her palm, sending Margit's two gentle dogs into spasms of agitated barking and racing up and down the room in search of the invisible baby.

When we departed into the night, I refused even to set foot in Lillian's car until she had managed to get it up onto the road and ignored pleas that my weight would help. Lillian handily accelerated back up the driveway, leaving me standing there feeling foolish and I was actually grateful when she stopped and let me get back in.

Nonetheless, when my neighborhood came into sight, I wanted out. Lillian looked hurt and argued that she wanted to come and look at my house. I said no, I wanted to just get out and walk the rest of the way. *"En annen dag, en annen dag!"* another day, I insisted. My two friends cajoled me to return, but I hardened my heart to their pleas. They simply hated to see their glass-smithereen catcher walk away while they still had a few slippery miles to go.

All *vanskeligs* and *glatts* aside, the evening had been an unqualified success for we had managed to get there and back without getting killed. And *kveldsmat,* or supper, in Margit's home would go down as one of my favorite memories of Norway.

Only one small thing had gone wrong. Earlier I had popped down to the basement looking for a rest room with its typical Norwegian logo of a cheery potty sitter. Unfortunately I managed to trespass into several rooms and storage closets before coming across the correct place. How was I, a ding-a-ling *kjerring*, to know that a little red heart on a door also meant "rest room"? It stung a little to realize I was not as smart in Norwegian ways as I thought I was, but only my *gubbe* would hear about this one.

23

Seasons & Changes

On snowy winter nights the ancient, rocky island exuded a pure, white wedding cake beauty. Snow was still a novelty to me, and unlike people who had drive to work everyday, I could enjoy it on foot, taking all the time I wanted. Still, could it all have been my imagination? Karl told us, right at the beginning, that Karmøy didn't get snow. When five inches appeared overnight which had to be shoveled out of the driveway, I wondered if he had noticed. People you would pray for as jurors also insisted they did not have snow there. It took me three winters to understand their communal snow blindness.

It turned out that Karmøyans were snow connoisseurs and ashamed of theirs. Only the dry mountain variety, Lillehammer and Oslo kind of snow, deserved the name, and they dismissed Karmøy's moist snowflakes as hybrid irritations. Real snow should grow meters deep and permanent so people could ski straight out their kitchen doors onto trails. It had to be firm and well packed, swathing roof lines like wide strips of marzipan.

Months of bone-chilling temperatures matured it to cement-like consistency impervious to rain.

This created yet another Karmøy weather fact. Genuine Norwegian snow cannot be washed away with rain. Quality-control restrictions such as these placed the island's snow under a distinct disadvantage because it never lived up to the lofty expectations of the residents. To save face, they tried to ignore it except when it became nuisance snow—too puny, too wet, too little, and not deep enough—it stayed too briefly and melted on top a little each night, making the roads slick and dangerous. The real, good snow still lay over the mountains.

Only children under the age of five reveled in it because they knew no better. They thought it was wonderful. I thought it wonderful too, sharing my dreamy comments with a lady as we stared outside watching gigantic, feathery flakes bumble against a window. She looked at me as though I were crazy. "Oh, I hate it! It's wet snow. If you have kids, they go and play and get wet. Then they have to come back inside and change. Then they get sick!" I got the message—not for her the delight of a crystal-lace curtain.

Even elementary-age children received early indoctrination. "Now school is over, what are you going to do?" I asked some, certain they must be bursting to run home to change, ready to play snowballs in Kopervik's glowing, Colorado ski-resort ambiance. "Eat!" came one girl's improbable answer. "We're so hungry!"

"Yes!" came a noisy assent, but I pressed on doggedly. *"Skal du gå på ski?*—are you going skiing?" Their faces showed the familiar baffled expressions I had come to expect of some very ordinary questions in Norway, as though I had suggested they wash their hair in treacle. *"Nei!"* cried one boy and everyone agreed. How could it be "no"?

Fortunately young Jarle from our street, sportily attired for winter, appeared on his skis. I knew he would provide me the right answer. Our neighborhood soccer field had been his private practice area for the past hour or so. "What do think about this snow? *Liker du?"* I asked, nodding yes in advance.

"*Nei! Det er kaldt!"* he answered, adding a pained look to back up his aversion to cold. It was hopeless. Tots and I were the only ones who appreciated fluffy, fascinating snow.

After three days of snow which came one year and stayed, Kopervik had a genuine winter postcard look about it. Real snow, thick, powdered, and dry, fell like a veil in blinding sunshine. Mothers pushed and dragged children in all sorts of vehicles. One woman pushed a baby carriage with twins inside—the island seemed to have more twin babies per capita than any place I had known. Her groceries hung from the handle, and she towed another child who was hunched over a little pair of skis. The group commandeered the width of the path, pausing every time the little skier fell down. "*Opp igjen!"* his mother encouraged and, after a few gyrations with skis and legs angled in the wrong directions, he scrambled "up again" and the entourage continued along the waterfront. Sea gulls fidgeted on a slushy layer of water on Kittilsbotn inlet looking confused and out of place. The town's elegant resident swans extended their long, lithe necks out across the water, curling them up and down like miniature Loch Ness monsters.

When they are not ignoring the snow, Karmøyans complain about the rain—so much so that even when it is not raining, they will it into existence by complaining about the rain last week, last fall, or due soon. "*For mye regn!"* too much rain, is how one retired gentleman put it as we chatted across his fence on a sparkling dry, sunny, snowy January morning under a rainless sky. My post office friends shared his fatalism. "Yes, it is pretty and quiet," one agreed, admiring the snowy landscape of the high street. "But it will rain next week—next Monday," she added with a satisfied air of certainty. Even my neighbor, rolling his eyes warily toward the blue sky ringing with bird song and redolent with blossoms one magical late spring morning, greeted me with the same dire news, "Probably next week we'll have rain."

Conversation focuses on rain, denying snow, and fantasizing about tropical sunshine. Television reporting is partly responsible; it keeps Norway's residents in general, and

Karmøyans specifically, meteorologically dissatisfied by reporting high temperatures from around the globe. My passion for the island was ever evaluated in the context of the perennial spoiler by the locals.

They tested my truthfulness, resolve, or madness, by fixing me with a penetrating gaze and asking the 64,000 *kroner* question. "You love it here? But the rain!" Even my dentist stopped his digging to stare into my face instead of my mouth and whispered incredulously, "You really love it? Even the weather?"

Friend Astrid finally rebelled when I reminded her about our recent lovely sunny weather. She looked as though I must be talking about some other place. She, like Karl, ignored inadequate weather aspects. Three weeks of sun did not warm her heart or tan her shoulders or lessen her frustration with seven or eight months of rain, wind, and storm. "It's okay for you to say that you don't mind it," she steamed. "You haven't lived here for thirty years!"

Certainly the look of desperation on a teenager's face when April rolled around proved how primed for good weather people were by then. "If there's some sun, we want to go away this weekend, but the weather report says wind and rain, maybe snow inland. We're waiting until tomorrow before we decide whether to go to the *hytte*. But not if there's no sun! I want some sun!" Karen cried, staring at me imploringly as though I could make it happen.

Only a miracle would bring sun to the slopes that week, but her attitude confirmed what I had long suspected. Whether the skies produced rain, snow, or sun, there was no pleasing a Karmøyan when it came to weather; the unevenness of quantity, duration and distribution were the heart of the problem. The heavens owed them.

Before long Karen got her wish; the sun returned. A symbol of the season were the newborn animals. We were fortunate to be invited to friend Torgeir Hårberg's farm to see his new calves. Torgeir's family owned a dozen or so cows and raised grass and turnips for feed. Two shiny, stainless-steel milk containers with stirring wands held the herd's creamy milk. Their barn was tall with a high, sloped roof, built in typical Norwegian rural style, and consisted of two levels with an attached silo. An exterior earth ramp, used by tractors, led to the second level which housed farm equipment and hay. The cows were kept below. The silo measured twenty-five feet in depth and was filled to overflowing with hay. A pulley lowered foodstuffs from the silo's central shaft down to the animals. The family had built the barn themselves many years before, and it smelled sweet and full of new life.

Norwegian cows were big-eyed, long and lean, with thin skin and shining flanks, brown or black, dappled with large, white spots, making them look more like artists' fanciful interpretations than the real cows I had seen in Oklahoma and Texas. When they wore canvas collars, they looked even more so. They wintered inside where they also gave birth. Our friend explained that calves were nursed only until they could drink from a bucket. I rubbed their stubby, coarse heads while they lunged across the bars of the pen to get mouthfuls of my jacket.

We strolled outdoors past where ruins of an ancient house, more recently used to shelter the calves, lay crumbling. A seven-foot-high weed took advantage of the sun and sprouted in the center. At their private cove Torgeir showed us his boathouse, its roof peppered with the previous year's swallows' nests. More would be built when the swallows returned. Another bird had taken up residence in a nesting box over the door. Along the path the first primroses of spring tilted their yellow smiles, reminding me of when my friends and I used to pick them as children in England. Torgeir's grandfather used to watch for mackerel from the cove. I sat on a couple of rocks hewn like a bench, surprised at their smoothness, and how comfortable the day's heat felt in their warmth. How many hours had the men waited, hoping, needing the catch? And how could I be sitting in their old place, viewing the same sound and same dark outlines of the mountains, three generations and a whole different culture later?

"When the water began frothing in the distance, it meant the mackerel were swimming up the Karmsund. As soon as grandfather and his friend saw it, they would run like hell, get in their boats, and set up their nets!" he told us, laughing.

Days had changed, though, and most families no longer depended on fishing. Torgeir just fished casually when he took out his pleasure boat. So much had changed; even small farming's days were numbered. Time and labor intensive and not profitable enough in milk and cattle production, they were losing viability, he explained. European Union membership, which, he predicted, would eventually be ratified, would deliver the final blow. "We have already decided that when my father retires, we'll get rid of the cows," he said. "We'll just have some sheep."

He showed us a large collection of ancient farm implements and antiques in his basement. A small, fading, framed document covered with signatures hung crookedly from a nail. A pass issued by the occupying troops during the 1940s, the document had to be presented each time his father carried goods back and forth to Haugesund. Looking at the yellowing scrap of paper, filled with signatures of people long since dead and whose manipulative power died with them, I shared the farmer's disgust with the injustice of occupation where a man running a family farm had to ask approval to buy and sell enough to support his family.

Upstairs we sat down to coffee and cake under the gaze of a fluffy family cat which dozed near the fireplace. Our hostess leaned across and lit the candles "for the guests." Before Norway, I had used candles mainly for birthdays, but now Mike and I enjoyed their both soothing and cheerful influence almost every dinner time.

In our friend's farm kitchen I felt at home. The country felt familiar; I had been raised in the countryside in England, where two of my childhood friends were farmer's daughters. I sat in their kitchens, watched tractors ploughing the land, heard noisy combine harvesters, scooped and tasted handfuls of sacked animal meal, peered over metal gates at giant hogs, felt life in a warm new egg, bolted over fields and five-bar gates to escape feisty cattle, carried pond water to thirsty cart-horses. Country living in Norway had brought me back to earth, where life moved at a slower pace, where everything had its own moment, no rushing past before feeling the beauty of now. I felt part of that circle of life. Lambs, people, primroses, we all had our time, and it had to be that way.

A week or two later I interrupted a bike ride to watch another farmer send his cows back to pasture. They scattered like fifteen released prisoners, drunk with fresh air, cantering down the slopes toward the cove. Tossing their heads, dashing in one direction then running back, running toward one another then backing away while trying to reacquaint themselves with their old field made them as frisky as horses. Most looked no worse for wear although their ribs protruded under their naturally thin hides and some wore canvas strapping around their udders, giving them a bandaged appearance you do not expect to see on a cow. Later I learned this prevented other cows from nursing.

The farmer watched intently from the fence, alert for any hitches, his neighbors alongside. Today he worried that his cows might hurt themselves in their joy to be free. Two were already butting heads after enforced close quarters had made them enemies. All the snide mooing, the critical nipping, and crotchety kicking had come to a head. The lady on the left shoved her barn mate aside and hurried toward a juicy patch of grass. Not to be pushed around, the other one cantered alongside and gave her a good bump. In response the lady lowered her head and shoved back. Trying to topple her to the ground didn't work either. Her unrepentant stall mate just leaned inwards, determined to hold her ground. Ungluing themselves briefly, they changed tactics and charged headfirst at one another. "I've just about had it with you. Take that!"

"Back off, lady, you made my life miserable too. I'm sick of you." They pushed and leaned, challenged and charged, purging their own personal vendettas.

Eventually, distracted by spring air and sweet grass, the herd settled down. The unexpected lesson of country theater helped put things in perspective. I had to adapt, even if I didn't want to. We would go back to city life in Houston later that year, but in the meantime I would treasure every remaining moment on the green and gray rocky hills of Karmøy.

24

The Norway Quilt

By the end of our stay, I had acquired a number of good women friends, but we had not acquired many "couple" friends. That was not unusual where we lived; couples enjoyed separate activities. Women got together with girlfriends, many attended school and church activities for their children. Clubs abounded, filling a variety of interests—motorcycling, stamp collecting, photography, ceramics, sports, riding, theater. Retirees and singles had multiple places to go and meetings to attend, as did bird lovers, singers and quilters. Even humanitarian endeavors like the Red Cross and Amnesty International drew loyal members.

Karmøyans were almost too busy to entertain. On one occasion our friends canceled a special week-night activity in order to have us over, and we felt guilty. It was a good thing we didn't rely on that aspect of social life and were instead quite satisfied for me to have my friends to meet with during the day and for Mike to be able to relax at home on his days off. He had progressed from working ten-hour days, five days a week, to fourteen days in a row, on twenty-four-hour call. Heidrun was a strict taskmaster and deadlines had to be met.

Expatriate spouses learned early on that they needed to handle life on the home front as best they could. They made friends with others in the same situation, and those friends became family for the duration. Pauline and I had done that, but she and her husband had already transferred to Stavanger. Stavanger was home to organizations such as the American Women's and Petroleum Women's clubs, which offered the comfort of a common language as well as diversions: classes in cooking, exercise, French, art appreciation, sewing, and more, not to mention dinner evenings out to try new restaurants, trips, and, perhaps most important for many, an English-speaking community.

Restaurant meals were horrendously expensive, a real deterrent to dining out. A trip to a local Italian restaurant and a meal of lasagna, salad, dessert and two diet drinks cost us the equivalent of $35. One could imagine how local people felt about spending so much. Many Norwegian companies, if they offered a social night out, invited only employees, not spouses or significant others. For awhile American spouses in Oslo rebelled. They had supported their husbands, moved overseas, pulled children out of schools, only to be stuck at home in a new country while the men went out after work with colleagues.

Forcing the issue didn't really work. Once I insisted on being invited to a work-related reception, only to discover, to my deep embarrassment, that there were only two nonemployees there—me and my mother. Not that there were no parties with Mike's work colleagues; there were a few, and those were fun. But like most of the people we knew, we ate at home and went out for dinner only occasionally. Our lives centered around Mike's work, my writing, art, and art friends. Basically we operated much as we did in Houston; living overseas did not change much, yet living in a small Norwegian village had taught me the importance of connections and permanence. Where had they been in our old life in Houston? Since we left, only one neighbor had written, once or twice, and that was it. In retrospect it seemed that any sense of community back there had been a mirage.

Although I felt gloomy while my husband was away, it never turned into paralyzing loneliness. True loneliness was a lack of caring people to call on, a sense of being ignored, whereas time alone was a necessity. When I wanted them, there were people to talk to.

Besides by then I had come to grips with my language limitations. Norwegian moved too fast for me to stay up with it unless I was in a one-on-one situation with a patient person blessed with an open mind and a sense of humor. I would never automatically pick up a conversational tidbit as people walked by. When I entered a crowded place, the language closed me out like a wall, but so did Arabic, Chinese, Russian, or whatever one's mother tongue was not.

I had no real complaints. I loved where I was; my heart felt at home. But it would not last. The life of an oil company employee was transient. Along with the ups—the excitement of new job opportunities and places to see—came the downs: not getting too attached to anywhere, more importantly, to anyone, in case you left. We would be on our way again by fall, returning to fast-paced Houston. One had to be on one's marks to get back into that kind of life, like a trained athlete ready to sprint at the sound of the starter's gun. I doubted I could catch up with urban speed and crackle—the traffic, the superhighways, pace of life, abundance, consumerism, foodism, the twenty-five brands of cereal to pore over in the supermarket, the two-hour mall marathons, commodification of the citizen, the overwhelmingness of an American city like Houston.

Estranged from America and its news-generated anxiety, I had walked, driven, and pedaled my introspective, fairly contented way through Norway for almost three and a half years, oblivious and uncaring about the world I had left behind. One day I supposed I would return, but the change seemed impossible to imagine. Now that the time was closing in, I felt fatalistic. I hoped that the unpleasant affair would be as painless as feeling a pinprick of anesthetic, then finding your tooth had been pulled out while you waited, eyes closed. But out of the blue came a sign, literally and figuratively, that my detached life in another land was a temporary state of affairs and the dentist was checking his appointment book. My country recalled me from the window of Lundbergs Bakeri.

AMERIKA-BESØK, red letters called out. Had my eyes deceived me? No. It did say AMERIKA, and I translated the poster as "America Visit." Kopervik's Husmorlag, the local association of housewives, was inviting the public to attend a special meeting. The poster was the first handwritten news item I had ever seen on Karmøy containing the word "America." Despite the island's reputed strong ties with it, nothing ever appeared in print in English anywhere, including the Avis. Indeed the few references to America were sports related or little news reports on politics or commerce, silly slices of life, or gruesome murderous events which, to my puzzlement and sorrow, still trademarked the most advanced, liberal society in the world.

My friend Elaine called the Husmorlag and learned that a visiting American would be giving a talk. Excited that another American had detoured to our little, off-the-beaten-path spot, we sallied forth to meet her.

That's how we met Kitty from California. We had never set eyes on her before nor had she on us and our lives were all very different, yet Elaine, Kitty, and I immediately fell in with one another like long-lost friends. Perhaps those around us thought we all were old friends because we exemplified sociable womanhood in action. We bubbled with questions, hardly giving one another time to answer before asking another. But as we knifed and forked our ways through open-faced cold meat, shrimp, salad, and mayonnaise sandwiches followed by cream cake and coffee, I could hardly get enough of our freewheeling American conversation. Had we met at an airport, on a boat, or on a Greek isle, it would not have been unexpected, but at Kopervik's Housewives Group? The pretty tables with flickering blue candles and blue *Husmorlag* song books scattered not so discreetly around were an unusual venue, by any measure, in which to celebrate our common American heritage.

"What are *you* doing here? When did you arrive? Wow! Really? You've been here twenty-three years! So, let's see, we're from California, New York, and Texas!" Our exuberant exchanges reminded me of Helen Reddy's old song. "We were women; we were invincible!" But we had to watch our manners. We were all guests and shouldn't be loud. As we whispered our last questions, voices lifted in song to open the meeting. Our crash course in trying to find out as much as possible about the visitor next to you was ending; Kitty would soon begin her talk.

We had found out only that evening that it would be about quilting, but if I thought it would be limited to discussing their attractive designs, I could not have been more wrong. Her explanation of *why* women quilted in the first place, especially in America's early days, would shed light on things I had not thought about before. Certainly we would know more about quilts, but more importantly, I would learn why I had been writing.

Kitty began by explaining that American settler women, far from home and families, began using scraps to produce lovely and useful quilts. She quoted from a poignant journal entry: "In a most desperate time a woman took a scrap of material, remembering its source with affection, and then stitched it as if stitching would help hold her together, herself, until spring." Quilting filled hours, days, or weeks of waiting or crossing the prairie, and everything important found its way into them. A creative outlet, they helped women handle all the details of life which, taken separately, could overwhelm their spirits, and she saw that as a characteristic which has continued.

"In California," she continued, "after any major crisis—mud slides, jolts, or earthquakes—our quilting shop is packed with people and they all want to talk. It becomes a therapeutic place, and the sewing itself brings you back to reality. After the earthquake my friends and I worried about everything and eventually decided the only way to get through it was by making an 'Earthquake Survival' quilt." Kitty held up the vividly colored quilt. "Each piece represents the stresses and worries which prevailed in everyone's thoughts during that unsettling time.

"It is very busy-looking, but that's exactly how I was feeling. But as I sewed all those little pieces together, I felt I was making it into something calmer. Taking little pieces and making something orderly out of them, changing the disorder into something solid and positive, well, when you have finished, you know you have survived. Certainly it was like that for me."

She offered one more insight. "I visualized the quilt's design as I went along, never knowing what it would look like. If I *had* known, I would never have made it. I needed a surprise to keep me motivated!"

Our California visitor shared her disquieting conclusions about how life in modern America affected her, mirroring mine. "Life there has a way of draining our creativity because of our fears. You don't know how lucky you are to be living a quiet, balanced life in Norway. When I first came here, part of me wanted to stay here for it was the first time in years that I had felt safe, completely safe. Back in America, I wondered what had happened in the past twenty years to make it so dangerous, and when did the problem start?

"Karmøy was so different. All the energy I used just worrying about feeling safe back home could be used creatively here. I began working through this conflict by sewing a new quilt which I call my Norway quilt because of the colors I associate with Norway, differing shades of blue, with white." Holding up the magnificent patchwork, she went on, "My quilts are part of me and perhaps it sounds strange, but because I feel so safe in Norway, I feel that if I leave my quilts here with my cousins, part of me will stay safe too."

Safe. She felt Karmøy's power too.

Until then I had never seen my need to write about my

life overseas as having any connection with making a quilt, yet it did, for a page or a piece at a time, it was all the same, and for the same reasons. In the safeness of Karmøy I sewed my quilt with words, taking all the pieces, working through the new challenges and situations, trying to bring it all together into something positive and cohesive. The process was necessary for the results, and the results unfolded as I went along. And like Kitty, had I known what it was all supposed to look like at the end and what the pattern revealed, I would probably not have been able to do it either.

Being around an American straight from home was like drinking a glass of champagne fast: my Americanism bubbled to the surface despite myself. Kitty symbolized what made up an American: optimism, enthusiasm, and drive—those intangibles which seemed to urge you to rush out and do wondrous things with your life, almost obligated you, one could say, to excel in a country where both high-flying and modest dreams, pursued with persistence, all had a chance. Yet my quiet life in Norway had almost been perfect—with a different, more spiritual center and a deeper awareness of nature. Being with our new friend felt so heady though that the laughing, talking, exchanging information could mean only one thing. Deep down I had been missing America and the outgoing ways of her people.

I hadn't missed America's fear culture, however. And as much as I wanted to, I could not hide in Norway forever. A few weeks later, when the Håvik post office disappeared overnight, it was yet another omen that we would go too.

The windows were dark and Britt was gone. The gold trumpet post office sign and box had been taken down so cleanly, it was as though the post office had never been there. The place

had returned to being a private house, but I stared at the empty
window hoping to bring it back to life, worrying about Britt and
her job. And what about me? I had come to rely on the homey
little place where a friend smiled when I came in. It annoyed me
even more that I had not been able to read about it in the paper
for surely the closing had been mentioned? An upstairs curtain
fluttered as a gray-haired lady noted my pause, then she and the
ghost of the post office slipped back into the shadows of her
house. Would she miss all the people coming and going downstairs? I thought she just might.

Post offices bring people together. I had met children in
its parking lot; chatted with my old friend with her dog, Rex, on
the way there; discovered a sheep caught in a barbed wire fence
close by and went to inform the farmer—all when I was walking
or biking to that particular post office. I often used the post office
as a reason to walk across the fields, my only errand being to mail
one letter. Removing the post office removed a casual opportunity for human interaction, and the enjoyment and importance of
getting to know those around you.

One afternoon Elise and Karl finagled an invitation for
me to meet their long-term friend and neighbor, Knut, who had
lived in America. "He has lots of stories to tell about it," Elise
promised. Knut and his wife lived in a farmhouse surrounded by
dainty flowerbeds. Despite his eighty-five years, he was an
outgoing, lean-bodied man who loved cracking jokes and telling
funny stories. His wife wore her hair pulled back neatly and a crisp
white embroidered apron cinched her waist. After we got warmed
up, our host spoke about his emigration to California in the
1930s. He had been a fisherman on the island, then worked in a
herring factory, but his prospects were poor. "People didn't have
so much money between their fingers in those days, and there
weren't many jobs around. You had to look after what you had,"
he said. America offered the best opportunities, he decided, so
he followed his older brother and some relatives there and later
joined the United States Air Force.

"The most interesting thing about America was that people there had more of everything than we had in Norway, but it wasn't so long after I went over that the bottom fell out of the stock market," he recalled, bursting into laughter. "Herbert Hoover got blamed for it!" After moving all over the U.S. with the Air Force, he applied for citizenship. "I became a citizen after waiting five years, and learned about government for the citizenship test. I went to the federal courthouse in Los Angeles, and the fellow there asked me all the questions he could think of and pretty soon I had passed!"

As Knut, Elise, Karl and I ate heartily, conversation shifted to his first private airplane ride. "One of my friends had just got his pilot's license and bought an old German biplane, a two-seater, water-cooled," he began, eyes twinkling. "He asked me, 'Would you like to take a little flying trip with me? Then I'll show you San Pedro from the air.' Of course, I said, sure, and off we went. Well, after awhile we heard a loud noise and realized the plane was getting overheated. We landed on a little playing field and a side wind nearly got us, but we straightened up. My friend asked me, 'Do you want to go up again?'

"Oh, yes!" I said, and after we let the engine cool down awhile, we went up and back to where we came from!"

Everyone laughed at the picture and Knut couldn't resist adding a bit more. "My friend was Swedish-Finnish, and well, maybe you don't know, but years back they put the Swedish king's likeness in the outside toilets here in Karmøy! Ah, they put all sorts of pictures there—they even put Hitler's there, under the lid!"

Knut's family had lengthy and current ties with America. "My dad was on the Pacific coast somewhere and had a homestead in Canada, but I never traveled with him," he told us. "I have relatives in Minneapolis and Duluth, and once saw a place that was just started as a log cabin near Pequot, in an area of small lakes." Karl added his remembrances of the era. "You know, there were about fifty or so Norwegians in that area of the States around that time and there was a photograph taken of them.

Knut's father and mine and a lot of people from around here are in it. I'll have to find it for you," he told me.

In no time Knut recalled another tale. "Once these two guys and I went to Nebraska and stayed there for eight months prospecting for gold. Whatever we found we took to the buyer in Auburn. He paid so much per ounce and it was ninety-seven percent clean. The price then was only $32 an ounce in 1933 or 1934. There weren't many people out there, but one was from Texas. We decided he had killed someone back there and that's why he was up in the hills!"

Knut exploded with mirth, prepping us for the final part to the story. "The Texas fellow used to call me Barnacle Bill because, you see, we had agreed when we set out that none of us would shave or cut his hair while we were there. So with my long red whiskers and long hair … I looked like …" he left the scruffy picture to our imagination. "Well, that's what he called me, Barnacle Bill!" A second nickname had him chuckling. "I also got the name Rocker. Some guys called me Rocker after Knute Rockne, the Notre Dame football coach, whose family came from Voss here in Norway."

After the war, however, life took an unexpected turn. "My father back in Austevik contacted me and said he was giving up the farm. My older brother wanted to stay on in America, so all of a sudden it was offered to me. My father said I could take it or it would have to go to strangers." Keeping the farm in the family beat out his ambitions to remain in America.

"I don't regret it, coming back to Karmøy, because I needed a quieter life after the war to more or less get adjusted," he explained. "My doctor here said that I was like a racehorse straining to take off ."

Only one cloud darkened our cordial visit and that was my reference to Håvik as his neighborhood. "This isn't Håvik! It never has been and never will be," he snapped and Karl agreed. "He's right. It's *Austevik*. But when Norsk-Hydro first set up their office, it was in the Håvik prayer house the west side of the highway and the post office merged Austevik into Håvik. But what about Vorrå?—was that a legitimate name for the neighborhood since Vorråveien led into it? I asked. "No, this is not Vorrå either!" Knut exclaimed. "That's over on the other side of main road, farther down!"

Knut flushed as he defended Austevik, but I risked one more question. If he were in Oslo and someone asked where he were from, what would he say? "I would say I am from Karmøy." But what if they ask where on Karmøy? "Then I'd say I'm two or three kilometers from Kopervik," he continued evasively.

Karl jumped into the discussion. "For me, I say, if you're going to send me a letter, it's 4265 Håvik." I conceded the skirmish to superior opponents. Theirs was a well-practiced conspiracy. No matter what the post office decreed, they were from Austevik and nowhere else. Effective that spring, Knut's mail would no longer come via Håvik's post office. Instead it would be routed through Avaldsnes, whose association with the island's ancient and royal past would, I hoped, surely compensate for more recent inequities?

Knut still missed American food: American chili beans, ravioli, Swiss steak well done with gravy as well as tacos and chili con carne. He listed them off as though he were reading from a menu, and Elise cautioned, "Those are not so good for you, you know!" It was a moot point, so everyone laughed. Before I left, the old gentleman inquired after our former landlord, his long-time neighbor, who still worked away from the island although his wife and family had moved back into the house. "Do you know when Håkon is coming back?" I shook my head, no, and his disappointed look touched me because it reflected how just one neighbor's departure affected everyone in the hamlet.

Over the years Austevik had lost its very name and postal and map identities, and when it lost its people to offshore jobs, everyone waited for them to come back. Absences were assumed to be temporary, even if lengthy. "When is he coming back?" must have been asked a thousand times on the island. Whether they left to fish, work a rig, work internationally, or even when

they emigrated to America for a better life, the men were expected to return to Norway eventually, if only to retire. Small
neighborhoods struggled to remain viable, and when even the
post office left, it made it that little bit harder.

When far at sea remember me
And bear me in your mind
Let all the world say what they will
Speak of me as you find.

Writer unknown
(Written on an old milk jug)

Before leaving, I added my name to those in a guest
book filled with comfortingly familiar United States place names.
Knut spoke with an American-style accent, and I marveled that he
could turn the language on and off so easily since he rarely
needed English in his daily life. A contented man, he had long
since reestablished himself back home after his adventures. But he
had left part of himself overseas. His tone turned serious when he
told about returning to America for a visit in 1972, twenty-four
years after he had returned to Norway to take care of the farm.

"I spent all my youth in America. I had a lot of friends,"
he said, pausing. "Flying there, going to see people I had known,"
his voiced trailed off. He turned his head away from us, eyes filling
with emotion. "I felt I was going home," he said softly.

Going home. Knut's journey through memory took me
to that United States airport where I stood in the noisy crowd
waiting at Customs and Immigration. Words and comprehension

were my passport, protecting and arming me, guaranteeing me safe passage into America, past the lines of the hesitant and unsure, anxious and scared. As an American citizen I was home. No one would direct me to a separate, secondary line for nonresidents or visa holders where my very purpose of being in the country was suspect at worst, scrutinized at the least. "What brings you here? "How long are you staying?" In Norway, being merely a visa holder and always having to ask permission for entry at airport customs made me feel second rate. While my husband entered under the auspices of a large American corporation, I was just his spouse, an addendum. I shrank to the status of a child at customs, always aware I had better be a good little girl, wipe my nose, and pull up my socks every time the officer's eyes caught mine. If he didn't approve of how I looked and behaved, he could say no.

Just pretending to be back on American soil felt good. Everything was easy, even there by myself. I was in control, the mantle of first-class citizenship status around my shoulders. I could reclaim my rightful place in that promised land which both Knut and I had found to be good.

If Beth had been a reminder and Kitty a telegram, then Knut was the final summons. I wanted to be back in America where I belonged, where I was entitled to be. Someone else might take my place if I stayed away too long. If I could have jumped on a plane for the States at that moment, I would have, so urgent was my need to get back and feel that sure of myself again.

" ... Be patient toward all that is unsolved in your
heart and try to love the questions themselves like
locked rooms and like books that are written in a very
foreign tongue. Do not now seek the answers, which
cannot be given you because you would not be able to
live them. And the point is, to live everything. Live
the questions now. Perhaps you will gradually,
without noticing it, live along some distant day into the
answer."
—From *Letters to a Young Poet* by Rainer Maria Rilke

25

Island Soul

There comes a magical, liberating moment in a difficult and challenging experience where you finally have control of the situation, past and future integrate; everything feels suddenly easy. With the learning and striving over, you can risk a look back and see where you've been. For a long time I refused to do so, to admit there had been problems with living in Norway, but as the return to Houston grew ever closer, I found myself noticing them.

Perhaps the post office door swinging in my face started me off. It was probably the fiftieth time and infuriated me as usual. Why didn't Norwegians hold the door while another person was coming through? Once in a great while someone did, but that didn't make up for the lack of consideration the rest of the time. Then there was the surrender of my Texas driver's license. I still had not gotten over that. The licensing bureau held foreign licenses until the person was ready to leave, at which time they exchanged the Norwegian license for the foreign one. I felt vulnerable without that security in my wallet because it identified me as an American citizen.

The hardest part of my time was in Oslo. Expensive and misery-inducing quarantine stays are the punishment for bringing your canine and feline family with you, so you all suffer. Without the companionship of my pets and when the worry about them merged with the difficulty of not being able to communicate properly or understand the language around me, I seriously considered taking a cab to the airport, and leaving on the next plane west. Other countries manage to process healthy domestic pets in a day or two; not so Scandinavia, which insists that it is motivated by fear of rabies entering the country. First there had been the excruciating complex examinations and inoculations by our Houston vet before their trip, Norwegian vets afterwards, followed by extreme anxiety that the government would euthanize our animals if any details in the "animal import" documents were inaccurate. On top of this we paid an enormous kenneling bill.

After that our only input into their lives were half-hour, weekly visits to the quarantine station on the other side of Oslo, a facility surrounded by high, chain-link fencing like a prison. In fact, that is how I viewed it as I rang the bell for entry each week. Rudy was too small to be any trouble to anyone, ditto the cat. But Nicky was afraid of things, needed coaxing and proper handling, and I was the only one he trusted. He'd already gotten into trouble by snapping at a shampooer who spoke to him in, of course, an alien tongue. We trudged around and around the quarantine station yard in rain or snow. I kept up with his obedience training, telling him to be a good boy, assuring him everything would be all right, even though it was out of my hands. Sometimes I just sat on a rock, stroking him, praying he would be good and get out of the place with the other two. I counted off the sixteen weeks.

If that was worst, then most of the other issues were minor social ones. Why did it seem so hard for some students to get accepted into college, and why wasn't college promoted more? And why weren't more private jobs advertised in the paper? Someone once told me that an employment agency only accepted applications from people recommended by existing job-seekers. I couldn't imagine how people managed to get work in non-government positions. If it hinged on anyone writing a letter and getting an answer, I could see why that failed. Certainly most of my letters, written in English with a Norwegian translation below, still got no replies.

Passing the buck was something else I ran into although I wondered if this happened just because I was talking to someone in another language. Whenever I tried to get some information, the response was that I should call so-and-so instead. Once it took the best part of six months and at least six long distance calls and three letters to try to get a decision from someone who promised to return calls and never did. Trying to sound cheerful and pleased when you are about to pull your hair out with frustration was hard, but as long as I had chocolate handy, I could do it.

In Norway I encountered a lack of respect for personal privacy which felt uncomfortable. Incomes are public knowledge and people can go look them up, I was told. A person's photograph, age, income, and even the age and model of car they drove could be listed in a newspaper article. Papers even ran names and addresses of local "millionaires," making them vulnerable to burglars. Expatriates made these lists due to their high taxable incomes. These salaries looked monumental since they included allowances to compensate for additional Norwegian taxation and costs of living that were two to three times those in the States. Everyone had to get their piece of the pie, and the resulting tax reconciliations were so complex that a major U.S. tax service was the only entity skilled enough to unravel them. Intrusions like these seemed designed to eliminate any pleasure from working hard and amassing some wealth. I also heard, yet could hardly believe, that the income tax bureau demanded that citizens scour their pockets and wallets for loose currency and list it on their tax returns!

I missed courtesy titles like "Mr." and "Mrs." and found surnames alone too harsh, first names, too familiar, especially for older people I had just met. And I didn't care much for the term "*samboer*" which meant a person living with another. These *samboer* relationships acted like marriages and produced children. It took me awhile to remember not to ask, "And how are your wife and children?" and instead ask the innocuous, "How's your family?

All in all, though, I had been more than happy in Norway. Everyone had been so nice. And who was I to complain? America wasn't perfect either, far from it, and my disapproval of some things Norwegian was my problem, not theirs. My focus had been to get on with the business of living in a productive, positive way, blending into the community. The fact that, at the end of my stay, I could look back and say I had been able to do so, spoke volumes. Norway had been generous to me.

Still, despite my mission to make myself fit Karmøy and have her fit me, there had been times when even I had to admit that the fit was tight on both our parts. When Knut spoke, his words opened a dam which had been holding back an ocean. America was really where I felt accepted, where I could understand everything, and where, despite her faults, I belonged.

"*All landscapes have to be re-discovered and understood in the light of new experiences. The source has to be recognized and the roots found again to belong naturally in the ancient soil of some timeless existence. Sometimes we need to be exiled in order to find out where we do belong. It is only then that we realize how freely we enjoyed being part of a landscape, when we were not conscious of the influence it was having upon us and we expected nothing of it other than the daily pleasure it gave in making us aware of its presence.*"
—From *In Fen Country Heaven* by Edward Storey

America's immense size was part of it, oddly enough. Wide and spread out and still not filled up with people, it gave me three thousand miles one way, two thousand miles the other to run across mentally and see if what I had in mind to do worked. From a distance American life pumped along highways, through telephone lines, down the tiniest country lane, and through her energetic people like blood through a giant heart. In America nothing was small or small-minded and all goals potentially great. I needed America's physical space and unfettered future-oriented spirit, but mostly I needed her language.

Back in America I could read every scrap of material and make instant decisions about the information. Reading between the lines, discerning nuances, and understanding colorful Americanisms and anecdotes would be automatic. The history of the society and culture would not be foreign to me. I would fit in, belong. I would be back in the driver's seat figuratively, in one of the world's most mobile societies, yet the regret that I had to leave my personal sanctuary, my little island, was real. I wanted both worlds and could not have them.

Nothing could have been more different from the life I lived in Houston than the life I lived on Karmøy , yet even in its difficult moments, the experience had provided one of my greatest periods of personal growth. Not the least was my writing and resurgence of my desire to draw. But, importantly, the humbling experience of being an outsider unable to utilize one's intellectual skills as fully and easily as one normally did at home, as well as realizing that even tiny and enormous things escaped me, affected me even more. This was how an immigrant felt; frequently helpless, ever dependent on the good will and patience of others, perhaps sometimes viewed as stupid—all due to not understanding another language and culture.

Without Tor, my language teacher, I wondered if I could have made it. He helped me begin taking a few small steps toward linguistic and emotional control of my new life. The children, our special helpmates, deserved thanks as did my kind and patient Norwegian friends and neighbors who listened to my *dårlig,* awful, attempt at Norwegian. But for them all, I might never have learned anything about their world. If living in another country taught me one thing, it was the importance of language. When I returned to the United States, I would repay the debt and tutor others in English so that their children, especially, might obtain the American dream.

Language and culture are as codependent as a pair of shoes. If you have one without the other, you hobble; if you have both, you dance. In Norway I hobbled, but at least I managed to stay on my feet, and much of the time I simply padded around in what felt best, the old moccasins of my English and American culture. But as time ran out, I became lazy about Norwegian and, given that I still missed much of what was going on around me, I wondered why I had tried so hard to learn it in the first place. What were my motives? On the surface and initially it was to help me cope in a culture that spoke a different language.

But more than that had driven me, and the pieces began to fall into place. It had been that casually tossed, profound question from the restaurateur in Oslo. His words still seemed fresh in my mind. "How can you know the soul of a people if you don't know their language?" he had asked. His innocent challenge was responsible for all the seeking I had done on Karmøy. I had wanted to learn the people's language, listen to their stories, look at what they looked at, share their day-to-day lives, and come away expert in their foibles, beliefs, and attitudes. I would have them pegged. I would know their soul. Soul. It sounded so important and I would have found it from my hotbed of Norwegian culture, Karmøy.

But it did not happen like that. I became no expert in their ways. From knowing parts of people's lives, I drew conclusions which might or might not be accurate. In the end cultural patterns were always subordinate to the commonality of the human condition. Having so few years in their culture limited my access to the people, let alone their souls, which remained far, far beyond my capabilities of understanding. Besides, language alone did not open one's mind; you needed knowledge if your heart were to take understanding to a deeper level. By the time I realized what the soul of a people is and where language fits in, it was late in the game and surprised me with one more, not very attractive truth. My burning need to write, to learn while I lived in Norway was driven by yet another motive. I had been testing the fidelity of my American soul, and it was *that* I had been searching for all along. I wanted to find clues that the Norwegian soul was superior to the American one and would suit me better.

Ingratitude was not the reason because America had been good to me. Rather, it was the death and violence-obsession of movies and the news media and their related negativity that had worn me down before I left. Slick television reporting dished up gruesome news, and the public had either developed a taste for watching and listening to it, treating the stories like grim entertainment, or had forgotten to hit the "off" button. Sometimes I wondered which America television anchors were reporting on because their stories were of a place and people alien from mine. The America I emigrated to was not that way, my old neighborhood was not that way now, our town was not that way, and judging by the thousands of immigrants applying to enter, America was not that way to them either—or why would they want to come? As Chinese-born Nien Zheng wrote so eloquently in her memoir, *Life and Death in Shanghai,* "I hope in due course to become a citizen of this great nation of warm-hearted people and wide open spaces."

Americans *were* warmhearted, yet their valid and noble heritage was being eaten away by perceptions of fear of the unknown attacker, a man with a gun. Healthy, happy people enjoying a free life that millions envied worried and purchased weapons for self-defense and tuned into the television news to hear, once again, that danger lurked around the corner. "You walk that road alone?" a Houston neighbor once asked, surprised. "Sure, why not," I replied. "But … what if someone wants to *get you?*" No one wanted to "get me," I assured her, especially at nine-thirty in the morning as I zipped along in worn sweats. She, like many Americans, had willingly exchanged her personal freedom for gun access, the security of life in a civilized society for that in an insecure one. She knew that irate neighbors might turn a gun on each other after an argument, a child could pick up his father's weapon and accidentally shoot himself, teenagers could take guns to school and kill classmates and teachers in order to satisfy perverse needs. Even children learned things far too soon. My friend's two-year-old daughter pointed at an image on the television. "Gun?" she asked. "No, a stick," I lied, feeling sick that she not only recognized it but had already included the word in her baby talk vocabulary. By the time we left Houston, my perception of being in danger had eroded my creativity.

Karmøy's safety revived me and once I felt my creativity return, I never wanted to live any other way. I was looking to hang my hat on another rainbow and maybe Norway offered it. But just when I began to think that I could give up America, a disparaging remark lit up my darkest soul-searchings with a high-power flashlight. A group of us, Norwegians and Americans, had been talking about living and working in other countries and how it felt to stay there or go back home. One man had tried overseas life and didn't like it after awhile. His heart was in his own land. He had not enjoyed being an immigrant.

"Immigrants are rootless," he said, and the impact was like having him point directly at me and tell me *I* was rootless and could never commit to another country because there I was, thirty years after emigrating, undecided about the place I had chosen and looking to find some place better. The truth was he was right. Hardly a day passed that I did not despair of ever finding peace of mind and spirit again in America, and I wanted to stay where I felt perfectly safe, in Norway.

But somewhere in America there had to be a small, safe place and I would find it. It was my land, and while some things were bad, most were very, very good. I needed to give America another chance, and freshen my perspective. Perspective implied having traveled through something to get somewhere, and I had already found myself looking at America from afar, sometimes to idealize, other times to vilify. Even Norway, during my short time, was looking a little different as time went by. Perspective was like grandchildren—an easier ride than raising your own children. It was the final reward for having lived the days first, then thought them out afterwards, and afterwards.

What a journey that man in Oslo had sent me on with his casual remark. I often felt providence played a role for I was sent on my way like a mountain climber, to explore an unknown vista. My exotic trip fascinated me for almost four years. The long, quiet times on the West Coast of the country permitted contemplation of a small society as well as the larger one that was my own. I reached the end with a renewed appreciation of the power of language as it related to culture and a sense of belonging. His words and philosophy proved right. You could not understand the soul of a people without knowing their language. My little inroads had just scratched the surface, but I would have to be satisfied with that.

Soul, it seemed to me, meant people's central belief in themselves regarding where they stood and how they fitted into their particular culture and society—whether they felt individually accepted by the whole, communally cared for and protected. They knew how to meet its particular demands and what their responsibilities and lifetime prospects were. They felt a love and commitment to the community's welfare and protection. These components of individual belonging underpinned the communal soul of the people like roots anchor a plant. Cultural traditions wove a supporting lattice. But without language none of it could survive. The communications code—writing, reading, listening, and speaking—were the rain, sun, and soil which kept the people and culture alive and growing.

Because the language was not mine, the Norwegian soul was not mine either nor could it be. My language was English and my soul as I knew it was American. But Norway had left her mark on me. I would admire and speculate on her from a distance but would feel freer at home in America where individualism and independence were cultural presumptions. In America it was up to me, not her, to make life the way I wanted it to be.

"Finally, the gentle power of sanctuary does wonders to restore our peace of mind, perhaps the greatest gift that taking sacred time and space can give to us. In sanctuary that elusive peace we seek in all aspects of our life seems more easily attainable."

—From ***The Sanctuary Garden***, by Christopher Forrest McDowell and Tricia Clark-McDowell

26

Olaug, Hindenburg, & Me

By project's end there was only one expatriate Heidrun family remaining in the Haugesund-Karmøy area—a locale our former corporate headquarters office in Oslo had originally labeled "a remote site"!—and I was absurdly proud to note that it was ours. I hoped the company had forgotten about us, but not so; Mike came home excitedly waving a party invitation. We had been invited to the company's enormous Heidrun completion party in Stavanger. It was a good news-bad news situation. Mike viewed it as a public celebration of a job well done, and closure of one of his most exacting career challenges. I saw it as the unwelcome end of my enriching, peaceful life in Norway. I threw myself into what time was left. "Seize the day!" American tee shirts cried, and seize them I did, imprinting each into memory so I could recreate them later, when I missed that special life.

At the Stavanger hotel shortly after, the gigantic ball-room thundered with the near-deafening sound of hundreds of excited voices. Dressed in my first Paris-made creation, albeit one which had shared an unglamorous ride home earlier that week in my bicycle basket, I felt exuberant too—almost enough to forget my pinching shoes. Thanks to Heidrun, I had come to Norway and for that opportunity I was eternally grateful. I had been living on a beautiful little Norwegian island "far from the madding crowd" and writing about it. What better cause for celebration!

My desire to stay on Karmøy to the very end reflected my need to finish my job—trying to put everything I had experienced and learned into place and onto paper. That was brought home to me when I bumped into Olaug, Liv-Marit's aunt, at a crafts meeting just a week after the cocktail party.

Her face was one big frown. "One of my sheep is about to lamb. I must get back," she said, checking her watch for the umpteenth time. Out of the blue, I found myself asking if I could go over to her farm later. Since arriving on the island, I had nurtured a secret desire to see a lamb born, but I kept that to myself. Olaug agreed, looking unsurprised.

Olaug's cottage was tucked in a small farming neighborhood, as far removed from a hotel party scene as one could imagine. I drove cautiously past enormous sheep the size of calves sauntering around my car. Her flock, black ones and standard white, filled the pastures alongside her home, and the pregnant one was easy to spot. She was the only one unable to run away when she saw me. The rotund, dirty brown mother-to-be was plopped gracelessly in the field, looking very uncomfortable as she half-heartedly nibbled grass. When she saw me, she shot me a scared look, struggled onto her spindly legs and tottered off about ten yards where she lay down again, panting.

"Does she have a name?" I asked Olaug, hoping I could address the animal and make her feel better about me. "Oh, yes, it's Åla, but she has a new name now!" she said with an innocent little smile.

"A new name?" I replied seriously, quite sure I was about to learn some interesting old Norwegian custom I could add to my writings. My friend burst into laughter.

"Hindenburg! That's her new name! You know, because she looks like she might explode!"

Laughing helped Olaug temporarily forget her woes and me realize that not everything I came across had to have some literary angle. Hindenburg was a perfect nickname for the sheep. She looked as round and pressured as a balloon, and while I sympathized with her situation, I kept a respectable distance. She was a lady who needed a wholesale account with a throw-away, moist towelettes distributor. My friend Olaug was a braver woman than I to get close to the animal's disagreeable back end. Still, she had the situation under control and wouldn't call the veterinarian. "It's too expensive. I'll be helping her myself," she told me. How exactly did that work, I asked, almost afraid to hear too many details. "It's very messy, but I have some very long gloves," she said with an air of someone who had long ago discovered nature would take care of the production if she could help steer. Mess was incidental to the larger picture, and rubber gloves took care of the cosmetics.

Long gloves, no matter how long, seemed inadequate to the job. A full rubber suit and goggles followed by an hour-long shower would have suited me. Any yen to witness a lamb's birth rapidly disappeared. On second thought, maybe I had watched too many romanticized versions of births seen through a soft cinematic haze, accompanied by music. Reality and pain were not for one who had once fainted in a hospital while simply visiting a patient. Feeling increasingly squeamish, I was glad I had kept my ulterior motive to myself. I would be free to go if lambing seemed imminent and things looked tricky.

We squatted down, surveying the hills, feeling night fall. Olaug's expression relaxed. "This is not very much, 103 *mål*, but it's mine! I'm very lucky my brother didn't want it, so I got it. You know, when you have land," she looked at me with bright eyes, pressing her right hand against her chest, "it gets into your soul!" We lapsed into silence, watching the lazy curl of blue water in the distance, smelling decidedly sheeplike by then. I looked across at poor Hindenburg still struggling around and tried shooing away armies of midges and insects whirling about us. Then I glanced at my old shoes which were covered in mud and sheep droppings and felt supremely happy.

My feet had to have a sense of humor. Certainly if they could have laughed they would have been hysterical. A week before at the big party they had been pink and nice and in high heels while the rest of me wafted perfume. Right now my feet and shoes smelled, and no one would have welcomed them into a hotel ballroom. But if my feet had no qualms about where my path in Norway had taken me, nor had I because I was finally doing something I had always hoped for—standing on the land appreciating the outdoors with a Norwegian farmer, hearing about what was really important to her, and feeling she could use my company. I was in seventh heaven. And if asked to choose between looking elegant in a crowded hotel in town or standing in a muddy Karmøy sheep field watching evening fall with Olaug, the second won hands down.

Olaug's land had gotten into her soul, and the island had gotten into mine. While I would never, ever, be a Karmøyan and could not claim to be, I knew the rocky little island would always draw me back. The fresh wind whipping at my hair, the sound of bleating on the breeze, jingling cowbells, sheep dogs barking me away from their property lines, rough soil, heady fertilizer. The ever-surging ocean, spitting sand dunes, wind-whipped waves slapping the beach, washed gray rocks and screeching seagulls. For such a quiet place there was noise and activity all right, but the right kind—and peace and safety.

I would take my walks again, absorbed in the scenery of sky, water, and mountains, happily lost in the deep places of the mind where you can run without legs, soar like a bird, wonder and create, never tire of the questions nor of trying to find the answers, and hear the spirit-filled silence of God. When I did return, and I could not imagine not returning, I hoped it would be as an old friend and not a stranger.

My friend invited me in for coffee with a hint of a dare in her eye, an unspoken invitation.

No, I had to get home, I lied. The truth was I was too
nervous about what I might see if I stayed around. I drove home
to Kopervik smiling, toes wriggling in my dirty shoes. The next
day Olaug called to tell me that Hindenburg, nee Åla, had delivered two big lambs at 11 p.m. I felt a twinge of regret at not having
had enough courage to stay, to experience something amazing.
But my city life had not prepared me to cope with anything as
natural, and possibly as difficult, laborious, and emotionally
exhausting as attending a lambing. Olaug had been up half the
night and sounded worn out and I understood why. She was
quite a woman, and I knew I had only barely escaped a role as
reluctant midwife.

FIN STAS
Etne Bunad
Patti Jones Morgan
1994

27

Back to America

When the April 16, 1995, *Houston Chronicle* arrived, it marked a change in our philosophy of where home really was. Until then Mike and I had read the paper together on Sundays as distant observers of the city's scene. The headlines that screamed, people who got shot, politicians who got into trouble, schools that fell behind or got ahead, social programs that were tried, the everything that composed four million people's lives and interests filled a hundred pages. Little seemed to relate to my life on the island of Karmøy. In fact I felt that the chasm between that life and ours was so broad as to be two different worlds. But Houston would be our home again and I read the paper to prepare myself for it.

Reading the *Chronicle* was easy even if irritating. Too much to absorb, but enough useful information to fill a book. Too many products to browse through, yet nice low prices on food, clothes, furnishings. The effect was a bountiful offering of everything a city person was supposed to know about, have, and buy. I took it along when a Haugesund teacher invited me to talk to his students about Houston. For good measure I included a multi-page fax of statistics and information a journalist friend provided to cover the most complex governmental and societal questions they could throw at me.

What they were really interested in, though, surprised me. They bypassed headlines in favor of a full-page advertisement offering a twelve-pack of popular colas for ninety-nine cents, about six or seven kroner. In Norway they spent about two dollars, just for a one-liter bottle on sale. Their eyes widened on hearing that the Houston area's population exceeded that of their whole country. Once they became accustomed to the excesses of America, they got down to the basics. Did we have poisonous snakes? Had I seen anyone from Hollywood? My file of educational and social statistics and useful information about American life gathered dust as the question and answer period puttered along. They were nervous about using their English in front of their friends and in front of a real-live American. I was a mine of information which few were ready to exploit.

My only success that day was really with the boy who asked about snakes and followed with a couple more questions. His teacher confided that he was generally withdrawn and it had been quite unusual for him to open up and ask questions, displaying both confidence and curiosity. Knowing the boy had been able to be himself with me was my reward.

I tried jollying the children along with a little kidding, but this raised only one or two cautious smiles. Time dragged and towards the end I held out my newspaper for someone to take as though I were handing over a birthday present. No one rushed up to take it. The children weren't yearning to read it after all. When the bell rang, the youngsters hurried out of the room, probably as relieved as I to call it quits. I placed the newspaper on an empty desk, sorry to abandon it so heartlessly after it had traveled such a distance. How come the children weren't just dying to pick it up and read it and learn about America?

Of course, I expected too much. Regardless of its fascinating contents, the newspaper's secrets were safely locked inside paragraph after paragraph of the English language. Even if the youngsters had wanted to "read" it, they really couldn't have handled much. I understood that feeling all right. Just reading the easy parts of Norwegian newspapers took effort and a dictionary. The *Chronicle's* 100 pages could take the lifetimes of all the children combined to decipher. That the written word is transformed from a conduit for knowledge and understanding to a physical barrier when the language is different presents a certain irony. We all use our own codes to transfer thought to paper, and nations will never know one another as well as they could because of it.

For me, though, soon words and language would be my old, comfortable friends again and my labor with Norwegian would be over. I left the *Chronicle* to fend for itself and hoped some kind person would take it home.

Our final year had moved by too quickly. Easter week holiday had come again, then National Day and another folketog at Avaldsnes. Tulips sprang up; lambs tumbled across the meadows like cotton puffs; ocassional sleek, white cruise ships slipped across the backdrop of mountains and water. Summer got its official welcome with June's Viking Festival. Karmøyans and "Vikings" from York, in Northern Britain, reenacted life from those ancient times in small campsites. A beautiful hand-carved repica of an old Viking harp lay half-hidden in a dusty corner of one of the tents, and our friend Dagfinn, knowing how it had caught my eye, presented Mike and me with one as a memory of Kopervik.

I felt myself slipping away from daily life, preoccupied with leaving. My friends shared their plans and I felt sad, knowing I would not be around to see how they went. "I dreamed about you last night, and you weren't leaving," Cecilie assured me one morning and part of me wished it were true, but on a deeper level, I knew the time had come to go. After years of saying I loved living peacefully in Norway instead of living with Houston's city tensions, I found myself uttering the unthinkable. I was actually looking forward to going back.

We said farewell to our children from Liarveien again. They were too young to understand their contribution, but everything they were, and all that they had done, had helped me adjust and live contentedly in their country. Once when they had marched into the building where we were holding a art show, I burst with pride at my little support team. They had taken a fancy to art and often checked out my makeshift art studio, inspecting ongoing and completed pictures with the air of connoisseurs from the Louvre or the Tate Gallery. Then they would settle down to their projects, drawing, sighing, and sharpening their pencils industriously as they went, squabbling over colors, giggling over the results. Their major themes were faces and people, houses and landscapes with an occasional basket of fruit. Quite a number represented Mike and me and various dogs. I tried not to worry about ones of a peculiar-looking woman who was supposed to be me. Maybe I did look like that? Each creation was as treasured as a Monet, and dozens covered our kitchen walls.

As a result, Liv-Marit invited me to her school art show. *Velkommen til kunstkafe,* came the handwritten invitation from her fourth grade class, celebrating Edvard Munch's art. At their "arts café" I could buy coffee or tea and *noe å bite i,* something to eat, *veldig billig,* very cheap. Some of the students' artwork would be sold too, so I went clutching a 100 kroner note, but had no luck whatsoever. Either I didn't hear when the picture was held up for "auction" or the pleased parents just snatched them up. I had to be satisfied with my coffee and roll, expertly served by Torgeir Hårberg's son.

My own artistic development had been affected by the children. "They would look much better in color," Monika insisted one afternoon, carrying off my sketches while Kristine armed herself with crayons. "No, they are supposed to be black and white!" I implored, tugging at my drawing pad. Monika's eyes spoke volumes and, once the girls had gone, I experimented with colored pencils. She was right; the sketches did look better in color.

Liv-Marit paid a last visit. We saw Mike off on the fast

boat one Sunday together, and her eyes lost a little of their
contentment as her usual computer game partner waved us
goodbye. "Can *you* play Gorilla with me instead?" she asked. I
declined on "Gorilla" but offered her a Checkers game. She beat
me twice. Mike had shown great firmness in refusing her whee-
dling requests to play Checkers earlier, and I wondered how he
did it. "It's easy," he told me. "I have to say 'no' all day long at
work!" Unpracticed, I stayed with what suited me, "yes," most of
the time.

In the kitchen, waiting for some frozen pizza slices to
reheat, she decided this was a good time to ask a question.

"Patti, do you believe in Jesus and God?"

"Yes, I believe in Jesus and God," I answered. She nodded
and wound her legs around various parts of a stool, listening for
the final buzz of the microwave.

"Do you believe in the Big Bang?" she continued. I
weighed my words carefully, reluctant to disagree with anything
her parents believed or her teachers told her. "I . . . I don't know,"
I said, sounding a little uncertain, but able to be convinced, if she
had a good argument; after all, she was ten.

"I don't know either!" she sighed. Leaving the matter up
in the air, as it were, we moved on to matters less complicated
and closer to home: eating pizza and drinking orange juice,
drawing, and playing the awful computer game, Gorilla. She
hugged me hard before we parted. "You are my *best* friend!" she
assured me with a loving smile, blue eyes dancing. I humbly
accepted her generous compliment. She did not know it, but Liv-
Marit had been my best friend first.

Our other, older little group from Kopervik—Beth-Iren,
Alice, Elin, and Judit without an *h*—stopped by a few days before
our movers came. "We have something for you!" they giggled
nervously as Beth-Iren handed us a handmade card decorated
with Disney character cutouts and a crayoned Norwegian flag.
They had managed to invent yet another version of my name, but
the sentiment of their goodbye message outweighed everything.

Dear Mike and Paty,
We hope you'll find a beautiful and a nice place in Texas.
We wish you good luck with the new people and the new place.
From Alice, Beth-Iren, Judit, and Elin.

They slipped their photographs and addresses inside so we could try to find them Houston pen friends, and penciled a big "Goodbye" on the back.

Once more Karmøy children led the way in communication. When we arrived, children had reached out to us, supporting us with their friendship, teaching us their language, asking nothing in return. Now that we were leaving, others a few years older wanted to reach out to American youngsters way across the ocean. Helping them do that was the least we could do.

They were right, in a way, that we going to a new place, with new people, and we certainly needed their good luck wishes. We would be strangers coming back to a different Houston neighborhood, and where we knew no one. Starting over, even in our old culture, would take work and would be in a place where the closest ocean was fifty miles away, the nearest mountain five hundred. Walks among brick houses instead of hills and fields would distract from creative thought, and finding words would be a daily fight. But differences and changes notwithstanding, we would face the challenge once again to try to make more friends and make where we lived home.

Up until the last, it was hard to believe we were actually leaving Norway, but the reality sank in after we sent our advance guard, Calypso, ahead. He bothered no one in the eighteen- hour trip across the Atlantic, tucked away safely in baggage holds. A new admirer at our Houston pet shipment company reported that our cat had exited his carrier purring, tail twirling skyward with a "No problem, I can handle this" look about him.

All that was left was for Mike and me to take the fast boat to Stavanger and fly back to Houston the next day. Some of my special friends joined me for a light meal at a hotel while Mike politely disappeared, purportedly to check out downtown Kopervik one last time. Elaine read me a poem, and we all swallowed lumps in our throats as she struggled through it. She and her mother, Eva, and Lone, Sigrun, Beth, and Cecilie smiled at me from around the table, and I felt blessed.

Despite my initial feelings of isolation and inability to cope, my sojourn in Norway had turned out to be the experience of a lifetime and Karmøy, in many ways, had become my second home.

On move-in day on Karmøy my only possessions fit inside a moving truck. Now packed again, they were already on the way back to America. As I was leaving, however, it was my Norwegian friends whom I valued the most. Their warmth and friendship were my real possessions and most treasured souvenirs, and these were going home in my heart.

About the Author

Patti Jones Morgan's freelance profiles and articles have appeared in *Southwest Art, Southwest Profile, ARAMCO World, Victorian Homes,* the former *Houston Metropolitan* and other magazines. Her work was also chosen for inclusion in *Writing about the Arts and Humanities,* edited by Paxman, Black, Jackson and Rushforth, published by S & S Educational Group. She began **ISLAND SOUL: A Memoir of Norway** during her stay in Norway (Oslo and Karmøy) from early 1992 until late 1995. The author loved life on the beautiful little island of Karmøy where the cold wind blows off the North Sea and rough waves race into its rocky coves, and regenerates herself there as often as she can.

Particularly interested in the American immigrant experience, Morgan is thankful that she was spared learning a brand new language when she emigrated to the U.S. from southern England in the 1960s. However, because learning to read, write and speak English well is essential for foreign-born people seeking various versions, modest or mighty, of the American dream, she periodically enjoys volunteer-tutoring adults in English as a second language.

She and her husband, Mike, and their assorted pets divide their time between Houston and the refreshing vistas of the Texas Hill Country.

PERMISSIONS

The author gratefully acknowledges use of John Masefield's poem *Sea Fever*. Published by arrangement with the Estate of Louis Untermeyer, Norma Anchin Untermeyer c/o Professional Publishing Services Company, Connecticut. This permission is expressly granted by Laurance S. Untermeyer.

Excerpts from *Letters to a Young Poet*, by Rainer Maria Rilke, trans. by M.D. Herter, Norton, copyright 1943, 1954, included by permission of W.W. Norton, Co. Inc.

Grove/Atlantic Inc., New York, kindly permitted use of an extract from *Life and Death in Shanghai* by Nien Cheng, copyright 1986.

Christopher Forrest McDowell and Tricia Clark-McDowell graciously allowed me to excerpt from their book *The Sanctuary Garden*, Simon & Schuster, copyright 1998.

Edward Storey permitted me to share passages from his copyrighted works: *The Winter Fens*, Robert Hale, London, copyright 1993, and *In Fen Country Heaven*, Robert Hale, London, copyright 1996.

Thanks are also due to the following: Dreyer Bok A/S., Stavanger, Norway, for permission to quote from *Norseman Follow the Trail* ; North American Heritage Press, Minot, North Dakota, for permission to quote from *Skis Against the Atom* by Knut Haukelig; Aleksander Hauge of Visnes, Norway, for permission to publish his lyric poem *Song to Karmøy*. Fru Hagny Thorsen, Karmsund, Norway, for permission to publish recipes from '*Velkommen inn i våre kjøkkener.*' by Kirkeringen, Norheim church; Marit Synnøve Vea of Karmøy for her contemporary version of Nils Aarøy's original *Karmøy Song;* and singer Mari Boine of Finnmark for graciously sharing the lyrics of *Goaskinviellja* from her *Ørnebror (Eagle Brother)* compact disc. Thank you all for contributing your creative endeavors to this book.

Martin Pope's English translation of Isak Saba's *The Saami Anthem* (1906) was reproduced by arrangement with Davvi Girji o.s, Karasjok, Norway.

PLEASE ORDER DIRECT:

islandsoulbooks@cswebmail.com or
islandsoulbooks@msn.com
ORDER BY FAX: (713) 937-3740

Or write to: **ISLAND SOUL BOOKS**
                        Post Office Box 843
                        Wimberley, TX 78676

Quantity discounts available to businesses and corporations. Limited edition, early ordering recommended. Prices subject to change without notice. Please include $4 shipping/handling in U.S.A.; international rates vary. Autographed copies by request. Books shipped promptly.

Also available through Amazon.com; and islandsoulbooks2 at Amazon.com's Marketplace books, new and used category. Distributor: Baker & Taylor Books.